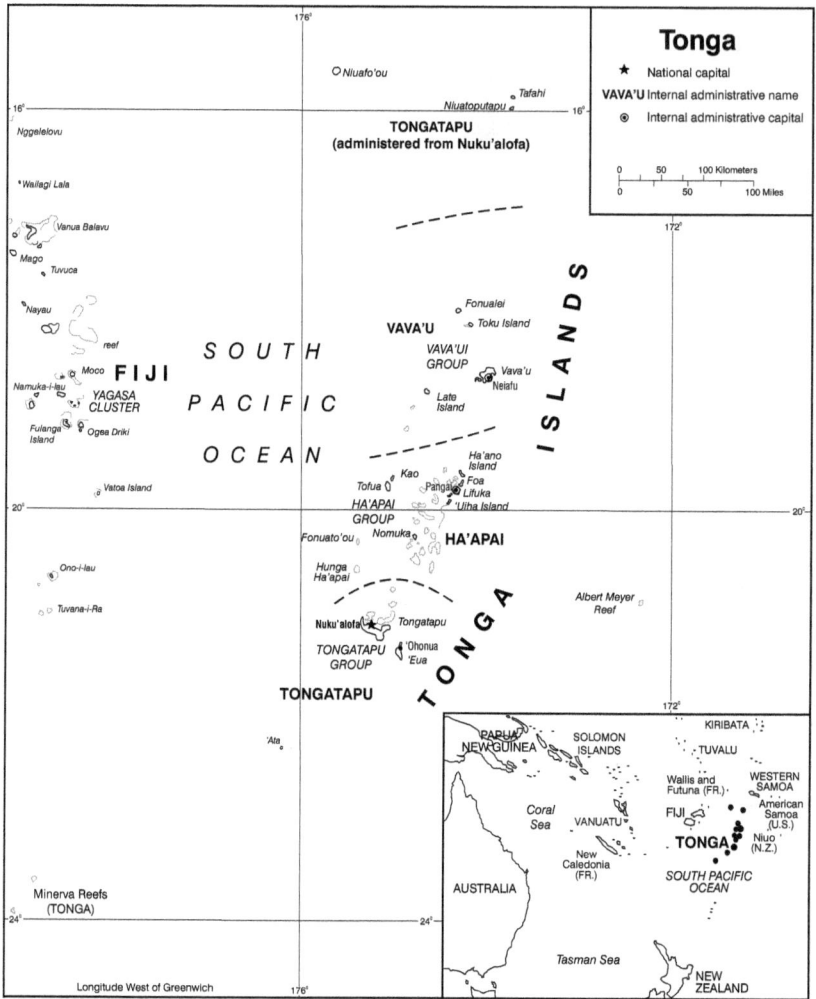

Map of Tonga

Persistence of the Gift

Tongan Tradition in Transnational Context

Persistence of the Gift

Tongan Tradition in Transnational Context

Mike Evans

Wilfrid Laurier University Press

WLU

This book has been published with the help of a grant from the Humanities and Social Sciences Federation of Canada, using funds provided by the Social Sciences and Humanities Research Council of Canada. We acknowledge the financial support of the Government of Canada through the Book Publishing Industry Development Program for our publishing activities.

Library and Archives Canada Cataloguing in Publication

Evans, Mike, 1961–
    Persistence of the gift : Tongan tradition in transnational context

Includes bibliographical references and index.
ISBN 978-0-88920-369-3 (cloth)
ISBN 978-1-55458-214-3 (paper)
ISBN 978-0-88920-944-2 (e-book)

1. Ha'ano Island (Tonga) – Social life and customs. 2. Ha'ano Island (Tonga) – Economic conditions. 3. Ceremonial exchange – Tonga – Ha'ano Island. I. Title.

DU880.E92 2001   306'.099612   C2001-930471-4

© 2001 Wilfrid Laurier University Press
        Waterloo, Ontario   N2L 3C5
        E-mail: press@wlu.ca
        Web: www.wlupress.wlu.ca

Paper edition 2009.

Cover design by Leslie Macredie. All photographs, including the cover photograph, courtesy of Mike Evans.

Contents

List of Figures and Tables

Figures

Tables

Acknowledgements

To the people of Ha'ano Island I wish to express my profound gratitude for their hospitality and generous contributions to this research. Without exception people patiently answered my questions and gave of their time to help in this project. Had it not been for this *'ofa* (love) and assistance I simply could not have completed this book. In particular I wish to thank Vili and Toa'ila Maeamalohi, Sione and Loutoa Talia'uli Fifita, 'Ika and Viola Katoa and their families for taking such very good care of me and my family over the course of some challenging times. My thanks also to Fanguna Vaitohi and Siofilisi Hingano for help with translations.

Thanks to the government of King Tupou IV for allowing this research, and in particular to the director and staff of the Ha'apai office of the Ministry of Agriculture and Forests for their unstinting support. The kind assistance of Mele Polutele of the Statistics Department, George Moengangongo of the Tonga campus of the University of the South Pacific, and Professor Futa Helu of the 'Atenisi Institute, was also important and appreciated. The hospitality of David and Val May, Langilangi Vī, and the staff of the Beach House made my stays away from Ha'ano congenial and productive.

I would also like to express my gratitude to the Social Sciences and Humanities Research Council of Canada who generously supported this research, and the School of Graduate Studies of McMaster University who provided significant funds to finance my fieldwork.

My debt to the Department of Anthropology at McMaster University stretches much farther back than just this book. I am grateful for the collegial atmosphere and attitudes of faculty, staff, and students, and wish to thank those who, over the course of the years, contributed to creating a space in which intellectual growth is enhanced by the sociability of everyday life. A number of people have supported and affected this work in other ways, some intellectually, some emotionally, and most both. My thanks to Carl Bertoia, David Burley, Matthew Cooper, David Counts, Jacques Critchley, Harvey Feit, Jennifer Gustar, Jasmin Habib, Henry Ivarature, Chris Justice, Martin Kendrick, Lucille Lanza, Jackie Low, Eudene Luther, Tom Miller, Chris Morgan, Jane Mulkewich, Janet Mayr, Paul Roberts, Mark Schuler, Matthew Sendbuehler, Pum Van Veldhoven, Wayne Warry, and Steve Worthington.

To Heather Young Leslie, I am indebted in ways I cannot even describe. While I have written what follows, what is written is in many ways not mine alone. Not only were we together throughout the fieldwork period, but through the years of preparation as well. (She also suggested the title for this book.) So much of what I think and what I have written is tied up in our mutual experiences and our conversations that it is, at times, impossible to assign authorship. I can only recognize my debt, and offer my deepest thanks.

Chapter One

Introduction — Recentring the Periphery

> After their prayer they came up to another landing, and they
> used that landing to come up to the island, and George I used
> that landing to look down on the whole area of Ha'ano, and
> he recognized that it is a small island, and he said that the
> name is *"Ha'ano Si'i Fakalahi ki he Lotu mo e Ako."* That means
> Ha'ano is not a big island, but it can be enlarged by religion
> and education. And that is why our population here now in
> Ha'ano is too small, because most of the people work to that
> model, go through religion and education.
> — Semisi Valeli Vake, January 1992

These are the words of the late Semisi Valeli Vake, a *motu'a tauhifanua* (old one who takes care of the land/people), of the village of
Ha'ano. Vake is explaining why the village, once about six hundred people, now hovers at a population of 150 full-time residents. Ha'ano has
become paradoxically smaller and larger over time since the first modern
King of Tonga, Siaosi Tupou I, named a small landing *Ha'ano Si'i
Fakalahi Ki He Lotu Mo e Ako*. For Vake, and for most others living in his
village, Ha'ano has grown to include populations in Tonga's capital,
Nuku'alofa, and overseas communities located in New Zealand, Aus-

---

Notes to chapter 1 start on p. 175.

tralia, and the United States. Though linked to a variety of other places, in terms of the "centre/periphery" dichotomy often used in political economic analyses of the contemporary world, Ha'ano itself is about as far as one can imagine from the main centres of political and economic power. Indeed, if the Western Polynesian Kingdom of Tonga is "the extreme periphery" (Marcus 1981, 48), then Ha'ano is even farther than that.

The island of Ha'ano (commonly referred to as Kauvai) consists of four villages: Fakakakai, Pukotala, Ha'ano, and Muitoa. It lies in the Ha'apai region, at the geographic centre of the Kingdom of Tonga, but at the periphery of the governmental and market structures that permeate this Polynesian nation. This monograph, working within the tradition of ethnographic description and analysis, uses a case study drawn from the Kingdom of Tonga in the South Pacific to explore the interrelationship between small-scale village based social and economic relationships, and the engagement of villagers with the modern World System. The monograph embraces the anthropological practice of in-depth analysis of culturally specific intentions and actions, but seeks to understand these in the context of the wider regional and global contexts in which they occur. My goal is to demonstrate ethnographically the operation of local agency in the context of the overarching structures of power that make up the World System that enmeshes us all.

The case of Tonga is a particularly illustrative one because the long-term economic linkages between the Kingdom and world markets (mainly in the form of copra or dried coconut kernel production) were not accompanied by direct colonization. Rather, internal social, political, and economic processes mediated, and continue to mediate, the manner in which Tongans face external markets, and market-oriented relationships and ideologies. This continues to be the case today, in spite of the fact that Tonga is not only entwined in a web of regional and global relationships, but Tongans themselves are now scattered across the Pacific and beyond. The Tongan diaspora has been purposeful, the result of many individual decisions taken within a cultural frame rooted and reproduced in particularly Tongan sensibilities. Tonga, Tongans, and Tongan culture exist in a transnational context (see Appadurai 1996; Hannerz 1996), but for many Tongans their behaviours and beliefs have been instilled by the day-to-day sociality of village life. In Tonga, in spite of superficial appearances to the contrary, non-capitalist forms of social organization continue to function effectively (and via their own rationales) in articulation with the capitalist world market.

Since the 1960s, political economists within an emerging "World System" approach and the associated "dependency theory" perspective (see especially Wallerstein 1974, but also Frank 1967, and Wolf 1984 among a host of others) have worked to analyze and describe the contemporary geopolitics of the globe. A centre/periphery model, which assumes that the actions and processes located in key European colonial nations have profoundly affected other less powerful peoples, has typified these approaches. To some degree, scholars operating within the World System approach hold that the concentration of technology, capital, and productive capacity leading to and coming from the colonial period has given rise to a system in which political and economic domination of peripheral areas directly benefits the central nations, and facilitates the reproduction of relations of domination and subordination over the medium and long term. While the general approach has been tremendously productive, recent critiques have stressed that the centre/periphery model is at risk of representing non-European peoples as passive victims and dupes of colonialism, and thus systematically under-represents the agency of so-called peripheral peoples. In the words of Marshall Sahlins, within World Systems approaches:

> other societies were regarded as no longer possessing their own "laws of motion"; nor was there any "structure" or "system" to them, except as given by Western Capitalist domination. . . . World System theory becomes the superstructural expression of the very imperialism it despises — the self-consciousness of the World System itself. (1993, 3)

As a part of an ongoing and constructive critique of earlier works within the World System frame (see Appadurai 1996; Fitzpatrick 1980, 1983; Gregory 1982, 1997; Sahlins 1988, 1992, and 1993), in this monograph I invert the centre/periphery model by recentring the actors and institutions under study, moving them from the periphery of the modern World System, to the centre of both specific attention, and explanatory relevance. In a manner reminiscent of the actions of the inhabitants of the islands themselves, I seek to understand the contemporary situation by starting on Ha'ano and working outward. Though peripheral geographically, politically, and economically in terms of the global systems, Ha'ano can be seen as the centre of another, uniquely Tongan system.

This system, like the larger overarching World System, is a product of history. In the analysis of historical events and processes which follows, it becomes clear that the manner in which Tongans are integrated into the World System comes directly from social relationships mediated through longstanding (one might even say "traditional") social and religious institutions. Behaviours within these institutions, which are linked to the flow of people off the island and economic resources onto the island, are themselves supported by an ideological system contrary to capitalist notions of rationality. Yet both the ideological system and social institutions effectively allow people to access overseas resources. Tongan villagers not only have a clear idea about how to garner overseas resources but ample evidence that their intentions can be realized. While the current system of migration and overseas remittances many not be sustainable over the long term, it is clear that Tongan values and intentions are effectively served by the system in the short term, and thus that local agency can be realized, rather than suppressed and remade, in the context of world markets.

There is no question that Tonga (as a nation) and Tongans (as individuals) operate within wider global and regional economic systems, but there is much to be said about exactly how people like Vake operate within these systems. Viewed from the village, what is notable is not the power and intrusiveness of global markets and capitalist relations of production but the provisionality of these forces.

Market-oriented production and labour migration provide important material inputs in the village economy, but the way that material, money, and people flow into and out of the village is governed as much by the practice of the traditional gift exchange system as it is by global or regional markets. In both material and ideological terms, the ramifications of the gift economy on the lives of villagers are direct, immediate, and ubiquitous; the World System and the demands of commodity markets are, in the first instance at least, peripheral. For the most part the people of Ha'ano Island articulate with markets at arm's-length. Market structures have relatively little direct impact on the relationships between people within the village, and relatively little direct effect on the relationships between people located in the village and their kin living elsewhere in Tonga, or elsewhere in the world.

Although gifts, not commodities, form the basis of exchange relationships between people, changes in the structure of Tonga's economy have transformed the context, meaning, and results of the gifts emanating from and filtering back to Ha'ano Island. The gift economy is integral to the continuity of traditional social organization and culture, *and* to the participation of households and individuals in the structures and institutions of the modern nation state and global markets. While wider economic structures and processes are important, the actions of Tongan villagers must be viewed in their own terms if we are to understand how it is that they affect, and are affected by, the integration of Tonga into the global economic system. Tongan villagers are linked to the World System and capitalist development by their commitment to, and use of, a uniquely Tongan gift exchange system, and not, or at least not yet, by the erosion or destruction of that system by the introduction of capitalism or capitalist relations of production. This commitment motivates and shapes the decisions villagers make about how and when they participate in the wider economy. The most telling means of integration into the regional economy today is through migration, but the action of migration and the values and intentions expressed in the decision to migrate are, once again, specifically Tongan.

In the language of one stream of development studies, the people of Ha'ano Island are "uncaptured peasants" (Hyden 1980). At the level of day-to-day subsistence, the households on the island can and do refuse, limit, and choose to participate in commodity exchange of various types; these choices are not dictated by global markets. The relative autonomy of villagers means that their actions and decisions are not easily explicable as a product of the World System. In order to understand exactly how it is that people's lives are constituted, we must look to local level processes, politics, and economics, albeit in the context of wider, but not determinate, structures.

Although the Tongan situation is in some ways unique, in others it is directly comparable to other Pacific microstates, and indeed significant portions of the rest of the world. Dealing with and within the modern World System is a problem we all face in one way or another. What follows is a description of one solution. Limited and provisional as this solution may be, it is one developed by people acting in their own terms, in pursuit of their own values, and for the people they care about both in the village, and across the globe.

Where Does Autonomy Come From, and Where Does It Go?

Part of the problem, identified by Sahlins earlier, is how we are to recognize and account for the impact of the World System while at the same time ensuring that not all local actions are reduced to the simple and inevitable results of this system. Tonga has long been embedded in regional political economic structures and, for some centuries now, the wider system that grew from European colonial efforts (see Bollard 1974; Sahlins 1988). To understand the current context it is vital to know something about the history of Tongan articulations within the emerging World System, and to trace the development of the Tongan social system from the precontact polity, through the institution of the modern Tongan state, and the integration of Tonga into world markets through the production of cash crops and labour migration. Some authors, notably Gailey (1980, 1981, 1985, 1987), have argued that the transformative effects of capitalism and the World System were felt very early on, and that Tongan society was fundamentally remade to the benefit of external powers. Others (for example Cowling 1990a, 1990b; James 1993a, 1995), though with some cautions against the rather radical reading of historical material promoted by Gailey (see especially James 1988), suggest that contemporary Tongan society is gradually being transformed into one dominated by capitalism and its institutions. While there is no question that profound transformations have occurred (Marcus 1977, 1980), there is much to say about the directions and sources of these transformations.

A variety of institutions worked to introduce limited amounts of cash into the Tongan economy, but did not fundamentally alter the way social relationships were constructed. Rather, cash became a medium for some types of gift exchange, and part of a more extensive and elaborate system of exchange. The original polity, an almost prototypical Polynesian chiefdom, altered under new political conditions. Old kinship structures, once the template linking chiefly and non-chiefly people, gradually eroded, to be replaced by increasingly fluid, and apparently nucleated configurations of close, cooperating, but isolated households. However, Tongan households are not isolated, but rather have forged relationships that now span the globe. They form these relationships as they always have, through gift exchanges that reproduce not only their social groups, but Tongan culture itself. The appearance of atomization, nucleation, and isolation, is just that, an appearance. The autonomy of Tongan villages and villagers described in the following pages is generated from a particular historical context that has allowed the extension of kinship and sociality from the village outward, and not its elimination or suppression by the ideology of capitalism and individual gain.

It is, however, possible to obscure rather than elucidate the relationship between what individuals choose to do within the village, and the village-level effects of the integration of the Tongan nation and national economy with global markets and international politics. Like many of the economies of the microstates of the Pacific, the Tongan situation is more or less described by the so-called MIRAB model (see Bertram and Watters 1985). This model is a description of an emerging pattern widespread in the Pacific, in which much of the cash economy is derived from MIgration and associated Remittances, international Aid donations, and the waged employment generated by the use of aid and remittance monies in government Bureaucracies.[1] In Tonga, as elsewhere in the Pacific, there is also an intact and vital traditional economy, consisting of both subsistence production and indigenously manufactured exchange goods.

The structure of the national economy today has several implications for people on outer islands like Ha'ano. The most striking of these is the concentration of resources (Sevele 1973) and (subsequently) people in the capital, Nuku'alofa, and its environs (Walsh 1970), and a corresponding depopulation of the outer islands as people move to the centre in search of education, jobs, and access to modern conveniences (Cowling 1990a). Migration to New Zealand, Australia, and the United States has also drained people away from Tonga as a whole.

Associated with this shift in population is an emphasis within the village on acquiring the means to participate in the opportunities available in the capital and beyond, specifically by providing educational opportunities for children. Many see education as the means to migration, both internal and external. The education of children requires cash, but it is a way of acquiring cash as well. However, that cash is valued primarily for its utility within the traditional exchange system. Furthermore, the costs of educating children are often borne through reciprocal ties created and maintained within the traditional exchange system.

At the same time, out-migration has created such a labour shortage within the village that for most households many alternative sources of cash (such as cash cropping or fishing) are difficult to access, even given what limited market opportunities do exist. Data collected from households on the island make it plain that wealth differentiation is a result of a Chayanovian cycle[2] in which a household's out-migrating children play a major role. These wealth differences are enacted through the traditional exchange system, and are clearly evident to all. Thus, in spite of people's recognition that out-migration has resulted in negative effects through depopulation, the utility of migration in providing material for gift exchanges continues to support decisions to leave the island. This is a direct result of the articulation of Tongan social organization and values with the wider regional economy.

For villagers on Ha'ano Island, their participation in the World System presents a serious paradox. The decisions people make are rooted in a distinctively Tongan cultural frame, based in and around traditional notions of appropriate social relations. While people's intentions and actions are only explicable in terms of their culture (Gregory 1982; Sahlins 1988), the ultimate results of these decisions may well be the erosion of the social and material basis of the relative autonomy that facilitates the long-term cultural reproduction. This book then is partly about a paradox. The villagers I describe have succeeded in forging their own way within the World System, and they have done so as agents rather than victims. But there are problems, limitations, and potentially disruptive side-effects to this success. Though people may well make decisions on the basis of cultural autonomy, these selfsame decisions may well result in a kind of undoing of their independence at the same time.

A Note on the Use of the Term "Tongan"

Throughout this book I use the word "Tongan," and implicitly typify Tongans as a result. As in any and all societies a great deal of variation in the attitudes and actions of individuals exists in Tonga. Furthermore the island of Ha'ano, its residents, and their lives are probably significantly different in some ways from other Tongans in other places and other contexts. Throughout our stay in Tonga we[3] were often told that Ha'apai people were different, more traditional, less concerned with money, than people in Tongatapu. People on Ha'ano Island would often lament the loss of culture and tradition occurring in and around the capital Nuku'alofa.

By far the bulk of the social science literature on Tonga is written from data collected in Tongatapu, the largest island in the group and the location of the capital and most infrastructural development; to a lesser extent the Vava'u region, the main northern region, is covered in the literature. Ha'apai, a collection of much smaller islands located between Tongatapu and Vava'u, and much more difficult to reach, is regularly ignored. Yet the people of Ha'apai are as much Tongan as those of Tongatapu or Vava'u. Representations of Tonga rarely admit the possibility of significant cultural variation from region to region, and thus Tongatapu is taken (usually by virtue of the lack of explicit recognition of difference or the possibility of difference) to be typical of all Tonga. This it is assuredly not. There are huge differences in the material realities faced by Tongans in the various regions; this is of course the most easily discernable difference, and frequently commented upon, if not dealt with systematically. I am rather more concerned with the variations between regions (and for that matter islands and villages) due to history and that most tangible of intangibles, culture.

The tendency of ethnologists working in Polynesia to assume connection and similarity, as opposed to the narrative of difference and discontinuity found in Melanesian ethnology, has been noted (Huntsman 1995; Thomas 1989). Here I simply point out the assumptions of sameness within the Kingdom of Tonga which are played out in much of the literature. I have no intention of trying to suggest a systematic challenge to these assumptions; I wish only to note that I hold the question open, and highlight that in this monograph, much of what is taken to be Tongan is based on intensive knowledge and experience of one island. My usage of the term Tongan, then, must be understood to be a construction rooted in a limited experience of Tonga, and thus it is a provisional representation.

The use of the term Tongan is further complicated by the ranked statuses which made up Tongan society in the past, and continue, albeit in a transformed manner, to order Tongan culture and society today. Tonga is commonly referred to as an example of a Polynesian society with decidedly hierarchical tendencies. Modern Tongan culture is normally conceived of as one stratified into three categories: the royal family, nobles, and commoners. The prerogatives of the first two categories are enshrined in law, and additional privileges are commonly observed according to custom. The social practices of commoners, although based on the same principles as the practices of the two higher strata, differ significantly on the ground (Decktor-Korn 1974, 1975; Kaeppler 1971, 1978). On Ha'ano Island, there are no nobles or royalty in residence, although there are a number of people who act as *hou'eiki* (high or chiefly people) in a variety of circumstances. The practice of the Tongan ranking system within the village is explored more fully later in the book; here it is sufficient to note that all of the data and conclusions presented are drawn from a population of commoners.

Where Does Data Come From, and Where Does It Go?

The major vehicle I use to examine and situate Ha'ano Island within the world is the village economy. During my fieldwork I collected a wide variety of microeconomic data which provides an empirical, if partial, picture of the structure of exchange and production on Ha'ano Island. This data is presented explicitly. The overt presentation of my empirical data is not accidental.

While there is no doubt that issues of power and control over the representation and interpretation of "reality" in contemporary anthropology are pertinent and even pressing (Clifford 1988; Said 1978), any interpretation can only occur in relationship to some empirical base (O'Meara 1989). All interpretation is, of course, positioned socially and politically, but it is also positioned empirically. How an interpretation is constructed in relation to some sort of accounting of the ground is at least as important as the theoretical or political orientation from which it comes. I do not mean to separate the processes of investigation from interpretation here (clearly there is, or at least should be, an hermeneutic relationship at work), but I do mean to suggest that anthropological analysis must admit the possibility that error might be exposed through empirical investigation.

My concern over the relationship of interpretation to empirical accounting is not simply the result of an academic debate. At a few junctures in this monograph I offer critiques of some of the literature written on Tonga, based largely on empirical grounds. While we might well accept the widely held notion that no interpretation, no matter how grounded in data, is "true" in a complete or final way, this does not require that all interpretation is thus even partially true. Some commonly held and repeated "truths" about Tonga or parts of Tonga are simply *not true*.

Conversely, I offer the data as a clear and contestable basis from which my own claims are made, and from which critique can be generated. A thorough account of the empirical data is also justified in the interests of comparison. It is my hope that when the theoretical issues which motivate and inform this work are revised and reworked in the future, the empirical data contained within will be of continuing use to those interested in Tonga and Tongan economic history.

All of the direct data collection was undertaken in the villages of Ha'ano Island. Thus most of the strongest claims put forth here are based on a village centred view. At the outset, however, it is necessary to note that, unlike other Polynesian societies (for instance Samoa), the village in Tonga is *not* a particularly meaningful social unit (see Decktor-Korn 1977). The village is, however, a major geographical forum in which individuals and other culturally significant social units interact and overlap. The village is a particularly intense locus of interaction for all persons, if for no other reason than the constant opportunities for reciprocity, cooperation, and competition present within the village in the course of daily life.

In addition to this microeconomic data (which was collected through directed interviews, surveys, and investigation of government records and registries), I also collected data of a more general nature through participant observation. The knowledge gained through some nineteen months of church attendance, kava drinking, formal ritual participation as a *matāpule*,[4] and the day-to-day processes of living in the village are crucial to understanding the village economy. Knowledge gained in this way, and from a wide reading of pertinent literature, is the foundation for contextualizing and interpreting the material gathered in survey form.

This sort of background is crucial for both data collection and any subsequent interpretation of Tongan social practices. One of the surveys I employed during my stay on Ha'ano Island was a long-term fishing harvest survey involving the villages of Ha'ano and Pukotala; in the end I completed the survey in only Ha'ano village. In part this was simply a function of time constraints. I also found, however, that the quality of the data collected was directly related to the social and geographical distance between myself and the respondents.

My attempt to carry out the survey in Pukotala was unsuccessful because I found that too much of the data reflected people's sense of humour rather than their harvests. There was, in my experience, a direct relationship between the social relationships of researcher and subjects, and the accuracy of the data collected.

My family and I were residents of Ha'ano, attended church and other social events, and maintained several cross-cutting reciprocal relationships with people in the village. While we did have personal ties to others in other villages, these ties were not as thick as those in Ha'ano. The quantitative data collected in the surveys I conducted do not qualify as "thick description" (Geertz 1973), but the nature of Tongan social relations is such that any description, whether qualitative or quantitative, must depend on thick personal connections for accuracy (Evans and Young Leslie 1995; see also Korn and Decktor-Korn 1983).

Information from the general surveys was cross-checked in a variety of ways, and while I am quite suspicious of the fish harvest data collected in the village in which I was not resident, I am relatively confident about the accuracy of the other data collected there and from the other two villages. Perhaps fish stories in Tonga, as elsewhere, are particularly prone to exaggeration.

Chapter Two

Economic Development in Polynesia

The history of Tongan interaction with the colonizing powers of the West was characterized by a degree of self-imposed isolation and a Tonganization of the structures and institutions offered by the West (see Marcus 1980, 1981). During the period of decolonization, however, the isolation of Tonga largely disappeared. While Tonga's history is unique, the patterns of the Tongan economy over the last twenty-five to thirty years have come to resemble many other of the small island nations of the Pacific, and thus a general introductory discussion of economic development in the Pacific, and more specifically Polynesia, is in order.

The term "development" is itself a contested one, and I use it here with caution. The assumptions embedded in development theory and practice have been discussed in considerable depth by Escobar (1995). Escobar shows convincingly that "development" underlies the creation of the Third World as an object of investigation and for transformation by Western interests. Remarkably resistant to critique, the notion of development contains within it the assumptions that there is one basic path to achieving a developed economy, and that this path is not only to be encouraged, but is inevitable as well. I understand the term development (and its usage in the general literature) to refer to processes which result in an increase in levels of market participation, capital investment, and

---

Notes to chapter 2 start on p. 175.

productive activity in the pursuit of national economic growth. Of all the possible trajectories of change, this is a very specific one, and one shaped by Western assumptions about not only what is desirable, but rational. Given this, the pursuit of other, perhaps contradictory, goals by peoples undergoing development are frequently considered the result of tradition-bound institutions and inherently irrational. Others have shown that this is not the case (see Gudeman 1992; Gudeman and Rivera 1990; Gregory 1982, 1997), and that the actions of Indian or Columbian small farmers (for instance) are clearly rational, but not based on the same model as development practitioners.

Nonetheless, a recurring concern in the literature on development in Polynesia (as elsewhere) has been the role of traditional social practices and institutions in the relative success or failure of development generally, and various development initiatives specifically. In Polynesia, work centred on Samoa (previously Western Samoa) has been among the most important in this debate.

Early authors working in Samoa, notably Pitt (1970) and Lockwood (1971), reach generally similar results from studies focussing on rather different phenomena. Lockwood's work is an attempt to empirically test Fisk's (1962, 1964 cited in Lockwood 1971) general propositions about the transition of "primitive" economies in articulation with markets. Briefly, Fisk's thesis is that the level of development (read market participation) will vary according to the incentives operating on producers; market linkage is held to be of primary importance. Lockwood finds that this thesis holds for the Samoa of the 1960s. He finds a rank order of market participation, substitution of modern for traditional goods, and participation in the cash nexus between four villages according to their ease of access to markets. The variation between villages was not great however; in all villages he finds high levels of unexploited land and labour (Lockwood 1971, 206). For Lockwood, although Fisk's thesis is supported, it seems that cultural factors may be more important than market access in limiting the demand for modern goods and services in rural Samoa. He finds that traditional exchange, land tenure and leadership patterns are disincentives to market participation and economic development.

In the most general of terms Lockwood suggests that rural Samoans "have little interest in the outside world which intrudes on them in the form of the market sector. They likewise have little evident concern for the future, little interest in productive investment, little willingness to 'develop'" (ibid., 206). Specifically, Lockwood finds that because of the strong link between specific lands and the *matai* titles (traditional leadership positions) which control usufruct rights to those lands, there is little incentive to bring lands into production when the transmission of title cannot be guaranteed from father to son or son-in-law.[1] The demands of the traditional exchange system to distribute material wealth through gift giving and ceremonial exchanges constrain both the desire and ability of people to accumulate both capital and productive resources. The real incentive to productive activity, both traditional and modern, says Lockwood, is effective participation in *fa'aSamoa* or the "Samoan way of life." Access to cash income is important insofar as this cash is useful in acquiring *matai* titles, via participation in the ceremonial distributions that mark a successful Samoan person.

Pitt (1970) comes to very similar conclusions. Although he sees land tenure patterns and traditional leadership structures as well able to adapt to the demands of cash cropping rather than the reverse, he too suggests that the lack of interest shown by rural Samoans in the expansion of market activity is a direct function of culturally derived limits. For Pitt, while Samoans may well be interested in increasing production in order to acquire Western goods, the reasons are again linked to their wish to be successful in terms of *fa'aSamoa*. The intent is to participate in, rather than fundamentally change, the Samoan way of life.

Shankman (1976) offers an evaluation of development in Samoa based on economic criteria that directly contradicts those of Pitt and Lockwood. He suggests that the heavy streams of migration from Samoa and other Polynesian nations must be understood as economically driven responses to the underdeveloped state of their economies. Overseas migration exacerbates this underdevelopment by draining labour resources from rural areas to finance consumption patterns while doing little to increase levels of productive activity in Samoa itself.[2]

If, Shankman argues, rural Samoans are so enamoured of *fa'aSamoa* and life in Samoa, why do they leave Samoa with such regularity? The level of overseas migration indicates Samoans' "very real concern . . . about their future and a sound appraisal of the results of their own efforts in an underdeveloped economy" (ibid., 102), not an enduring satisfaction with an idyllic South Pacific lifestyle. Using the "development of underdevelopment" (or dependency theory) approach pioneered by Andre Gunder Frank (1967), Shankman is explicitly changing the focus of economic studies of Samoa away from Samoan culture to Samoa's position in a wider regional economy. Migration in this view is a rational economic response to the relative rewards offered by various economic activities; Samoans migrate to wage labouring opportunities because they pay more than cash cropping (ibid., 100).

The result is an increase in remittances which underwrites consumption, but a series of negative effects also occurs which ensures the continuing underdevelopment of Samoa. The drain of labour away from rural areas causes a rise in dependency ratios and a decline in export earnings for the nation as rural people turn toward subsistence activities rather than cash cropping[3] (see also Connell 1986, 47). This inhibits the nation's self-reliance and can cause a serious balance of payment problem for the state. Migration stunts the growth of the indigenous economy and creates a dependency on labour receiving areas which seriously threatens the long-term health of the Samoan economy. Migration, in Shankman's opinion, is both the result of underdevelopment, and a cause of continuing underdevelopment.

O'Meara (1990) takes up this sort of argument with reference to cash cropping in Samoa. Shankman (1976, 75-6) notes that reliance on remittances as a major source of income has no impact on the response of cash cropping to price incentives or interest in new crops; even those families receiving substantial portions of their income from remittances respond enthusiastically to new agricultural opportunities. O'Meara offers an extended argument which also emphasizes that cash cropping activity is sensitive to price incentives generally rather than tied to particular goals (cf. Fairbairn 1985, 304). Using data gathered from a microeconomic survey, he shows that agricultural activity nets considerably less per day than wage labour. Due to the need for cash and the scarcity of wage labour, Samoans must continue to turn to coconut and copra production. The levels of production are tied directly to the levels of return. The problem is that the levels of return are very low and diminish with the intensification of labour (1990, 189-92). O'Meara writes:

> Instead of finding a "pathetic" response to economic incentives . . . the evidence shows a reasonable response to pathetic incentives. The villagers' response has been to direct their search for money away from their plantations and toward local wage labour, business, and overseas migration, where they see better economic incentives. (Ibid., 192)

The levels of agricultural development then are tied to poor commodity prices rather than cultural conservatism. Indeed, cultural conservatism in the form of sharing, gift giving, and ceremonial exchange is a response to scarce cash rather than the cause (ibid., 193-216).

The arguments of Shankman and O'Meara clearly put to rest earlier broad statements regarding the cultural causes of a lack of development in Samoa, but to a certain extent they also beg the question. Such arguments show clearly that economic rationality rather than traditionally based recalcitrance explains the actions of rural Samoans. But, regardless of why Samoans distribute remittances, wages, and cash from wage labour, the fact remains that substantial pools for capital investment are generally not realized. Remittances from overseas do not generally go into investments in productive inputs, mechanization, or the like (cf. Brown 1994). The point here is not to blame rural Samoans for not pursuing capital accumulation or for not engaging in intense self-exploitation in their copra plantations, but to recognize that generally they do not.

This is not to suggest that Samoan culture actively inhibits innovation or investment by enterprising Samoans, rather that it encompasses such activity. Macpherson (1988) suggests that Samoan village society is "neutral" regarding agricultural change and investments in business activity. He describes the activities of a number of individuals who were able to invest capital in productive equipment, like chainsaws, and create profitable business enterprises as a result. In the cases analyzed, the individuals involved did not suffer interference or censure for their activities, nor did they face intense financial demands for gifts or contributions to disperse their working capital. All, however, continued to participate in redistributive activities. Eventually all the individuals involved were granted *matai* titles[4] and began to spend more time on politics and community affairs than business. According to Macpherson:

> The difficulty for those who seek to increase production in the [agricultural] sector on a permanent basis to attain national economic and political goals may not be in finding entrepreneurial villagers to adopt innovations that improve productivity, but in persuading the same people to maintain productivity after the innovations have served their aspirations. (Ibid., 19)

Like it or not, we are back to Samoan culture as a limiting factor in agricultural development. There is, I think, a very simple reason for this. For village planters, agricultural production is not about sustained export growth, it is about the continuing viability of Samoan village life and their place within it. Individual villagers attend ceremonies, give speeches, or work occasionally in wage labour because they want to, and because they can. They are relatively autonomous.[5] Given that access to the means of production is not definitively structured by market relations, material necessity cannot compel villagers to sacrifice either their cultural or economic autonomy.[6] Like the Ni-Vanuatu described by M. Rodman (1987), self-reliance for villagers is rather a different thing than self-reliance for the state. If we return to Shankman's treatment of the economic factors causing underdevelopment with this in mind, it seems clear that migration is, at least in the short term, rather more a problem for the state than for the families receiving remittances. Migration is an economic practice which leads to underdevelopment because remittances allow villagers receiving them to refrain from the intensive self-exploitation in agricultural activity, and still participate effectively in Samoan life. It is quite an assumption that given the "rationality" of balanced import-export levels, villagers should or would prefer increased agricultural growth no matter what the cost to traditional social activity and the quality of their lives.

MIRAB Economies in Polynesia

In their article "The MIRAB Economy in South Pacific Microstates," Bertram and Watters (1985) put forth the thesis that the processes of economic change in several Pacific nations have operated in a manner which has suppressed agricultural intensification. When viewed from the perspective of those who would promote development, this result is decidedly negative. This situation, according to Ogden (1989), is due to a paradox of development in the Pacific. Given the range of choices available to Islanders, actions and strategies that might lead to increasing capital investment and export growth are rationally precluded, rather than embraced. Regardless of the model of economic decision making embedded in the concept of development, the structure of the economy, and the model of economic behaviour ordering people's actions lead to very different, though still rational results. As in Samoa, overseas migration and remittances, foreign aid, and the growth of government administration have provided other, more economically attractive, alternatives to agricultural growth in spite of the fact that the rationale for aid and administration remains "development" in the classic sense. The postwar flows of "rents" from remittances and aid "entitlement" have created the conditions for increased consumption levels in spite of a lack of economic "rationalization" in the agricultural sector. Individuals operating in this context make rational decisions which do not entail persistent agricultural innovation. Bertram and Watters speculate that the levels of consumption thus achieved *could not* have been reached through agricultural growth (ibid., 510); the implication is that these levels cannot be achieved by development geared to national self-reliance either.[7] This argument is directed specifically at very small states like the Cook Islands and Niue where the number of island born people who reside outside of state boundaries is sometimes greater than the actual residents (see Bertram 1986, 813), but has since been applied to other microstates as well (see for instance Shankman 1990).

Connell writes that this situation "is viewed with concern and dismay by many in [these] countries" because it "has nothing to do with self-reliance" (1986, 49). Bertram and Watters (1985) suggest that the situation is not reversible via agricultural development and rather than fitful and frustrating efforts to achieve this, policy makers should turn toward ensuring economic stability (ibid., 515-16; see also Ogden 1989, 371). Connell's position comes from his work as the primary investigator of a large South Pacific Commission-International Labour Organization study of migration in the Pacific. The policy recommendations of this study directly contradict those of Bertram and Watters (see Hayes 1991). Like Shankman, Connell is working from a dependency theory perspective, which suggests that the economies of the South Pacific are shaped, indeed misshaped, by the wider regional economy. Migration in this view simply transfers human resources to the central economies in the region (especially Australia and New Zealand), leaving the sending nations bereft of the capacity for growth (i.e., development). A key problem with this position, though, is the focus on the nation state as the frame of reference. Those working within a MIRAB perspective still tend to recognize the nation state as important, but also look to ties between nations, including those mediated by people outside of official state sanctioned channels as significant.

The place of kinship and social ties in MIRAB economies is central. It is important to note that the stability of the situation is dependent on remittances and aid. The flow of remittances is ensured in MIRAB economies by the continuity of the stream of migrants, and by the long-term strength of ties between migrants and their remaining kin. Indeed Campbell (1992) argues that in Tonga, remittances are more significant in terms of economic stability than foreign aid. Transnational kin ties knit migrants to their homelands in a variety of ways (see Marcus 1981). Continuing connections between migrants and their kin located within sending communities are framed within a common understanding of Tongan culture, and ensure continuing emotional ties, even where the intent to return permanently is lacking (Macpherson 1985). For the most part it seems that migrants from Polynesia do not disappear into receiving societies even when the migration patterns are not circular (Ahlburg 1991; Brown 1994, 1996, 1998). Migration is linked to cultural continuity to the extent that the kin groups are (Bertram and Watters 1985, 499), because migration helps maintain traditional social life in which the kin groups are embedded. Social practices understood in traditional terms are thus both the motivation and beneficiary of migration.

The causes of the lack of development in MIRAB economies, including Samoa, are at once cultural and economic. The levels of migration and foreign aid common to many Polynesian nations have created an economic situation in which economic rationality reckoned at the level of villages and villagers dictates that agricultural intensification is only one (generally poor) economic option. There is, I think, little doubt that cultural factors do impede development in the classic sense; but on the other hand the vitality of traditional culture is linked to the active and effective maintenance of ties between people dispersed by migration, and these ties are paths through which remittances flow. There is no need here to redefine development, simply to revalue it. Indeed it is necessary to recognize that when rural producers are willing and able to combine subsistence production, limited market production, and overseas remittances to meet their material and social desires, economic development is not enhanced. Given the sheer practical limitations to sustained agricultural intensification which bear on almost all of Polynesia to one degree or another, it is doubtful that current consumption levels could be met by any enforced program of national self-reliance (see also Stevens and Evans 1999). With this in mind, it is also doubtful that the destruction of traditional culture in the interests of development would serve any practical or economic purpose.

If development processes are viewed from the perspective of rural Polynesians, economic and cultural factors *cannot be separated*. The reasons people choose one or another economic option, and how they go about exploiting their opportunities, are inherently connected to their aspirations; that these aspirations are culturally constructed is an anthropological truism. As long as aid and migration continue to be viable sources of income, the likelihood that villagers will choose to intensify agriculture is limited by both economic and cultural factors.

The way that Tongan villagers view migration derives from a very specific analysis of the economic structures with which they interact. The MIRAB model is interesting partly because it leaves room to try to understand how it is that Tongan strategies and sensibilities have shaped the system. People choose to encourage their children to migrate overseas or seek employment in the bureaucracy rather than develop plantations or fishing enterprises; these decisions both shape and are shaped by the economic and political context in which they live. Perhaps even more important are the decisions that people make about consumption, especially the tendency to direct resources to social reproduction rather than capital accumulation and investment. *The pattern described by the acronym MIRAB is indeed the result of development ideology, market structures, and the like, but it is also the result of the purposive actions (i.e., agency) of Tongans and other Pacific Islanders.* The bulk of the rest of this work is in fact devoted to understanding this agency through a very specific treatment of the actions and intentions of the people of Ha'ano Island. Before moving on to this substantive work, however, it is necessary to clarify another aspect of the theoretical framework I employ; that is, just what is a "gift"?

Gifts and Commodities

"Gift and Commodity," is the central conceptual dyad I employ to explicate the manner in which the people of Ha'ano Island have experienced development. The current interest in and usage of these terms derive from the work of Mauss and Marx. The distinction between gift and commodity is found in the exchange context, and is a product of the recognition or denial of an ongoing social relationship between the transactors. A gift, or an object exchanged in which the value of the object is based on, and part of, the social relationship between the transactors, can be transformed into a commodity by simply exchanging the object in a context which eliminates the relationships between transactors.

For Mauss "the gift" was totalizing. Referring to the Polynesian "institution of 'total services'" (1990, 13), he writes:

> All these institutions [of exchange] express one fact alone, one social system, one precise state of mind: everything — food, women, children, property, talismans, land, labour services, priestly functions, and ranks — is there for passing on, and for balancing accounts. Everything passes to and fro as if there were a constant exchange of a spiritual matter, including things and men, between clans and individuals, distributed between social ranks, the sexes, and the generations. (Ibid., 14)

In Mauss' view the transactors in these exchanges were groups, not individuals (ibid., 5). "Contractual gifts" were to some degree contracts which not only related groups, but constituted them; that is, the structure and ideology of gift exchange and the society in which they occurred were reciprocally constructed in the processes of exchange.

In a similar manner Marx viewed the commodity form as both totalizing and ideological.[8] Marx saw commodity exchange and capitalist production as intrinsically linked within the capitalist mode of production. Producers are systematically and ideologically separated (alienated) from their products by the ideological construction of exchange[9] as a depersonalized process occurring between things, thus fetishizing the commodity. Commodity fetishism refers to the appearance within market exchange that value is a function of the equivalence of goods. A good exchanged for another,[10] or a certain quantity of money, is valued in and of itself rather than in and of the labour subsumed within the good. A commodity transaction denies the relationship between the transactors (and producers), and thus fetishizes the commodity or good, creating a situation in which "relationships between people masquerade as relations between things" (Parry and Bloch 1989, 7). Gift exchange, by contrast, is all about the relationship between the transactors, whether hierarchical or egalitarian, and rather than denying a social relationship between the transactors (either individuals or groups), it expresses that relationship.

While it is easy to overdraw the differences between capitalist and non-capitalist societies on the basis of the gift/commodity dichotomy (Appadurai 1986),[11] it is also easy to minimize the distinction between gifts and commodities by assuming that the encapsulation of a society within the World System, a system dominated and ordered by the capitalist mode of production and commodity exchange, necessarily results in the transformation of a society to meet the demands of the system.

The distinction between gifts and commodities, and the importance of that distinction in Papua New Guinea (PNG), is well developed in Gregory's 1982 monograph *Gifts and Commodities*. Gregory's intent is to develop a political economy approach from which the nature of the emerging relationship between gift exchange and commodity exchange in PNG can be conceptualized. Specifically, he attempts to rectify the assumptions of modernization theory about the nature of the transformation from traditional to modern economies. He writes, "the problem to be explained in PNG is not the demise of the 'traditional' sector and the rise of the 'modern' sector but rather the simultaneous rise of both commodity production and gift production" (ibid., 115). This requires the specific treatment of the processes through which productive inputs (land, labour, and capital) are acquired by production units. In societies engaged in simple commodity production (SCP), these inputs can be garnered *either* as gifts *or* as commodities. How resources are acquired has everything to do with *both* gift exchange and commodity production.

The term SCP, as it is used here, is an analytical category of productive forms, distinct from, yet operating within, a capitalist mode of production (see Friedmann 1978, 1980; C. Smith 1984; G. Smith 1986). Where capitalist production uses commodities (land, labour, and capital) to produce commodities, SCP relies on non-commoditized productive resources to produce goods (commodities) for the capitalist market, and goods (gifts) for traditional exchange. A fully capitalized form of production is one which relies solely on commoditized inputs in the productive process. While the reproduction of a SCP form relies on the market for certain inputs acquired through commodity exchange, the extent of dependence on markets may vary greatly. SCP usually implies that some degree of subsistence production still occurs.[12] The "competitive edge" for simple commodity producers is their access to sources of productive inputs which are outside of market conditions (G. Smith 1986). Access to such non-commoditized resources is dependent on social ties between people.

The incursion of capitalism into tribal or peasant economies over the last few centuries has, through the conversion of social relationships to their commodity equivalents, transformed many of these societies. The adoption of capitalist relations of production by tribal peoples is problematic because of the denial of felt social ties that this requires. The commoditization of social relationships that capitalist relations of production entail is antithetical (at an ideological level) to gift economies and those engaged in gift economies (Comaroff 1985; Taussig 1980). SCP on the other hand, entails the intensification of social ties because these ties facilitate production through the provision of gifts of labour, land, or cash. Various authors (notably Meillassoux 1981; Wolpe 1975) would argue that it is capital which, for its own purposes, preserves non-capitalist modes of production in the process of capitalist expansion, but such a position strips agency from all but capital itself (Fitzpatrick 1980, 1983).

SCP is a productive form which, while dependent on markets for its reproduction, is not a product of markets. The character of relationships within the form is a function of *both* internal dynamics and the market conditions which it faces (C. Smith 1984). Social relationships within SCP have the potential to effervesce, because social ties, maintained by the gift economy, are essential, and thus exploited and intensified by individuals within communities engaged in SCP (G. Smith 1986). In this sense it is *because* the intensification of the gift economy is an asset in commodity production, that gift and commodity production may flourish at the same time, *but the reverse may also be true*; commodity production is embraced because it facilitates gift exchange.

The development and use of the concept of SCP has been largely restricted to people severely challenged by historical circumstances in which colonialism and neocolonialism have resulted in the commoditization of significant aspects of their lives. The use of non-commoditized social relations is one way that such people can continue to survive in a political economy otherwise dominated by capitalism. In many areas of the Pacific however, where capitalism is experienced primarily as market relationships (not as capitalist social relations of production), people may operate in a SCP form but in ways determined primarily by historically specific and locally controlled circumstance. Linkages between markets and social dynamics may have more to do with prestige than survival.

Material wealth, its acquisition and its distribution, has both ideological and material significance. For the people orchestrating the linkages between the gift and commodity spheres, both material well-being and personal prestige are intertwined. Examples drawn from the Highlands of New Guinea helps to illustrate the tensions involved. For instance, when describing the growth of indigenous *bisnis* (business) and entrepreneurial activity in the Goroka area, Finney writes:

> Where an entrepreneur has relied heavily on labour contributions or pooled money to get his start, he must pay attention to two levels of management. On the one hand, he has to operate or direct the operation of his coffee plantation and whatever other enterprises he owns. On the other hand, he must keep his following of contributors and other supporters in hand by means of direct cash payments and gifts and by seeing they share in the prestige associated with his commercial activities. Because of this dual allegiance there is a danger that if a man pays too much attention to the management of his enterprises and to his bank balance, he may neglect to reward his followers sufficiently, or, conversely, that if he devotes most of his time to keeping his followers happy, then his enterprises and financial position are apt to run down. Either way a man stands to lose — by financial failure, or by the loss of his following. (1973, 173)

This need for balance is also expressed by Warry in reference to Chuave *bisnisman* (1987, 139-44). Warry suggests that businessmen in Chuave who are able to gain prestige as well as wealth in the course of their careers are those with the ability to manage the tensions between the demands of business and the demands of kin until the business interests produce enough revenue to satisfy both. In Chuave few are able to achieve the necessary balance. In both Goroka and Chuave, those involved in *bisnis* run the risk of losing prestige by not paying enough attention to redistribution of wealth, and the prestige of the group in relation to their personal status. This prestige is tied to community values, and derived from relationships within the community. The loss of prestige, for whatever reason, thus has both political and economic consequences.

Gift Exchange in Village Tonga

The situation on Ha'ano Island in the early 1990s is slightly different from those described by either Finney or Warry. The manner in which Tongan villagers have integrated into the regional economy alone has, to a certain degree, suppressed direct commodity production on the island. Nonetheless the model suggested by those working with the concept of SCP is still applicable. People do have particular cash requirements, and they do consume a limited amount of goods accessible only as commodities. The vast majority of cash and commodities is however, destined for, or processed through, gift exchange. Furthermore, the vast bulk of production is accomplished with noncommoditized sources of land, labour, and capital.

Since the colonial period, and increasingly since the 1960s, development processes have shaped Tongan social life, but so too has Tongan social life shaped the way that Tongans participate in regional and global economies. Sufficient material autonomy exists for people to make choices, and their choices have been in pursuit of goals explicable only in terms outside those mobilized by neo-classical economics and the ideology of development. As in the PNG examples above, personal and family prestige on Ha'ano Island are maintained and enhanced by participation in traditional and ceremonial exchange activities. "Tradition" here, is taken to refer to customary activity rather than a timelessly continuing or unchanging pattern of activities (see Shils 1971). The point here is not that Tongan society and culture have not changed, but rather that these changes are not easily read off the patterns of the World System, then or now.

The changes initiated by King Tupou I in the mid- and late nineteenth century brought about a significant shift in social organization. The introduction of Christianity in the mid-1800s also had a profound effect on both social organization and the ideological constitution of the Tongan family. The institutions of church and state promoted a subtle but significant shift of emphasis within the kinship system, which has strengthened the smaller units of social organization (the nuclear family and household), at the expense of the larger kinship groups. There has been a steady erosion of the corporateness of kinship groups in general, and the household and family groups which now form the base of the social landscape are neither corporate nor the locus of unified interests which can be played out in production or exchange.

Regardless of the changing constitution of the kinship and social system, linkages within continue to be constructed through gift exchange practices operating within a particular construction of traditional social relations. Furthermore these practices have material significance in terms of how people access the means of production. The relative autonomy of Tongan villagers in the face of the pressures of the World System is integrally linked to the maintenance of these practices. In order to understand the changes and continuities in Tongan social organization, it is necessary to place the discussion into a historical context.

Chapter Three

Social Structure and Organization during the Contact and Early Post-Contact Period

M ost analyses of pre-contact Tongan social organization are concentrated on political structures and processes among the ruling elite. Our knowledge of how political power devolved to the lower levels of the social order is scant. This monograph is primarily concerned with local-level social and political processes as they bear on the economic development of the Kingdom, and thus the lack of good historical material on the lives of the bulk of the population (the commoners or *tu'a*) is somewhat problematic. Nonetheless, below is a reconstruction of political and social change in Tonga since contact, with a particular concentration on the effects of these changes on the social lives of commoners. In the interests of both historical continuity and coherence this chapter provides a review of what is known about Tongan society of the contact and immediate post-contact period.

While the local level political and social processes of this period are somewhat obscured by the nature of Tongan historiography, I have tried to reconstruct both the vertical and horizontal linkages of the social system in the pre-contact polity. My interest is in showing how pre-contact social relationships were transformed during the contact period. It is in the expansion of horizontal linkages at the expense of vertical ones that the current gift exchange system is founded. It is crucial that this be

Notes to chapter 3 start on p. 177.

understood as a transformation rather than transmogrification of the pre-contact Tongan social organization. A central question need be the source of the pattern of change; that is, are we to understand change as patterned by autochthonous phenomena, or ideas and relationships introduced with World System linkages? The simple and obvious answer is that both indigenous and external forces played a role, but as we will see, the basic patterns of change are contiguous with a Tongan past, rather than the disruption and replacement of the cultural patterns of that past.

Ethnohistorical and Ethnographic Reconstruction: The Sources

Information on Tonga in the early contact period comes largely from explorers' accounts, the narratives of European sojourners and, from the beginning of the nineteenth century, the writings of missionaries. The best written source of information on early contact Tongan society is Mariner's 1817 (Martin 1991 [1817]) account. Mariner was a clerk on the privateer *Port au Prince*, which was captured and destroyed by the forces of the Chief Finau 'Ulukalala at Koulo in the Ha'apai region in 1806. Mariner, one of several members of the crew to survive the burning of the *Port au Prince*, was eventually adopted by 'Ulukalala, and lived some four years in Tonga. The account of his stay was elicited and compiled by the physician John Martin, and stands as the primary Western-authored source of information on early historical Tonga. George Vason (1840 [1810]) provides an account of his experiences from 1796 to 1801. A member of the first missionary landing in Tonga, he later abandoned the mission and integrated into Tongan life. His narrative is a valuable but less structured and detailed source than Mariner's.

In addition to these two works are several missionary accounts of varying quality and detail (see Lātūkefu 1974 and Urbanowicz 1973 for a thorough accounting). Unfortunately none of these early works provides much insight on the daily lives or social experiences of commoners except insofar as commoners are seen as subordinated to chiefs and their retainers. For instance, Mariner's account deals with Tongan society as a whole in considerable depth, and is by far the most exhaustive and comprehensive of these early materials, but deals with commoners or *tooa [tu'a]* as a residual category consisting of the "lowest order of all, or the bulk of the people" (Martin 1991 [1817], 293), and pays them very little direct attention.

The first professional anthropological work in the islands fell to E.W. Gifford who resided in the Kingdom for some nine months in

1920-1921 as part of the Bayard Dominick Expedition of the Bernice P. Bishop Museum.[1] While the three volumes which came out of Gifford's research (1923, 1924, 1929) are useful, the central sociological work, *Tongan Society* (1929), is a rather bizarre mixture of material from the oral histories of pre-contact Tongan society, and material drawn from Tonga of 1920-21, with some considerable confusion as to what data comes from which period.[2] It appears from Gifford's introduction (Gifford 1929, 3-4) that his purpose was to produce an ethnography of pre-Christian Tongan society.[3] Like the earlier work of Mariner and the various missionaries, Gifford's sociology of Tonga concentrates on the social organization of Tonga at the highest levels and occludes possible variation between chiefly and commoner people by virtually ignoring the commoners as a stratum.

Bott's *Tongan Society at the Time of Captain Cook's Visits* (1982) is the most complete and exhaustive accounting of early contact Tongan politics. This work was produced using oral histories collected by the Tongan Traditions Committee in the 1950s and 1960s, the accounts of early explorers (as the title suggests, from Cook's Journals in particular), and from conversations with Queen Sālote Tupou III. Bott's work is similar to Gifford's in that it is a reconstruction; both Bott and Gifford rely on oral histories and *tohi hohoko* (genealogies, originally oral, but recorded with the advent of written Tongan in the early 1800s). Bott does attempt to achieve a temporal clarity lacking in Gifford's monographs, but like Gifford, she is overtly concerned with elite politics and tends to treat commoners as a residual class.

Christine Ward Gailey's monograph, *Kinship to Kingship* (1987), is notable within the scholarship on Tongan history for a number of reasons. First it is an overtly Marxist-oriented analysis that traces the effect of the introduction of Western ideas and goods on Tongan state formation. It also offers a sophisticated conception of the significance of gendered roles and statuses within the historical transformation of pre-contact Tongan polity. Gailey attempts to describe the shifting relations of production and exchange, not only between genders, but between commoners and chiefs as well. This necessarily involves an attention to the commoner stratum lacking in other historical works. Unfortunately there are substantive and empirical problems with Gailey's treatment of the activities of commoners (discussed later) which effectively shift her focus back to the elites of Tonga so that *Kinship to Kingship* remains trapped within an elite paradigm.

'Okusitino Mahina (1992) has recently written a reconstruction of Tongan political history based on his analysis of *tala ē fonua* (lit. telling of the land and its people, ibid., vi), or Tongan traditional history. Mahina's work may also be viewed as elite oriented insofar as his subject matter, "*tala ē fonua* is, more often than not, mostly about great people (heroes, gods, kings, queens, etc.) and their great deeds (diplomacy, war, marriages, adventures, etc.) . . . (ibid., 3). Furthermore, in his own words, his work is "a study of the *tala-ē-fonua*, as used and understood by a privileged few in Tongan society, little attention has been paid to alternative or fragmented traditions[4] of Tongan early history that do not derive from received traditions (ibid., vii).

By "received traditions," Mahina refers to what he later terms the "collective/heroic/*hou'eiki*" (chiefly) or societal level traditions of Tongan vernacular history as opposed to the "fragmented/populist/*tu'a* (commoner)" ones based in specific locales (ibid., 28-29). Indeed, his analysis is focussed on the relationship of myth and oral history to politics at the highest levels of Tongan society — the so-called heroic history typical of Polynesia — and rarely devolves to commoner social life; in this he is in good company (Sahlins 1981, 1985). Mahina's recognition of two levels in the oral history of Tonga is refreshing and important, but his subsequent concentration on the received, perhaps dynastic, history is consistent with both the treatment of Polynesian history[5] generally, and significant portions of Tongan oral tradition specifically. Thus, like Bott and Gifford, and indeed like one face of Tongan oral history itself, Mahina focuses on chiefly history and politics.

Unlike, and in many ways opposed to, the works discussed above are village oriented works which began with the Beagleholes in 1938 (1941). Aoyagi (1966) and Morton (1972) also produced analyses of village life which challenged some of the assumptions of earlier elite inspired works. The work of Shulamit Decktor-Korn (1974, 1975, 1977, 1978) and Garth Rogers (1975, 1977) problematized the representation of commoners in Tongan ethnography. Their descriptions of kinship and social structure at the local level stand in direct contradiction to earlier works which took elite structures as typical for all Tongans. The analyses of Decktor-Korn and Rogers now form a benchmark in terms of the study of social organization in the villages of Tonga, but because all of the works centred on villages deal with contemporary Tonga, problems continue to plague understanding of how exactly commoner life ways in the mid- and late twentieth century correspond to those of the past. In part these problems arise because of our inability to determine the exact sources of variation between analyses like Gifford's, and those of Rogers or Decktor-Korn. Three general factors could come into play: (1) elite versus commoner focussed data collection

(2) significant historical transformations in Tongan society, and (3) variation between specific localities within Tonga. Even before considering the possibility of differences in the theoretical basis of a particular interpretation of the Tongan data, any or all of these factors may have lead to the obvious contradictions present in the literature.[6] Nonetheless it is vital to work through these contradictions in order to build up a picture of pre-contact Tongan society, for this picture forms the baseline from which subsequent changes are conceptualized.

Reconstructions of Tongan Society

Pre-contact Tongan society is generally understood as one of the most stratified Polynesian chiefdoms. For instance, both Sahlins (1958) and Goldman (1970) place Tonga among the largest and most highly stratified polities in the region (see Kirch 1984, 36-37, 219). This view of Tonga comes from Gifford (1929), and the ethnological literature shares some of the confusions of the ethnographic literature insofar as Gifford's reading of Tongan political structures obscures the relationships between commoners and chiefs. The above cautions notwithstanding, the broad outlines of pre-contact social structure are best set out by Mariner (Martin 1991 [1817]), Gifford (1929), Bott (1981, 1982) and Mahina (1992). The following synopsis is drawn largely from these sources.

Politics, Power, and Authority

The highest ranking title in Tonga was that of the Tu'i Tonga, literally the King of Tonga. The first holder of this title descended from the God Tangaloa and a human woman (see Biersack 1990, 49; Bott 1982, 90-91; James 1990, 1991a, 1992; Mahina 1992, 91-92 for versions of this myth and analyses of its significance); subsequent titleholders and their descendants were held to be sacred and semi-divine, and ideologically at least, the political power of the line derived from this divinity. Tongan traditions recorded by Gifford (see also Ve'ehala and Fanua 1977, 29-30) trace some thirty-nine Tu'i Tonga from the first, 'Aho'eitu (about 950 A.D.) to the last, Laufilitonga, who died in 1865 (Gifford 1929, 49-52). The origin of the *Tu'i Tonga* and the origin of the traditional Tongan polity are coterminous. All other *'eiki* (chiefly) titles are held to descend genealogically from the central Tu'i Tonga title as cadet lines hive off from the senior one. The ranking of titles, again ideally, was held to be "determined by the genealogical derivation [from the Tu'i Tonga] of the first title-holder" (Bott 1982, 67; Gifford 1929, 122-23), but the shifting balance of political power could, and apparently did, result in changes in the rank of titles in relation to one another (Bott 1982, 67-68; Gifford 1929, 30).

Operationally the relative ranking of political titles was quite complex. Although titles were ranked according to the genealogical connections of a particular title to the Tu'i Tonga title, the power of any one titleholder was much more complicated. Political titles and the power associated with them were generally passed through patrilines,[7] but the social rank of a person was a function of the rank of both parents, with the rank of the mother having as much or more effect. Over time, titles rose and fell in importance as political alliances shifted, and the fortunes of war[8] and reproductive success varied (Biersack 1990; Bott 1982, 67-68; Morgan 1989).

The political situation at the apex of the political system became even more complex during the reign of the twenty-fourth Tu'i Tonga Kau'ulufona I (about 1470 A.D.). At this time the sacred and secular powers of the Tu'i Tonga title were split.[9] The Tu'i Ha'atakalaua title was created and vested with administrative authority over the Kingdom.[10] Eventually another administrative title, the Tu'i Kanokupolu, came to contest supreme administrative power with the Tu'i Ha'atakalaua, and it was this title from which Taufa'ahau, or King George I (the first modern king) arose. These three titles, the Tu'i Tonga, Tu'i Ha'atakalaua, and Tu'i Kanokupolu form a distinct stratum of chiefly titles (that is paramount or *tu'i* titles), above a range of localized but still chiefly or *'eiki* titles.[11] This *tu'i* class of titles was recognizably distinct in marriage patterns; they in fact formed a marriage connubium, in which cross-cousin marriage was practised (Bott 1982; Gailey 1987, 63-84; Mahina 1992, 179), and were set apart from both lesser chiefly lines and commoners by the use of a distinct set of linguistic conventions as well (Gifford 1929, 119-22; 'O. Taliai 1989).

These titleholders and their close kin are sometimes distinguished from other *'eiki*, as *sino 'i 'eiki*, or aristocratic chiefs (Bott 1981; Marcus 1980). Similar distinctions can be found in the early ethnohistorical sources. According to Martin (1991 [1817], 293), several broad categories of people were recognized. The royal lines, both sacred (the Tu'i Tonga) and secular (the Tu'i Ha'atakalaua and Tu'i Kanokupolu), were a higher ranking subset of the *'eiki* class, established by virtue of genealogical distance to particular titles, and ultimately to the Tu'i Tonga line. The *'eiki* stratum was followed by a class of ceremonial attendants or *matāpule*, their close kin, called *mu'a*, and then the commoners or *tu'a*. A final class of war captives, *popula* or slaves, is also mentioned but seems to have been quite small and neither politically or economically significant.

Although these different strata had distinct rights, privileges, and responsibilities, the main organizing dyad was probably the *'eiki/tu'a* or chiefs/commoner pair (see especially Mahina 1992). The boundary between these two categories is not now, and probably never was, all that distinct, for many individuals would have been able to claim some degree of *'eiki* status.[12] Furthermore title and *'eiki* status were not coterminous, and most *'eiki* did not possess titles (see Bott 1982; Marcus 1980). According to Marcus, prior to the establishment of the constitutional monarchy in the late nineteenth century (discussed later) individuals of *'eiki* status often refused titles conferred by the emerging Tu'i Kanokupolu kingship, and instead passed them to junior lines, preferring to derive their authority from their regional status instead (1980, 61-62). Biersack (1990) refers to the distinction between *'eiki* status and title holding as one of "blood and garland"; the former was based in individual social rank and intrinsic, the latter a political distinction which was removable and extrinsic (see also Bott 1981, 38). Social and political rank were of course related, but not in any simple structural way. If at a particular juncture the relative ranking of titles was more or less agreed upon, the relative rank of the titleholders was also informed by their social rank, and social rank derived from the kinship system.

The fundamental principles of social ranking were: (1) sisters rank higher than brothers; (2) elder ranks higher than younger; (3) father's side ranks higher than mother's side. For political alliances the first principle was extremely important, and involved what Mahina terms a "socio-psychological deference" (1992, 172). For example, the highest ranking titleholder (i.e., the Tu'i Tonga), was subordinate in social rank to his sister (called the Tu'i Tonga Fefine or female Tu'i Tonga) and coincidentally her sons and daughters, regardless of her children's position in the title system. As a result an individual might be subordinate according to the rank of the title held, but superordinate in kinship and social rank, and therefore able to demand resources etc., and accrue political power as a result. This institution, called *fahu*, allowed a sister's children to make significant political and economic claims upon their mother's brother and mother's brother's children, and thus to transform social rank into political and economic power — power which could ultimately reflect on the title of the sister's husband and children (Biersack 1990; Morgan 1989, 8).

According to Bott, "sisters have a right to be respected by their brothers and a right to ask them for food and support, though they cannot command . . . (1982, 58).[13] Nonetheless there are several instances in Bott's text, which show clearly that this limitation (that is on the right to

command), did not effectively negate the material and political consequences of the *fahu* relationship (ibid., 59). Titles and thus political rank
generally passed through men; "blood" or social rank was passed through
both men and women, and in this the rank of the women was more significant (Bott 1981, 19). Even if political title and social rank conferred
different types of power (Bott 1982, 56-59; Mahina 1992, 168-74), it is
clear that processually, political and social power overlapped in the politics of the chiefly stratum. There was a built-in ambiguity in the relationship of social rank to political rank which limited the concentration of
political power (Biersack 1990; Bott 1981,1982; and especially Gailey
1981, 1987) within any particular chiefly group and its associated title(s).

At the highest levels of the Tongan polity this ambiguity was resolved
to some degree by the custom of removing the children of the Tu'i Tonga
Fefine from the title system through the marriage of Tu'i Tonga Fefine to
foreign chiefs, more specifically, to members of the *fale fisi*, a royal house
derived originally from Fijian high chiefs and thus *tu'i* in rank, but somewhat removed from contention for the central titles of the Tongan polity
(see Bott 1982; Gailey 1987; Kaeppler 1978; Mahina 1992, 177-78).

Political and Social Organization

The first attempt to describe how the title system was integrated into the
social organization of Tonga was Gifford's (1929). The picture of Tongan
society which emerges from his account is a highly structured one in
which the political title system is conflated with the basis of social organization. Gifford identifies the largest unit of social organization as the
ha'a, which he translates as "tribe, class, family." These *ha'a* (that is
tribes) says Gifford, are patrilineages, and "each consists of a nucleus of
related chiefs about whom are grouped inferior relatives, the lowest and
most remote of whom are commoners" (ibid., 30). In Gifford's view the
ha'a were directly related to the title system; he in fact views them as
clumps of patrilineally related social groups clustered around titles[14]
transmitted from father to son or younger brother.

One of his most important and problematic claims was that these *ha'a*
incorporated commoners; that is that commoners belonged to *ha'a*, and
were simply lower status members. Gifford's image of patrilineally
defined *ha'a* membership was also problematic.[15] In spite of his patrilineal model, Gifford recognizes that both "matrilinear" *ha'a* reckoning, and
political realignment of lineages occurred (1929, 30; see also Bott 1982,
78-85). It is a testament to Gifford's empirical rigour that he does so in
the absence of the more comprehensive theoretical understanding of
ambilineal kinship systems which emerged in the 1950s and 1960s

(Keesing 1975, 91-92). It seems that the attribution of patrilineal transmission holds only for the highest ranking titles, and although it may have been an ideal, the ability to meet this ideal was "a direct function of political strength" (Goldman 1970, 293).

The first clear recognition that Gifford's 1929 representation of the Tongan kinship system was limited came in Ernest and Pearl Beaglehole's 1941 monograph. They note that "Previous description of this society [Tonga] has not always made it clear whether the reference of social custom or fact is to the society as a whole or to the chiefly class only" (ibid., 3). While they seem to accept Gifford's reconstruction of Tongan society as relatively unproblematic,[16] they sought to "record something of the life of the village-commoner" (ibid., 3), presumably in order to balance the previous concentration on the chiefly elite.

Although their study of Pangai village in the Vava'u region must be viewed with some caution due to the brevity of their fieldwork,[17] it was nonetheless the first village level study done in Tonga, and valuable for that fact alone. Indeed, the Beagleholes' work marked not only the first empirical testing of Gifford's general claims about Tongan society but the first finely grained accounting of daily life among commoners.

In the course of the Beagleholes' monograph several areas of disagreement arise between their observations and statements made by Gifford. Of particular note is the Beagleholes' claim that none of the Pangai villagers "knew their lineage" (ibid., 71). That is, none of the villagers claimed membership in any of the *ha'a* identified as encompassing patrilineages by Gifford, and the villagers had "no strong lineage-feelings . . . nor any strong lineage-groupings" (ibid., 71). To the best of my knowledge, this observation has been repeated in almost every village level study since (cf. Cowling 1990a, 119-25); it certainly coincides with my own observations on Ha'ano Island.

The Beagleholes' opinion of the source of this contradiction is difficult to discern. They note, in a roundabout way, that Gifford's informants were primarily from the chiefly class, and that his work is a reconstruction of past Tongan society, but nowhere explicitly offer comment on whether Gifford has overextended his knowledge claims, or whether there has been a shift over time in the knowledge of, or membership in, *ha'a* by Tongan commoners. The issue is further complicated in that Pangai village is located on a royal estate. Gifford notes that commoners would usually claim membership in the *ha'a* of the chief on whose estate they reside (Gifford 1929, 30), but the Beagleholes state that in Pangai village a commoner would not "dare" to make such a claim in relation to the Royal family (ibid., 71). Although this could be a situation specific to villages like Pangai (that is villages on the lands directly held by the *tu'i* stratum of the *'eiki* category, or perhaps a royal estate today), the bulk of the ethnographic literature suggests otherwise (cf. Rogers 1975, 243). Whether this situation is a result of post-contact transformations or not must remain an open question due to the lack of available data on pre-contact commoner social life.[18]

Chiefs and Commoners

Ironically the observations of the Beagleholes and others which contradicted Gifford, led Kirch to suggest that:

> The division of commoner and chiefly classes was, at the time of European contact, sharply drawn. Contrary to the statements of Sahlins (1958) and others that Tongan society was organized on a ramage structure throughout, it is clear that ranked lineages (ha'a) pertained only to the class of chiefly title-holders and their immediate descendants (Bott 1982, 157; Decktor-Korn 1974, 1978). Commoners were affiliated with chiefs *not* on the basis of descent from a common ancestor, but through residence on the lands or estate (*tofi'a*) of the chief. (Kirch 1984, 232)

The problem with this statement is that while it is probable that commoners did not belong to *ha'a*, it is not clear, as Kirch claims, that Tongan society therefore lacked a ramage structure. This is an important distinction, for Kirch's reconstruction allows his further statement that Tonga had developed "true class distinctions" by the time of European contact (cf. Bott 1982, 57). Kirch's use of the term *tofi'a* (land controlled by a chief) is germane here. According to Bott, *tofi'a* is a post-constitutional term. Prior to the constitution a chief's hereditary estate was called *fonua*. This is significant in that the linkage, between a chief and land implied by the use of the term *tofi'a*, as opposed to those ties between a chief and specific groups of people located on the land implied by the term *fonua*, is probably related to provisions in the constitution (Bott 1982, 69) and not, as Kirch claims, a facet of pre-contact, or for that matter pre-constitutional, Tonga. It is on the basis of the claim that chiefs held title over land rather than controlling the kinship group which held land, that he contends that chiefs and commoners formed separate classes. The issue is further clouded because it is clear that kinship, or at least the idiom of kinship, encompassed the relations of chiefs and commoners at the local level.

In reference to the question of whether or not chiefs and commoners formed separate classes in pre-contact Tonga, Gailey contends that:

> Where everyone's access to labour and resources is through kin connections, no matter how ranked, there can be no class differences — so long as kinship determines use rights. Only where a non-producing group depends upon a producing one, *and can deny the producing groups continued subsistence* — its existence as a group — can class relations be discerned. In pre-contact Tonga, these conditions were only partially fulfilled. . . . Chiefs allocated land and access to other resources in their capacity as guardians of Tongan fertility and prosperity (Gifford 1929, 76, 144, 171); but could not refuse to allocate such resources. (emphasis in the original, Gailey 1987, 52)

The difference in the conclusions drawn by Kirch and Gailey is based on empirical grounds rather than theoretical ones. Gailey's argument turns on two substantive issues: (1) at some level land was held by kin-groups, not chiefs, and (2) access to land was based on kinship connections. These two points are actually intertwined in the Tongan context, and are reducible to how localized relations between commoners and chiefs were organized. Although Kirch is correct in saying that Tongan society was not organized in an encompassing ramage system centred on the *ha'a* identified by Gifford, local organization was nonetheless largely built on a series of kinship based connections between chiefs and a range of subordinate kin groups.

Local Organization

The term *kāinga* was central to both political and social organization at the local level. One meaning of the word refers to *any* individual's (including, but not exclusive to, titled chiefs) bilateral kindred. It also had a "quasi-metaphorical" (Bott 1982, 57) usage, in which it referred to the groups and individuals subordinated to a localized chief; that is they would be referred to as his *kāinga*.[19] According to Bott (ibid., 69), most but not all of those living under a chief would be related through kinship. Thus in terms of membership, a chief's political and personal *kāinga* would have considerable overlap. It is unclear if there was any consistent or generalized pattern of subdivision within a chief's political *kāinga* (ibid., 70), and there is considerable disagreement within the literature as to both the nomenclature and the exact nature of the localized groups subject to a chief.

Gailey, for her part, uses Maude's (1971) description of local organization as the basis for her argument.[20] According to Maude, local organization consisted of a series of corporate groups (called *fa'ahinga*[21]) headed by the senior ranking male, or *'ulumotu'a*. The *'ulumotu'a* held minor titles which were associated with the chief's title, usually as either *tehina* (younger brother), or *foha* (son) titles; that is the original lower titleholder would have stood in a corresponding relationship to the chief of his generation (Bott 1982, 69-70).[22] The relationship of *tehina* and *foha* titles to the *'eiki* titleholder was ramified; the *fa'ahinga* under such titles originated in junior and therefore subordinate lineages. The men holding these titles were sometimes called *motu'a tauhifanua* (lit. old one who looks after the land/ people). The titles were *'eiki*, but subordinated (ibid., 57).

There is some confusion in the literature about this class of titles. Bott calls these titles *motu'a tauhifonua*. [23] Marcus refers to *matāpule tauhi fonua* (1980, 44, 59) in a few different contexts; first to refer to the small subset of the Tu'i Kanokupolu *matāpule* who were granted *tofi'a* by King George I after the constitutional monarchy was established (and so are "*matāpule* who cares for the land"); and second to refer to a set of *'eiki si'i* (petty chiefs) who are no longer recognized as such and are now referred to as *matāpule*. I never heard the phrase *matāpule tauhi fonua* in Ha'ano, and to the best of my knowledge this is almost a contradiction in terms. *Matāpule*, or more correctly *matāpule tufa* (*matāpule* who distribute kava in a kava ceremony) have *fatongia* (duties) to a particular *'eiki* title and are active (see Bott 1982, 65-66). *Motu'a tauhifanua* are *'eiki*, and may sit for the *'eiki* titleholder, but are not active, that is perform no duties for the titleholder although they may substitute for the titleholder, and are clearly distinguished from the category of *matāpule*.

It seems that *matāpule* also sometimes headed *fa'ahinga* (Maude 1965, 51; Maude and Sevele 1987, 116). *Matāpule* are not *'eiki*, but rather attendants to particular chiefs or chiefly titles. It should be noted that originally only the *tu'i* titles and very high ranking *'eiki* had *matāpule* (Bott 1982, 66, 97-98). The nature of *matāpule* titles is significant in terms of the issue of pre-contact class formation. *Matāpule* translates literally as "the face (*mata*) of power/authority (*pule*)." As a stratum they are significant in that they may have formed a non-kin based source of support for the highest chiefly titles. According to Gailey the prevalence of *matāpule* and the roles they played (as warriors and overseers of production):

> indicate an estrangement between the highest-ranking, titled chiefs and their lower-ranking chiefly kin. By the late eighteenth century, only district chiefs were nominated from the ranks of chiefly people: all others were titled, but non-chiefly matāpules. (1987, 81)

While this is almost certainly an overstatement (that is *all* others were not non-chiefly *matāpule*) which grows from a lack of understanding of the difference between *matāpule* and *motu'a tauhifanua*, it does suggest that a process of incipient class formation was occurring;[24] the *matāpule* titles associated with the royal lines were historically and ritually held to be of foreign origin (Biersack 1990, 49, 52; Bott 1982, 66;[25] Mahina 1992, 166-67). Widespread creation of *matāpule* titles by other lesser chiefly lines appears to be a later, possibly post-contact phenomenon (Bott 1982, 66).

In Ha'ano, there are some *motu'a tauhifanua* titles derived from kin groups which married into the area; the titles are in fact the names of the brothers of a chiefly woman who married to the Tu'i Ha'angana (the highest ranking local title). According to oral histories these brothers accompanied their sister to "look after her" and were subsequently grant-ed lands. These titles are considered *'eiki* titles, not *matāpule* ones, and are still distinguished from *matāpule* titles by people today.

This passage from Mariner (see Martin) indicates that he at least rec-ognized two possible origins for titles within the stratum he calls *mata-booles [matāpule]*:

> Their [*matāpule*] rank is from inheritance; and they are supposed to
> have been, originally, distant relations of nobles, *or* to have descended
> from persons eminent for experience and wisdom, and whose acquain-
> tance and friendship on that account became valuable to the king, and
> other great chiefs. (1827 [1817], II: 89, emphasis mine)

Given that Mariner was well aware of the distinctions between the royal lines and the other titled chiefs (which he calls nobles here), his com-ments are consistent with my contention that the strata of *motu'a tauhi-fanua* and *matāpule* be differentiated. The first part of his statement thus refers to *motu'a tauhifanua* (that is *tehina* and/or *foha* titles associated with "nobles" or non-royal chiefs), and the latter to *matāpule* connected with the royal titles or great aristocrats.[26]

Within the *kāinga* of a local chief then, were *fa'ahinga* headed by men holding titles in some way related to the chief's title. The relationship of the other *fa'ahinga* to the title-holding chief were conceived of in terms similar to that of the bilaterally constructed kindreds of individuals. The relationship between the *'eiki* and the *'ulumotu'a* were conceived in kin-ship terms, the terms referred to the relationship between the titles, *not necessarily* the individuals holding the titles (Bott 1982, 69-70). The political *kāinga* of a localized chief was organized through the idioms of kinship; it is however important to note that intermarriage between a chief and members of his direct *fa'ahinga*, with members of the *fa'ahinga* under his control, was common and thus formed another layer of interre-latedness. The relationship between the chief and his *kāinga* was characterized by an asymmetrical reciprocity. Goods, such as pigs, yams, pandanus mats (woven from the leaves of the pandanus tree) and bark cloth, and some corvée labour flowed upwards to the chief from those in his *kāinga*, and then were channelled to higher-ranking chiefs until finally reaching the Tu'i Tonga. In turn, chiefs were supposed to redistribute wealth garnered from external sources, and generally treat their people generously (ibid., 160).

For an individual the *fa'ahinga* was an intense locus of social ties, crystallizing the options implied by their own bilateral kindred. Access to land probably devolved from the local chief, to the head of the *fa'ahinga* (that is the *'ulumotu'a*), and then to the members of the *fa'ahinga*.[27] It is significant to note that participation in the *fa'ahinga* was to some degree or another, optative, because any individual could activate ties to several different groups through both cognatic and affinal links, that is to any of their *kāinga* or the *kāinga* of their spouse (note that postmarital residence was generally but not exclusively patrilocal). Nonetheless, the *fa'ahinga* were probably still corporate groups, controlling both land and knowledge (see Evans and Young Leslie 1995), and having specific obligations and duties to the local chief. Within the *fa'ahinga* were subgroupings, called *'api*, which were extended family units, and probably the minimal unit of production and consumption (Maude 1965, 29). Social rank within the *fa'ahinga* and the *'api* was determined according to the principles set out above, regardless of the relative rank of the *fa'ahinga* to other like groups. Indeed, one of the *fa'ahinga* would be the direct descent group of the chief.

Still, the *fa'ahinga* were under the political control of the chief, and according to the chiefs at least, held land at their pleasure, although it seems that chiefs exercised the pleasure of eviction only rarely (if ever), and that lands once granted were retained by the *fa'ahinga* through time (Maude and Sevele 1987, 116). Ideologically, the power of chiefs over particular areas devolved from the Tu'i Tonga. According to Maude and Sevele, "ultimate title to the land was considered to be vested in the Tu'i Tonga, and the position of a chief seems to have been more that of a ruler of an area *and its people* than that of a landlord" (ibid., 117, emphasis mine). This distinction is of the same order as that drawn above in reference to the terms *tofi'a* and *fonua*.

The primacy of the linkage between a chief and his people, rather than a chief and his lands, can be established on additional grounds. While emphasizing the power that chiefs exercised over their people, Bott notes that a cruel and capricious chief might find that "his people would begin slipping away to live with their wives' or mothers' people" (1982, 71). P. Tupouniua (1977, 12) suggests that younger men were actively encouraged to remain within the localized groups and within a chief's *kāinga*; by implication this suggests that commoners had some options available to them. While residence was largely patrilocal, it was not inevitably so, and it seems that people could and did activate the non-patrifocal, that is other cognatic ties, inherent in the kinship system (see Gailey 1987, 60-62). Furthermore the size, productivity, and willingness of a chief's *kāinga* to contribute surpluses for political projects had a direct bearing on the ability of a chief to participate in elite political processes (Bott 1982, 160; Morgan 1989; Tupouniua 1977, 12); land filled with and exploited by people, rather than land in and of itself, was materially necessary for chiefs to be such, and commoners had a limited but significant ability to vote with their feet.

Local Autonomy and Central Control

Bott (1982, 159-60) claims that although all land was controlled by the Tu'i Tonga *in theory*, there are no known cases in which he dispossessed people from lands. The control of the centre was usually exercised through marriage, not naked political or military power (civil war occurred between the assembled forces of *tu'i* class titleholders or claimants). The Tu'i Tonga, and later the Tu'i Ha'atakalaua and the Tu'i Kanokupolu would send close relatives out from their seats in Tongatapu to marry into the chiefly lines of other regions. The in-marrying scion of the royal line would thereby gain the support of his wife's *kāinga*, and by virtue of the higher rank he possessed due to genealogical proximity to one of the *tu'i* lines, either he or his descendants would absorb the original inhabitants into their own *kāinga*. The original chiefly line would then be transformed into a *tehina* (younger brother) line, giving them a place of importance in the new political structure, and limiting the possible tension between the old and new chiefly lines (ibid., 161; see also Mahina 1992, 171).[28]

While this process does not make sense if we assume a patrilineal, or even patrilateral pattern in the succession of titles, once the social ranking of individuals is factored in, a sort of coherence is evident. The sister of the original titleholder would be of superior rank to her brother, and so too her children (they are *fahu* to the original line); this in combination with the high blood rank of their father, could be, and obviously was, sufficient to reverse the more usual relationship between political and social rank,[29] and allow the localization of a new chiefly patriline. Nonetheless, the chiefly representative of the royal line *married into* the local area; high rank was insufficient in and of itself to establish control of an area over the long term. Kinship connections were also necessary to create linkages with the original inhabitants and absorb them into his political *kāinga*. Political support did not arise directly from control of land, or for that matter from the putative ability to alienate land from its inhabitants (see also Maude 1965, 32-33).

Thus, although local organization was not consistently or determinately related to the wider title system, and Gifford's image of the *ha'a* as encompassing patrilineages is likely incorrect, the relationships of local titleholders to their people were ideally ramified, ordered through the kinship system, and limited by kinship based obligations (see also Gailey 1987, 82-83). Individuals derived their rights to land from their standing within the *fa'ahinga*, which was in turn ordered within the wider local context by the *fa'ahinga*'s relationship to the local titleholder. It is also clear that membership within a *fa'ahinga* was optative to some degree, but it is unclear just how often such options were exercised.

Chiefliness and Social Organization

The *'eiki/tu'a* or chiefly/commoner distinction should be approached with caution in its application to pre-contact Tonga, for it may obscure as much as it describes. While it may be easy to distinguish the highest of chiefs from the most common of commoners, in the middle ranges the divisions are much less obvious. Within the *fa'ahinga*, kinship relationships would have been known, and traceable to the *'ulumotu'a* (in many cases an *'eiki* person, that is at least a *motu'a tauhifanua*). Thus chiefliness, at least in the local arena, would be fairly well diffused and devolved.

Mahina (1992) integrates this relativity of chiefliness into his reconstruction of what he calls the "complementary and opposed vertical and horizontal axes of the three dimensional Tongan social organization." He writes:

> The celestial or upward arrangement of people into hierarchies or stratifications (with *tu'i* at the top, *hou'eiki*[30] in the intermediary, and *tu'a* at the bottom of the social heap) forms the vertical aspect, while the terrestrial or earth-bound organization of people into categories or units (ranging from the smallest *'api*, through *famili*, *kāinga*, *fa'ahinga*, *matakali*, to the largest *ha'a*).[31]*Fahu* and *'ulumotu'a* are concepts of categorisation and utilisation, but *'eiki* and *tu'a* are principles of heirarchisation or stratification. (Ibid., 174)

The principles of *'eiki/fahu* and *tu'a/'ulumotu'a* articulate with the social organization of the polity by integrating social groups, while opposing them. Within the smallest group, the *'api*, the kinship correlates of *fahu* (*mehekitanga* or father's sister and *'ilamutu* or sister's children) and *'ulu-motu'a* (*fa'tangata/tu'asina* or mother's brother and *fakafotu* or brother's children) constitute the *'eiki - tu'a* dyad, rank individuals within the *'api*, and form the basis for the integration of the *'api* in the next level of social integration (i.e., the *kāinga/fa'ahinga/matakali* referred to by Mahina — see below).

The *'eiki - tu'a* dyad here is not one of simple rank. Mahina distin-guishes between the *pule* (authoritative status) of the *fahu*, and the *mafai* (political power) of the *'ulumotu'a*. Further:

> For every social unit headed by a (patrilineal) *'Ulumotu'a*, there is always a (matrilineal) *Fahu*; both positions in each unit become redun-dant as you move from one unit to the next, ie., from a smaller to a larger group, until you get to the largest unit. (Ibid., 175)

The *fahu* and *'ulumotu'a* are complementary and opposed at each level of integration, but disappear between levels. At the apex of the system the Tu'i Tonga is the *'ulumotu'a* of the entire polity. He stands opposed to the God Hikole'o (sister to the God Tangaloa 'Eiki, the father of the first Tu'i Tonga) who stands in the position of *fahu* to the Tu'i Tonga, and thus the entire polity. At all levels the performance of the duties of the *'ulumotu'a* to the *fahu* is the performance of power; that is the recognition of the chiefliness of the *fahu* through the provision of material goods and/or cere-monial elevation (i.e., authoritative status) has as its correlate the "consoli-dation of . . . secular/*tu'a/mafai* (political power)" (Mahina 1992, 183) of the *'ulumotu'a*. The Tu'i Tonga, *'eiki* and *fahu* to all others (especially the Tu'i Kanokupolu and Tu'i Ha'atakalaua), was also thus the *tu'a* part of the *'eiki/tu'a* dyad in some circumstances (that is in relation to Hikole'o).

Kinship and the Diffusion of Power

Ideologically at least, the actions of those symbolically designated *tu'a*, were not necessarily an expression of domination or powerlessness, rather they were indicative of secular power, and sacred subordination. Assumptions about the subordination of commoners to chiefs at the local level must be tempered with the recognition that this subordination was neither com-plete, nor completely unassociated with locally salient expressions of power however limited they might be. Although chiefly power and authority suf-fused the system, it was limited, constrained, crosscut, and diffused by the ideological and kinship systems in which this power was embedded.

Although the lack of detailed information on commoners makes it dif-ficult to make any definitive claims, some somewhat tentative conclusions may be drawn. First it seems unreasonable to suppose that commoners were in fact an undifferentiated mass, class, or category. There is every reason to suppose that within commoner *fa'ahinga* the kinship system itself coded differential rank and power. Further it seems likely that the ideological basis of political power and authority of chiefs was replicated, albeit through the kinship system, within and between *fa'ahinga*. Finally it is probable that the persons in *fa'ahinga* were related to and interacted with superordinate chiefly persons and groups as members of the *fa'ahinga*, and not as individual commoners.

In Ha'ano today there are several titles, some recognized as *motu'a tauhifanua* names related to the Tu'iHa'angana (for instance Peito and Hiko are recognized as *tehina* or "younger brother" titles, while Kienga is a title which came with the brothers of a high ranking woman who married to the Tu'iHa'angana line, and Pouvalu is one which is likewise associated with the brothers of an in-marrying high ranking woman from the Tu'i Vakano), some *motu'a tauhifanua* related to other titles (for instance Vake is related genealogically to the highly ranked Tungi title), and a number of *matāpule* titles linked directly to the Tu'iHa'angana (for example 'Ahi, Fisi'iniu and many more). In addition there are some *to'a* (brave man or warrior) names as well (for example Mahuniu). Each one of these titles has a complex genealogical and political history (Evans and Young Leslie 1995); the detailed explication of the specific titles is beyond the scope of this monograph. Here it will suffice to point out that each one of the extant titles (and perhaps any number of names which have disappeared over the last two hundred years) would have been associated with a *fa'ahinga*. For commoners within, subordination to the Tu'iHa'angana would be mediated through the title and titleholder of their *fa'ahinga*. Commoners were clearly, but not simply, subordinated because of the ramified title system and the coding of political relationships between groups (rather than as individuals on a class or class-like basis).

These points are pertinent in terms of how we conceptualize the reformulation of the social system which occurred following contact. From the perspective of local level politics and economics, the current practices of villagers in terms of the formation of groups through participation in gift exchange appears rather more consistent with the past (in terms of social organization and practice) than is sometimes admitted. The transitions in local organization which grew out of political and economic developments after contact involved a shift in the focus of commoner social life rather than a fundamental reformulation.

Chapter Four

European Contact and the Transformation of the Traditional Polity

The earliest European contact with Tonga was in 1616, when Schouten and Le Maire landed in the northern outlying islands of Niuatoputapu and Niuafo'ou. From that point on there were sporadic contacts (including Tasman and later Cook) throughout the group (see Wood 1932, 14-25; see also Herda 1983). The first missionary landing, undertaken by the London Missionary Society, was in 1796, but it was unsuccessful (see Vason 1840 [1810]). In 1826 a second mission landed at Tongatapu. This mission, of Wesleyan Methodists, eventually formed an alliance with the Tu'i Kanokupolu Taufa'ahau, and managed the conversion of the majority of the population.

The effect of the earliest contact by occasional ships and the people these ships left behind in Tonga was relatively small. Even the introduction of firearms seems to have had relatively little direct effect on the structure of Tongan politics. There does seem to have been an intensification of warfare, but the reasons for war remained tied to chiefly competition, and were not profoundly altered (Gailey 1987, 163-65). It is generally held that a period of frequent warfare and civil unrest began with the rise of Finau 'Ulukalala (Mariner's benefactor) and continued into the mid-1800s (see Burley 1994). The linkage between contact and this civil unrest is far from established. Burley (1995) reports that the movement

Notes to chapter 4 start on p. 179.

of people into fortified sites which is often held to be a result of an uncommon period of warfare (see for example Lātūkefu 1974, 22), in fact predates Finau 'Ulukalala, and thus throws into doubt earlier simplistic assumptions about the "peacefulness" of Tonga and the disruption of civil order arising from contact.

More significant social change began with the widespread conversion of the Tongan population by Methodist missionaries in the 1840s. From this period on, the history of Methodism and the history of Tonga were inexorably connected (see Lātūkefu 1974 and Rutherford 1971 for definitive treatments of the relationship of church and state in early modern Tonga). The mission's success, and the success of its most important convert, Taufa'ahau (the Tu'i Kanokupolu), came about after a series of wars and political victories which culminated in the elimination of the Tu'i Tonga and Tu'i Ha'atakalaua titles, and the ascension of Taufa'ahau to political supremacy as Siaosi (George) Tupou I of Tonga. In the course of his reign, both Methodist Christianity and a number of state institutions were borrowed from Europe, modified, and integrated into the Tongan social and political landscape.

By 1875, Taufa'ahau had effective control over the entire Kingdom, and had instituted a number of changes in the political, social and economic structure of the country. These changes were effected through a series of documents culminating in the constitution of 1875.[1] Among the most important changes were:

1. The establishment of the principle that all land belonged to the crown, and then the subsequent creation of a landed nobility chosen from a subset of traditional titleholders, to which "traditional estates" were returned, albeit on modified terms, and the establishment of royal and government estates on all other lands.

2. The "freeing" of the commoners from their traditional obligations to their chiefs.

3. The enshrining of the right of all Tongan males to be allocated lease lands from either noble, government, or royal estates. These lands were made heritable by their descendants according to the rules of patrilineal primogeniture. Lease monies from these lands were paid to either the noble or the government depending on the estate type from which the land was granted.

4. The enshrining of rules of patrilineal succession to the crown and to all noble titles.

5. The establishment of a constitutionally empowered legislature, including royal, noble, and commoner representatives at Nuku'alofa.

These changes had a number of ramifications. Here I am most concerned with the effects they had on local social organization. It is important to note at the outset, however, that the changes inscribed in the constitution *were not realized overnight*. In fact many of the changes were neither understood by the bulk of the populace (Lātūkefu 1974, 215; Wood Ellem 1981, 82), nor enacted for several decades.

Land, Local Organization, and the New Order

The construction of a new political orthodoxy and changes in conceptions of land tenure were linked in fundamental ways, and had a profound effect on the political and social structure. Taufa'ahau's reform of land tenure, specifically the introduction of leasehold lands, freed the commoners from their obligations to local chiefs. During this same period the creation of a class of nobles (*nopele*) from the ranks of the traditional chiefs transformed the relationships of chiefs to their people, and chiefs to the now solitary Tu'i Kanokupolu royal line.

The Vava'u Code of 1839, promulgated by Taufa'ahau when he was Tu'i Ha'apai and Tu'i Vava'u,[2] and before he had control of the rest of the Kingdom, had this to say about people, land, and chiefs:

> each chief or head of a people, shall govern his own people, and them only: and it is my mind that you each show love to the people you have under you, also that you require them to be industrious in labouring to support the government and in their duties to you their chiefs; and that you divide to each one of them land for their own use, that each one may have means of living, of supporting his family procuring necessaries, and contributing to the cause of God. (Lātūkefu 1974, 223)

The Vava'u code was written after Taufa'ahau's conversion to Methodism, and with the assistance of the missionaries, but it would be a mistake to assume that only missionary interests and agendas were played out in this or subsequent proclamations by Taufa'ahau. It is clear that Taufa'ahau's political agenda was not subordinated to the missionaries', although the two often coincided (ibid.). Two elements in the passage above are worth note here. The code calls for the division of land to individual households; and it restricts supralocal chiefly prerogatives to Taufa'ahau and his line, although it does not interfere with the prerogatives of chiefs over their own people.

The 1850 code of laws had little more to say about land,[3] but it did further reserve authority to the line of Taufa'ahau and his government, which now controlled the whole of Tonga although considerable localized resistance remained, particularly in Tongatapu. Under the section titled "The laws of the chiefs and those who govern," after the recognition of the right of chiefs (here for the first time restricted in print if not in practice to those appointed by the King) to demand corvée labour for their own support, is a passage demanding that chiefs "shall pay strict attention in seeing the King's work properly executed, but in case of his negligence [that is the Chief's to the King], his people shall do less for him" (ibid., 228). The intention here is clear; the authority and legitimacy of the local chiefs were to be understood in relation to their subordination and fealty to the new king.

The 1862 code of laws is an extensive document outlining the structure of the new government in considerable detail. In the section titled "The Law Concerning Tribute" (ibid., 247-48) commoners were "set at liberty from serfdom, and all vassalage," and chiefs were barred from appropriation of commoner's goods. This was a sharp break from customary practice, in which chiefs were entitled to some goods and labour from their people. This customary tribute was to be replaced by taxes (to King and his government) and rents (to local chiefs). As in the Vava'u code, chiefs were directed to distribute land to their people, but in addition, the 1862 code made it unlawful for any chief to dispossess commoners who had paid their rent and tribute (taxes). All unoccupied land was claimed by the state (ibid., 251).

The Constitution of 1875, written by the missionary Shirley Baker, but vetted and amended by Taufa'ahau himself (see ibid., 284), was an even more detailed document which set out not only the structure of government but redefined the relationship of the King to local chiefs, and government to all Tongans. It set down the way the legislature was to operate, and provided for the creation of a class of nobles drawn, by Taufa'ahau, from the ranks of chiefs. Inheritance rules of patrilineal primogeniture were also enacted for the first time. Only twenty nobles were recognized in 1875; ten more were added by Taufa'ahau in 1880; during the reign of Tupou II, two more nobles were recognized; Sālote, the third in the line of Tupou, created one additional noble. Taufa'ahau did not select these nobles only from his allies, but rather attempted to draw into the new structure both friendly and antagonistic chiefs in an attempt to quell opposition to the new state by drawing powerful chiefs within its orbit, and thus aligning their interests with his own dynasty (Lātūkefu 1974, 213; Wood Ellem 1981, 79; 1992, 4).

The Hereditary Land Act of 1882 granted specific lands to the nobles, and to six *matāpule* of the King as well (see Maude 1965, 98; Wood

Ellem 1981, 77-78). This however left a number of chiefs without formal recognition, and without legally recognized land holdings. Two classes of landholders were created as a result; a class of hereditary landholders (nobles and *matāpule* with estates or *tofi'a*), and a class of customary landholders without legal recognition of either their status as chiefs, or their customary lands.

By 1891 the outlines of commoner land tenure were also in place, and few changes have been made since (Maude 1965, 98-99). There are three types of estates in Tonga:
1. Royal estates controlled directly by members of the royal family
2. Noble estates controlled by individual Nobles but administered by the Ministry of Lands
3. Government estates controlled and administered by the Ministry of Lands.

All Tongan males over the age of sixteen were entitled to 8¼ acres of land for farming (called an *'api tukuhau* or tax allotment) and a house site in a village (called an *'api kolo* or town allotment). Land once granted, could not be reclaimed or repossessed except according to law. Furthermore the administration of all land grants was to be undertaken by the Ministry of Lands, and not individual nobles, although nobles were granted the right to be consulted about land grants on their estates in 1915.[4]

It is important to note again here that the provisions of the Constitution were not all either understood or enforced immediately. Some provisions, like the making of all town and village sites government land for instance, were never enforced and were subsequently dropped altogether (Maude 1965, 98). Land registration in particular was a slow process.[5] Even before the 1915 provision that estateholders be consulted on land grants, it is probable that neither chiefs nor commoners contemplated circumvention of the customary obligations inherent in the *'eiki/tu'a* relationship (Wood Ellem 1981, 78-79); that is a commoner probably could not, and almost certainly would not, register land without the consent of the estateholder. It is also clear that customary landholders who were not recognized as nobles did not simply disappear. The last years of Taufa'ahau's reign, all of Tupou II's, and the first years following Sālote's coronation saw considerable agitation by local chiefs who had not been recognized as nobles (Wood Ellem 1981, 1992).[6]

According to Wood Ellem, the effect of the reforms of the 1875 Constitution was to transform the subset of chiefs recognized as nobles into a class of landlords or privileged "chiefs" (see also Maude 1965, 98), while customary landholders remained "leader-chiefs" in the manner described above (i.e., as leaders of their *kāinga*). It would seem that if Taufa'ahau's intention had indeed been to shift the legitimacy of the nobles from their relationships with their localized *kāinga*, to the state under the control of the royal family, he was at least partially successful (Wood Ellem 1981, 78; see also Kaeppler 1971; Marcus 1980). The residual customary land-holders, although still a focus for the loyalty of their *kāinga*, and capable of causing problems for the state and the Tupou dynasty in the 1920s (Wood Ellem 1981, 79), were gradually separated from their lands as the land laws were implemented, and the customary holdings were thus dispersed[7] (Wood Ellem 1992).

As the new land laws were gradually operationalized, individual men (and a few widows) came to control their own lands. Although land on the estates of the former chiefly (but now noble) titleholders remained under the control of these chiefs, once land was granted and registered with the Ministry of Lands, it became the property of individuals, transferable over generations, and protected in law. The *fa'ahinga* under the *'ulumotu'a* lost its landholding role and, in the process, most of what corporate character it previously possessed. The pre-contact system, while ambilineal and thus flexible to some degree, was nonetheless composed of a series of social groups made corporate through exchange processes in much the same manner that Mauss suggested. The shift in the relations between nobles and their people, the material and political marginalization of the *motu'a tauhifanua*, *'eiki si'i* and other chiefly leaders who went unrecognized in the constitution, and the individuation of land holdings among commoners, caused a *gradual* erosion of the previous basis of local organization and land tenure (cf. Gailey 1987, who tends to write as if previous social and political relations were transformed at the stroke of the constitutional pen).

It would be premature, however, to assume that the kinship basis of local organization and commoner social life was destroyed, or that social organization is now atomized into nuclear family units. The *fa'ahinga* of old no longer function,[8] and indeed the most easily identifiable extant social unit is the *'api* or household, but this is not necessarily a result of the dissolution of social ties. Instead there has been a transformation of the older ambilineal system into a kindred system. Ironically, the remnants of ambilineal kinship are to be found in the ubiquitous connections between individuals which form the foundation of everyday commoner life, and the kinship connections which order the ceremony and hierarchy of chiefly politics.[9]

Christianity and Local Organization

In addition to these political changes the widespread conversion of the population to Christianity, and in particular to Methodism, was also of some significance for commoners. Within the practice and theology of Methodism was the notion that all individuals were equal (controlling for age and gender) before God. This was a significant departure from pre-contact religious belief.[10] Commoner participation as lay preachers and functionaries within the new churches brought them together with higher ranking people on a more egalitarian footing than previously. It also appears that the new churches structured the participation of individuals within the church in new and different ways from previous ritual and ceremonial practice.

The missionaries brought with them a conception of the family which differed significantly from Tongan forms. The Tongan word *famili*, clearly a borrowing from English, currently has several, sometimes contradictory and sometimes overlapping meanings, but its central and most frequent usage *within the churches* is to refer to the nuclear family (cf. Decktor-Korn 1977, 153-70; Marcus 1980, 15-17).[11] More and more, the *famili* became the unit of ceremony and exchange within the churches;[12] this is a distinct shift from earlier social processes in which the smallest unit of ceremony was probably the *fa'ahinga*. Furthermore, where previously chiefs were the focus for ceremonial exchange and ritual activity among commoners, the churches have gradually come to share this function. Today the chiefly political *kāinga* of old remain. Modern nobles continue to draw upon the resources of their kindreds (and now their tenants as well) for various projects (see Morgan 1989, 6). Nonetheless the central focus of most commoner gift exchange has undeniably shifted over the last century. Chiefs and their projects continue to draw some resources from commoners, but the vast bulk of the wealth publicly deployed by commoners is an expression of the vitality of social connections focussed on commoners themselves. Today the public performance of exchange is predominantly mediated by the churches, not the chiefs (Bott 1981, 63).

Commodity Production and the Role of Church and State

Both church and state were catalysts in the explosive growth of commodity production. New taxes and the demand for church donations created a need for cash.[13] Political and religious hierarchies had exacted tribute in pre-contact times and, according to Bollard (1974, 51), the use of cash in meeting new obligations to church and state institutions was a change in the medium expressing the relationship of people to the elites, rather than a change in the relationship itself (cf. Gailey 1987). Both the church (by facilitating market linkages and providing loans for donations), and the state (by imposing fines and taxes), made concerted efforts to draw people into market production and the use of cash. The uses to which cash was put however were very limited. According to Bollard cash was used to meet obligation demands, not transaction demands (1974, 25). This distinction is central in understanding the nature of the social transformations which accompanied the growth of commodity production.

It is not clear in any of the major syntheses dealing with the introduction of Methodism during the early post-contact period (i.e., Bollard 1974; Gailey 1987; Lātūkefu 1974) exactly how the social dynamics of exchange and production were played out within the churches. That is to say, we do not know exactly how social units within the churches were constituted during any one exchange event, or how resources flowed between groups in the course of producing and pooling the goods used for donations to the churches. We know that state taxes were levied on individual males, and on their registered lands, and thus might suspect that individual households ('api) acquired the cash necessary, but this is not certain.[14] It is also worthy of note that although there was some tension between church and state when one had its interests compromised by the tribute extraction of the other, the payment of taxes and fines seems to have generally been secondary to church donations in the allocation of commoners' resources (Bollard 1974). Today, church donations among Methodist churches, while generally made by nuclear family units, are sometimes organized into larger units, and almost always have a component of both public and private pooling to them. It is likely that the nucleation of families within the practice of Tongan Christianity was a long-term process, one that is by no means either complete or, for that matter, inevitable.[15] It is however generally agreed that the intensity with which people engaged in commodity production for the purposes of church donations, regardless of the exact constitution of the donating units, was tied up with competition for prestige between groups and individuals, and that this sort of competition was supported and encouraged by the church (Bollard 1974; Lātūkefu 1974).[16]

By the end of the nineteenth century there was a decline in the use of cash for both church donations and taxation. The Tongan church split from its Australian parent, and the levels of cash donations dropped (although contributions in kind may have increased). The burden of taxation shifted somewhat from individual men, to customs duties (Bollard 1974, 31),[17] and the general levels of cash use and commodity produc-

tion by Tongan commoners dropped for this and a number of other reasons (including the collapse of market linkages and the great depression).
It was not until World War II and afterward that commodity production,
for either internal or external markets, began a slow increase. From the
1960s on, there has been a steady rise in a number of market indicators.
The ascension to the throne of a modernizing king, Tupou IV, in 1967
was followed by a number of development initiatives, and a concomitant
rise in wage labour, migration, and market activity. Assumptions about
the effects of this increase in commodity production and market engagement on social organization must, however, be approached with caution.

The Questionable Significance of Commodity Production

While there is broad agreement on the outlines of economic change since
contact, there is considerable disagreement about the significance of these
changes. Gailey (1987) offers the strongest and most detailed argument
for viewing the changes in Tongan economic and social processes as ones
of "commoditization." Bollard's division between obligation and transaction demands points to the need to recognize a significant difference
between monetization and commoditization. The conflation of these two
processes plagues the work of Gailey. Exhaustive and detailed critiques of
Gailey's work are available elsewhere (see for instance Gordon 1992;
James 1988). Here I wish to draw attention to just a few issues. Gailey's
rather complex argument is that the emerging state and the newly introduced churches of nineteenth century Tonga each contributed to the
transformation of the Tongan polity by disrupting and replacing the
material basis of the reproduction of power and authority in Tongan society. Her underlying premise is that given the ambiguities of power and
authority in pre-contact Tongan society, one of the central validations of
power and status was found in the processes of production, appropriation
and exchange of *koloa* (or women's wealth — primarily bark cloth and
woven mats).[18] Gailey argues that the changes wrought in the early contact period resulted in the consolidation of political and economic control
in an uneasy alliance of the state, the churches, and merchant interests.
Further, she argues that these interests were true class interests, underwritten by the use of the coercive power of the state and the ideological
influence of the churches. Gailey considers that the transformation of
gender relations, specifically the erosion of the power of women as *sisters*
was crucial. *Fahu* rights, and the notions of rank which they expressed,
were part and parcel of the cognatic claims and privileges which crosscut

and thereby limited the patrilaterally vested political power encoded in the title system (Gailey 1987, 119-20). Women, previously independent of their husbands to a considerable degree because of the institution of *fahu*, were socially and politically marginalized when (1) Christian notions of the nuclear family, and the role of women within it were introduced, and (2) when the role of women's wealth and social rank was obviated in the succession of titles by the institution of patrilineal primogeniture and the rule of law. The reforms of Taufa'ahau removed the role of *koloa* in political legitimization, eliminated the ambiguities of rank, and substituted cash and commodities for traditional wealth items as the medium of tribute relations.

At this point, what Gailey calls the communal and tributary modes of production were subsumed by the capitalist one (ibid., 218). She writes:

> In Tonga, articulation of three modes of production can be detected, with a capitalist one dominating. Social reproduction not only involved the continuity of tribute extraction and — as a resistant residuum — communal production, but also a commodity sphere. The capitalist mode of production encapsulated both tributary and communal production, since the tribute extracted, in goods or labour, was destined for a capitalist market (cf. Van Binsbergen and Geschiere eds. 1985). Only part of the tribute amassed was consumed directly or traded for other, often luxury goods for consumption by the elite. Most of the tribute was marked for accumulation[19] and investment at home or abroad. The capitalist sphere determined what would be extracted through tribute relations. (Gailey 1987, 247)

Gailey's argument really operates at one level, that of the nation-state, and proceeds only by assuming that (1) the capitalist mode of production dominates and (2) that the commoditization has therefore occurred. While she recognizes the continuing existence of "a degree of communal control over production and distribution," this control arises from "the tribute system and the needs of mercantile capitalism" (ibid., 257). Gailey also writes:

> The coexistence and continuing accommodation of contradictory modes of production — communal, tribute-exacting, and capitalist — underscore the incompleteness of state formation in Tonga. The production-for-use sphere continues; kin and quasi-kin relations still organize a significant portion of social labour. Moreover, the persistence of the kin-based use sphere shelters producing people from the assertions of cultural determination by state-associated classes. The entrenched character of economic, political, and ideological resistance is testimony to the continuing efforts by Tongans to arrest the growth of exploitive relations. (Ibid., 260)

If this resistance is "entrenched," what is it entrenched within? In what way is the capitalist mode of production dominant, and what exactly has been commoditized?

It is interesting to note that like Marx (1971, 67 cited in Appadurai 1986, 8; Parry and Bloch 1989, 4), Gailey seems to use the term production-for-exchange to mean market exchange; that is commodity exchange, while her use of the term production-for-use includes both gift exchange and barter (1987, 246). Herein lies the rub: for Gailey, what characterizes commodity production seems to be the ultimate disposition of a particular good; that is it enters the market at some point in its circulation.

Another view of commodities however, takes a more transactional perspective, also founded in Marx, but in his treatment of commodities and commodity fetishism. Commodity fetishism refers to the appearance within market exchange that value is a function of the equivalence of goods (i.e., that a good exchanged for another, or a certain quantity of money, is valued in and of itself rather than in and of the labour subsumed within the good). A commodity transaction denies the relationship between the transactors (and for that matter producers), and thus fetishizes the commodity or good, creating a situation in which "relationships between people masquerade as relations between things" (Parry and Bloch 1989, 7). Gift exchange, by contrast, is all about the relationship between the transactors, whether hierarchical or egalitarian and, rather than denying a social relationship between the transactors (either individuals or groups), expresses that relationship. Clearly Tongan commoners produced large quantities of goods which were destined for commodity markets very early on. But, rather than expressing the radically transformed social relations implied by commoditization, copra and cash[20] continued to mediate social and reciprocal relationships which were not fetishized.

Clearly, the churches and the state in early modern Tonga extracted surplus production from commoners, and then used the market to convert this production into cash or other commodities which could be used for their own projects. Tonga was in fact integrated into world markets, but in fundamental ways the flow of wealth from commoners to church and state expressed old, rather than radically new, relationships. We must look at why it was that commoners were giving this cash and copra. The answer to this lies in the term "giving." What these commoners were doing was about gift relationships, and although these relations were mediated by cash and by copra (destined to enter commodity markets), these resources were not necessarily marks of commoditization, but rather really good gifts.[21]

In general terms the history of commodity production in Tonga is not about the subordination of gift exchange to commodity production, but rather the reverse. If the substitution of taxes for tribute commoditized commoner-noble relations, it is not clear that commoners ever realized it. There is little to suggest that cash was anything more than a new type of wealth utilized by commoners in asymmetrical exchange with nobles. The performance of the state in terms of tax collection was always inconsistent, and ultimately the state was forced to shift the burden of taxation into indirect taxes (Bollard 1974, 52; Campbell 1992, 73). On the other hand, provision of tribute in traditional goods by commoners to their nobles continues to this day. Church donations were never direct commodity transactions, but rather clear gifts. Although the new land system provided the state's rationale for taxation, it is again important to remember that the new system was only slowly implemented. It is not certain that the state ever really had administrative control, in spite of some appearances to the contrary (Bollard 1974, 51). Further the land leasing system did not commoditize land in any straightforward way. Land could not be sold by anyone. Large tracts could be leased by nobles or members of the royal family, but this potential did not result in the long-term alienation of much agricultural land (Simkin 1945, 112). Land, the basis of subsistence agriculture, remained accessible to the vast majority of Tongans; material necessity could not force people into either wage labour or commodity production.

In Gailey's own work, commodity production is linked with the intentions of producers. She writes that "commodity production refers to the making of objects for sale in national or international markets, with the goal of profit-taking and reinvestment for expanded production" (Gailey 1987, 77). But what if the intention of producers is otherwise? What if the goal of production is participation in gift exchange?

The centrality of gift exchange in Tongan social life was never obviated by commodity exchange. Gailey's reference earlier to "communal production" as a "resistant residuum," moves gift exchange to the theoretical margins. This actually inverts the relationship between gift and commodity exchange experienced by Tongan villagers today. Gailey has assigned analytical primacy to the commodity sphere in ways which Tongan commoners generally do not. The ideology and practice of gift exchange continues to have profound effects on people's lives.[22]

Tongan Gift Exchange

Gift exchange in Tonga is conceptualized in the same terms at all levels. The three core concepts which organize gift exchange are *'ofa*[23] (love and generosity), *faka'apa'apa* (respect), and *fetokoni'aki* (mutual assistance). All kin, quasi-kin, and political relationships are expressed in some combination of these terms. For instance, the brother/sister relationship was and is of central importance in kinship ranking and interaction. Brothers have *faka'apa'apa* toward their sisters; this is expressed in an avoidance relationship, and social deference of the brother to the sister. It is also expressed on ceremonial occasions materially in the giving of gifts from brother to sister. Sisters are *'eiki*, or of higher rank in relation to their brothers, and are treated as such. Similarly nobles (*nopele*) are *'eiki* to their political constituencies, and are treated with *faka'apa'apa*. This too takes the form of social deference, and the material provision of gifts from the commoners to their noble. Conversely the noble should have *'ofa* toward their people. While nobles can demand (an early law code referred to this as "authoritatively begging") material goods from their people, the noble should treat his people generously and fairly. A "good" noble treats his people generously, and demands things only occasionally, and only for specific types of events for which they are customarily entitled to support from their people.

Fetokoni'aki is often singled out by Tongans as the defining characteristic of good *angafakatonga*, or the Tongan way of behaving. It is the quintessential form of generalized reciprocity, and is often opposed to *angafakapalangi* (the European way) or *angafakapa'anga* (the way of money — read commodities).[24] Any and all social ties should be expressed through *fetokoni'aki*. Neighbours, fellow church members, friends, and all kinspeople should practice *fetokoni'aki*. To practice *fetokoni'aki*, is to show mutual *'ofa*, to fail to do so in appropriate situations or with appropriate people is to be without *'ofa*, and at best elicits pity, at worst contempt.

These three principles, *'ofa*, *faka'apa'apa*, and *fetokoni'aki*, operate within the household as well as beyond it.[25] At all levels of social organization however, there is a degree of freedom in terms of what people actually do. The concepts, and associated practices and attitudes, while patterned by the social and political system, are not determined by it. The realization, legitimation, and expression of social relationships occur through actions commensurate with the three principles. The primary way this happens is through gift exchange. Like the kinship system, gift exchange practices are optative; indeed in any particular instance the two are inextricably linked. Potential social relationships are actualized and maintained by mutual exchange. Even in asymmetrical relationships, like those of commoners to royalty or the nobility, some degree of *reciprocity is expected*. Any relationship which is perceived to lack appropriate levels of reciprocity, either material or emotional, is said to make one *ngaūe popula* or work like a slave. This epithet may be used in a number of formulations ranging from the excessive demands of spouses on each other, to the result of constant requests for aid by one neighbour on another without reciprocation, to wage labour for a demanding or unfeeling employer; the non-metaphoric use of the term refers to the lives of commoners before they were "freed" from the demands of the chiefs by Tupou I, actual slaves (a small number of war captives in the pre-contact and early contact period), and prison convicts today.

This notion of reciprocity is present in the context of people's participation in church as well. Of particular interest here is the importance of the *famili*[26] as a ceremonial unit in reference to patterns of feasting and gift exchange organized within the churches. The structural form of this feasting activity reflects the rise in the importance of the household/*famili* as a unit of production, consumption, and ritual, but the semiotic content speaks of fundamental continuities in the ideology of exchange, albeit articulated through the *famili* rather than through larger, more inclusive social groups.

The position of the Christian God is extremely important. Christians have *faka'apa'apa* for God, and God has *'ofa* in return. This relationship underlies not only the sizable church contributions which people make, but an intense and frequent participation in church organized feasts. Almost every household on Ha'ano Island, and especially those with children or grandchildren, sponsors at least one public feast a year and usually more. At these feasts food is offered as a gift to God, and those in attendance ask God to insure that the sponsoring family receive their *'inasi* (literally share or portion) of God's love and blessings (both spiritual and material); the feast is also almost always given in honour of a child who is named in the speeches, and who is the primary focus of the giving (to God) and receiving of blessings. Feasts of this type are extremely important on a number of levels. Not only does the family engage God in a gift relationship through the feast, but several other households as well. The households most closely associated with the sponsoring household will assist in preparation of the feast, and will often contribute resources as well. Once the feast is concluded, what food is left over (and there is always a great deal) is distributed throughout the village and sometimes beyond, in a pattern determined by the household's gift relationships with other individuals. Finally, but by no means least important, these feasts express a gift relationship between the child honoured, and their parents (or perhaps grandparents). The giving of a feast for a child is explicitly understood as a function of parents' *'ofa* for the child; it is part of the gift relationship between the parents and the child.

While the years after contact and the formation of the modern Kingdom resulted in a series of changes to the social organization of the Tongan polity, these changes are very poorly glossed as "commoditization." The flow of rents to the now constitutionally recognized nobility, and the flow of taxes to the state, and the flow of donations to the churches, all boosted the production of copra destined for markets in Europe, but this does not necessarily mean that any but the last step in the flow of these resources was commoditized. Rather a complex and sometimes ambiguous mixture of gift and tribute relations was responsible for the flow of material. While Gailey is justified when she claims that world markets determined what goods would flow through these relations,[27] the question of how or why goods flowed at all cannot be answered by appeal to the World System or state power.

Nonetheless, changes in the nature of the relationships between commoners and the noble elite had significant effects. Changes in the land tenure system and changes in the focus of ritual and sacred activity fractured the unity of the kinship and political systems, and inhibited the long-term reproduction of chiefly power and control. What was not inhibited, however, was the long-term reproduction of ties between commoners, or the centrality of either kinship or gift exchange in formulating and expressing these ties.

Chapter Five

Contemporary Social Organization among Village Commoners

A recurring problem in the various attempts to conceptualize social organization at the village level arises from attempts to ferret out social groups which correspond to Tongan terms, and build structural models of Tongan kinship. Applying indigenous terminology in an analytical frame may be difficult and, in the final analysis, of limited utility. One of the primary reasons for this is that kinship groups today are not generally corporate, but rather loci of overlapping interest and emotion, best understood as the result of the multiple practices of individuals rather than the subsumption of individual relationships into those of the group.

Construction of Social Groups

The terms *'api*, *famili*, and *kāinga* encompass the most important kinship based social units operating in the villages. In addition to these core terms are a number of others, some Tongan, and some the terminological result of the analyses of various authors; for instance *matakali*, *fa'ahinga*, and *ha'a* are still sometimes ascribed to contemporary organization, and analytical constructs like *maison* or family estate have been used to describe empirical patterns observed by anthropologists. Unfortunately

---

Notes to chapter 5 start on p. 181.

the use of these terms within the literature on contemporary Tongan social relations is both inconsistent and contradictory. Both the variety of terms used, and the inconsistencies in the way they are used within the literature are partially the result of the variation in the usage of the terms by Tongans themselves.

The term *ha'a* was discussed in reference to its historical context earlier; Kaeppler (1971) and Marcus (1980, 82) make the explicit claim that *ha'a* retained cogency into the 1970s. The direct relevance of *ha'a* organization to commoners is limited,[1] however, and thus ignored here. The terms *matakali* and *fa'ahinga* appear to be related, with *matakali* being a borrowing from Fijian (Kaeppler 1971, 191); the use of the term *matakali* is reported by Maude (1965, 51-53) and Morton (1972, 50-51), and mentioned by Kaeppler (1971, 191) and van der Grijp (1993, 134). The term *fa'ahinga* (described earlier) is more commonly used (Maude and Sevele 1987). However, neither term is particularly significant to commoners today although they may be known (van der Grijp 1993, 135).

Famili and Kāinga

Famili is arguably the most significant term of reference within the Tongan kinship system today. Cowling (1990a) lists the several meanings of the term:

    i. any nuclear family;
   ii. the members of an individual's natal household;
  iii. cognate kin, more correctly known as *kāinga*;
  iv. the totality of an individual's kin, both cognate and affines;
   v. members of the group of relatives with whom an individual works most closely in producing craft goods, feast tables (pola) for special occasions, or who work together on a regular basis in agricultural production for household subsistence needs or for cash sale, or to whom an individual could go to borrow money or other needs. (Ibid., 110)

In Tongan terms, *famili* can include a very large number of people, virtually all those to whom an individual is related by blood or marriage (definition iv.), although such usage is uncommon. Generally the term is used for the first two and last definitions given by Cowling.[2]

As is indicated in definition iii., the use of the terms *kāinga* and *famili* overlap. Decktor-Korn draws a rather strict distinction between *kāinga* and *famili*:

> Membership in the *kāinga* — if it may be called "membership" — is simply a matter of genealogical relationships; membership in the *famili*,

although founded on kin ties, is defined by participation in the activities of the *famili*. While *kāinga* is mainly a relationship category, *famili* is an action group which supplies members' households with goods, labour, and personnel when they are needed . . . while *kāinga* ties transcend local boundaries . . . the *famili* is essentially a localized group, most of whose members live in the same village. (1977, 153-55)

This is a useful distinction, and one with which many Tongans might agree in the abstract, although in common usage *kāinga* and *famili* are often used interchangeably, especially when referring to more distant kin.

Rogers suggests that the use of the term *famili* versus *kāinga* is indicative of a retraction of kinship obligations toward closer relatives; that is "the concept of *famili* reflects movement from the expansive sphere of *kāinga* ideology towards exclusive principles" (1975, 247). However he then goes on to discuss the "ideology of *kāinga*" using the term *kāinga* to mean *both kāinga* and *famili* because the usage of the terms is so flexible, and varies from village to village (ibid., 247).

The preponderance of usage on Ha'ano Island is as Decktor-Korn suggests; a *kāinga* is an ideal ego-centred kindred, while *famili* is generally used to indicate those relatives with whom an individual has more *active* material and social interests in common.[3] For individuals the most active material and social ties tend to centre on their natal families (including families of adoption), and on their families of procreation. The terms *famili* and *kāinga* merge somewhat at the edges even in Decktor-Korn's formulation however; *kāinga* relationships can be activated for specific and limited purposes, for example in acquiring short-term access to garden land, and thus *kāinga* is not simply an ideal "relational category" (Decktor-Korn 1974, 9-10; and see Aoyagi 1966 for a similar formulation using slightly different terms). What separates *kāinga* and *famili* in ideal terms, if not always empirically, is that contributions to the various projects of the households and individuals which make up the *famili* are made automatically and without overt requests (Decktor-Korn 1977, 169). Conversely "to ask *kāinga* for any assistance if they are not also members of one's *famili* puts one in a subordinate supplicatory position, which is not true for provision of assistance within the *famili*" (ibid., 164).

Decktor-Korn, and most Tongans as well, usually use the term *famili* to refer to localized kinship based social relationships that order and underlie mutually reciprocal exchange activity on a daily basis. Decktor-Korn's central thesis is that Tongan social structure needs to be understood as a "loose" one, in which the relative freedom of individuals to exercise a range of choices within the kinship system results in the highly variable composition of social units at all levels. Yet she insists that *famili* be understood as a social unit, one based on sibling sets or the descendants of sibling sets, although non-unilineal in membership (ibid., 155). Furthermore in Decktor-Korn's view, *famili* do not overlap (ibid., 161), that is they are discrete and exclusive at any one point in time, although membership tends to shift over time. Van der Grijp's concept of the *maison* (borrowed from Lévi-Strauss 1984, 190 cited in van der Grijp 1993, 131) very closely parallels Decktor-Korn's *famili; maison* refers to a kinship based action group, generally formed around ambilineally related sibling sets, and realized in a constant flow of goods and services[4] (ibid., 131-34).

Cowling disputes the analysis of both authors above; she writes:

> In my view no fixed rules should be formulated regarding the membership of a small kin-based group which cooperates on work tasks or which supports each other without question. Such alliances exist but the membership may simply be determined by the history of interhousehold relations of kin while children are growing up, or even by how many people can comfortably fit in the room of a house to prepare food or make mats, or are affected by personal preference. (Cowling 1990a, 115)

In fact Decktor-Korn's position is not much different, for she well recognizes the heterogeneity of *famili*. She writes:

> it must be understood that the criteria of membership in the *famili* are not at all rigid. A person could be affiliated with any *famili* to which he or she is able to claim a kin tie, even if the genealogical connection is not very close, provided it is accepted by the members of the *famili*. (1977, 155-56)

The source of disagreement between Cowling and Decktor-Korn can be seen in this statement from Cowling:

> Most individuals had a network of people to whom they would apply for assistance on various matters. Some of these members were kin and others were non-kin. In the case of kin the word *famili* was used as an *explanatory term rather than as a collective noun*. (1990a, 117, emphasis mine)

Although Decktor-Korn realizes full well that *famili* are not terminologically recognized as collective bounded entities by Tongans themselves, she seems to hold that individuals nonetheless recognize and distinguish *famili* relationships from all other types, including those based on genealogical ties as close or perhaps closer than those within the *famili*. It

is clear from Decktor-Korn's comments on her methodology for deter-
mining *famili* membership, that membership is an empirical question
which should be determined by direct observation of exchange patterns,
rather than by direct questioning (1977, 166). The problem here is that
while *famili* is a significant category of Tongan social reckoning, a *famili* is
not a social unit with defined boundaries, either over time or within any
one temporal instant. The term *famili* is a description of relationship; *famili*
is no more a defined social entity, corporate or otherwise, than is *kāinga*.

This leaves the issue of how valuable Decktor-Korn's definition of
famili is as an analytical and heuristic device. Clearly Decktor-Korn
believed it useful to describe kinship relations among rural commoners in
Tongatapu in the early 1970s. Cowling quite correctly points out that the
last twenty years have brought considerable change, however (1990a,
117-18). Ha'apai especially has been severely depopulated by out-migration (see Appendix I). This depopulation has resulted in gender and age
imbalances, and the fractionation of sibling sets. In the village of Ha'ano,
if there were intact and exclusive *famili* units in the past, they are largely
absent now. Instead most households rely on an array of relationships
rooted in kinship, neighbourliness (called *kaunga'api*), and common
church membership (*kāinga* lotu). Any or all of these connections may
constitute the basis for the generalized daily exchange relationships which
Decktor-Korn singles out as the defining characteristic of *famili* organization. Where genealogical and affinal ties may have been the primary path
through which particularly intense ties were formed, a considerably wider
array of relationships perform the same function today.

The rather ironic corollary to this is the extension of *famili* relationships beyond the locale that has accompanied increased levels of migration. Decktor-Korn stresses the localized nature of *famili* (see also van der
Grijp 1993, 136-37), in part because of the intensity of *famili* activities.
She writes:

> it is extremely burdensome materially and might well be impossible
> socially, either to maintain these obligations with more than one *famili*
> at a time or to have members of the same household involved in mem-
> bership of different *famili*. Similarly, it is difficult to sustain the obliga-
> tions of *famili* membership when members of the *famili* reside in differ-
> ent villages. . . . (Decktor-Korn 1977, 165)

Marcus, working primarily among the elite of Tongatapu during the
same period, describes a different pattern. Marcus too recognizes a high
degree of variability in *famili* organization, but explicitly rejects a solely
village focus as sufficient (Marcus 1977, 224). Instead he identifies *famili*,

famili groups, family estates all of which are synonymous for social units "established by repetitive interactions of mutual support among a set of kinsmen from different family units" (Marcus 1980, 113), the most likely basis for connection being siblingship. A close reading of Marcus' discussion reveals that the existence and vitality of these family estates are not universals, but rather more common among the elite whether commoner or noble; indeed Marcus sees "family estate development" as the "core process of elite formation" (ibid., 113), and the only empirically explicit discussion of family estates marshalled by Marcus is drawn from the elites.

The most obvious difference in the way Decktor-Korn and Marcus view the *famili* is in whether it is dispersed or localized. Their different experience of Tonga, one urban and elite, and the other rural and commoner, is probably the source of the different analytical constructs (see Decktor-Korn 1977, 168-70). Within a heuristic frame, and given the location and time of her fieldwork, Decktor-Korn's formulation was valid, but given the changes of the last twenty years, such a position is no longer supportable. On the other hand, conceptualizing dispersed family networks as corporate is also problematic.

Marcus frames his construction of *famili*, "*famili* networks," or family estates in terms of his "compromise culture," that is the result of the series of changes which occurred in post-contact Tonga. According to Marcus:

> The social transformation of the compromise culture perhaps did not make Tongan society more egalitarian in ethos, but it did somewhat equalize the opportunities and capacities for status competition and mobility among a greater number of more independently operating social units, which are the highly rank conscious and internally stratified *famili* groups. (1980, 15)

These *famili*, which become dispersed as individuals pursue various opportunities in education, employment, and land acquisition, are stratified internally as well as externally. Internal stratification is governed by both the norms of kinship hierarchy and by the achieved status of those within the network. Marcus suggests that a fundamental underlying tension is present within the *famili*; individuals within make decisions about the allocation of resources to either the group, or to their own individual projects. Individuals may use their personal resources to create ties of dependency with others, or share their resources within the group (presumably according to the dictates of kinship ideology). It seems that the most successful family estates are those which have used a common pool of resources through a corporate and stratified internal structure, to develop a wider network of client *famili* (ibid., 16). Marcus is thus distinguishing between family estates, and an even wider organizational form based on patron-client ties, while the family estate itself continues to be organized through kinship obligation and reciprocity. This wider structure of relationships, which Marcus calls "family estate configurations," is well beyond the ken of Tongan defined categories (ibid., 16), and for Marcus, seems to have replaced the old *ha'a* and chiefly *kāinga* systems within elite politics, in all but ceremonial situations.

Marcus's analysis is overtly focussed on the elite of contemporary Tonga. Like Decktor-Korn, Marcus has constructed an analytical unit for conceptualizing the way that Tongan social units form. But both the notion of *famili* corporateness, and that of a pattern of consistent patron-client ties, were found wanting for the analysis of the data collected on the island of Ha'ano. For the discussion that follows, I have used households to marshal my data. The use of the household has some of the same limitations as Decktor-Korn's use of *famili* or Marcus' family estates; that is, it binds into analytical units that which is not bounded in the course of daily life. One advantage of using households, however, is that because the household is clearly linked to people beyond through a variety of relationships, there is less of a tendency to assume the unity or exclusivity it clearly lacks.

Household and 'Api

The meaning of the term *'api* is somewhat more straightforward than either *kāinga* or *famili*; it refers *roughly* to the household. The *'api* is a co-residential group, which is usually but not always patrilocal or virilocal. It is important to note here that "the primary referent of *'api* is land" (Decktor-Korn 1977, 100), as in the terms *'api kolo* (town site) or *'api tukuhau* (garden or tax allotment), which refer to specific types of lands. *'Api* is *not* now translatable as either nuclear or extended family, and should not be conceived of as such (ibid., 102-104) in spite of the fact that most *'api* contain something approaching nuclear, stem or extended family units at their core.

Unlike most Tongan social terms, *'api* has a discrete referent rather than a relational one. The term applies to those who share a common residence, either in a single building, or in a clustered group of buildings, usually situated on a single town allotment. Relationships within an *'api* are characterized by common consumption (that is a common cooking pot), and some elements of cooperative production as well. Most *'api* are formed around primary kinship bonds, but may also include more distantly related kin, and occasionally non-related individuals as well.

Whether an *'api* may be considered a household is a difficult question. If "household (or domestic unit) refers to a co-resident group of persons who share most aspects of consumption, drawing on and allocating a common pool of resources (including labour) to ensure their material reproduction" (Schmink 1984, 89), then we may tentatively call an *'api* an household. Indeed the data collection process made the assumption that an *'api* could be considered a household, but it is necessary to make some initial comments before moving on.

Defining the household/*'api* in terms of geographical location is overly restrictive. In many areas of the country, especially the Ha'apai region of which Ha'ano Island is a part, levels of temporary migration have created dispersed households. Migration for the purposes of education can result in the seasonal and cyclical relocation of numerous people within Ha'apai, and throughout the nation. Pangai, the regional capital of the Ha'apai region, is the site of all the high schools in the area. Educational facilities in outlying villages and islands are restricted to primary school only. Children from those areas not connected by road to Pangai (that is the villages other than those on the islands of Foa and Lifuka) must move. The frequency of available marine transport from the outer islands makes daily commuting impossible, and weekly commuting tiresome. Many households are split between the village and the regional capital for much of the year. Typically one or more adults remain in the village, while the school-age children and one or more custodial adults reside within convenient distance of educational facilities. Household segments residing in the village continue to provision the entire household, and split their time between the village and urban residence.

Children fortunate enough to pass the entrance exams for the prestigious high schools located on Tongatapu may leave the region entirely. It is almost universally believed that the high schools on Tongatapu provide better education than those in Ha'apai. Children bright enough to gain entrance into Tonga High School (the only government-run high school, and the school generally considered the best in the country) will almost certainly relocate. The shift from Ha'ano Island to Tongatapu is much more difficult than that between Ha'ano Island and Pangai. The distance involved makes consistent provisioning from the village problematic and expensive. While some families may relocate in their entirety, a more usual pattern is to send the child to live with a relative in Tongatapu. Although in a technical sense this means that the child is shifting households, such children are included in the village based households in those cases in which the rural household continues to provision the child in some substantive way.

While the broad outlines of Tongan kinship patterns can be discerned in the ways that people bring together the three core concepts, 'ofa, faka'apa'apa, and feitokoni'aki, short of an exhaustive (and probably quite tedious) list, it is not possible to adequately represent the configurations of relationship existing in Tonga. From the preceding discussion it should be clear that the optative nature of Tongan social relations is the basis for the wide variety in the way in which people form and maintain social ties. A few short examples will serve to illustrate how these ties can coalesce into living arrangements on the ground.[5] The difficulty in constructing these examples is not in identifying the boundaries of the household; that is a purely analytical decision based on external criteria (primarily the notion of a common cooking pot). The real problems begin when trying to limit the linkages beyond the household that form part of the description. For the purposes of the aggregate analyses in the next chapter, some rather arbitrary choices must be made. However, it is important to remember that people do not generally view their potential social relations as bounded; they can and do seek out and establish new active linkages where possible. Indeed, both new and old relationships require active participation and care, and thus the social universe in which people operate is both an active and fluid one.

Sila and Sima are an older couple (in their seventies) who live with their grandson, Tevita (the oldest son of their daughter Mele), who has just left high school. Sima is an active and productive weaver, and Sila still gardens as well. Tevita also has gardens of his own. The household's weaving, gardens, and some limited fishing are used to support the three people who are full time residents in Ha'ano, and Sima and Sila's daughter, Mele, who stays in Pangai in a very small house, cares for two daughters (Mele si'i and Latu) and a son (Sila si'i) who are attending school there. (Mele's husband is a long term, perhaps permanent, migrant to Hawaii; he sends money home every year, but has not, and may not return himself). Sila or Tevita make the trip from Ha'ano at least once a week to bring provisions. On school holidays, or when special events demand, Mele and the children return to Ha'ano. The residence in Pangai is quite rough, and little investment is made in it by the family. Despite the fact that this household is dispersed, by my analysis it is a single household, because provisioning is done from a single resource base, people share a common cooking pot when possible, and the decisions they take reflect a broadly understood (but not encompassing) common interest. In some contexts, especially in terms of subsistence production and consumption, the household operates as a single unit. In others, for instance in terms of contributions to the churches, Sila and Sima form one unit, and Mele and her children another; in fact they belong to different congregations. While Mele helps Sila and Sima with their obligations to their church (and the reverse), she does so because of her *ēofa* to her parents, not because her interests are subsumed within the household or directed by the household head (i.e., Sila who is unambiguously the head of household by any reckoning that would make sense to people in the village). Again, in analytical terms the configuration I have described here forms one household, but there are clear lines of cleavage as well. In the next example, a series of households are described that are closely linked, but analytically separate.

Pila and Leti[6] live in a house on an allotment adjacent to that of Sila and Sima, with their primary-school-age children (two daughters, Seini and Saane, and a son Semisi). They also have one son named Finau si'i who stays in Pangai where he attends a church-run high school; in Pangai Finau is provisioned by Pila and Leti (and other close kinspeople), and stays with the principal of the school he attends. In addition, Timote (the oldest son) and Lolohea (the oldest daughter) attend high school in Tongatapu. Lolohea boards at the school she attends, and Timote stays with an older half-brother. In addition, Sela, Pila's father's sister (and the adoptive mother of Lolohea) also lives in the household. Sela frequently travels to Tongatapu to visit and help care for the two children living there. This household also has very close relations with three others; one headed by Pila's father Finau, one by his father's brother Sione, and one headed by Leti's maternal uncle Vili (note the wives of Sione and Vili, Lesi and Vina, are sisters). Members of all four of these households cooperate closely on a day-to-day basis. For instance Pila and Finau have separate gardens but harvest freely from each other; Finau, Sione, and Vili go to sea both collectively and separately, and supply fish regularly to all four households. Lesi, Vina, and Leti do weave together, but their production is held and allocated separately. These households do share widely amongst themselves because of the multiple and overlapping ties, but generally cook separately, and tend not to pool resources except in exceptional circumstances. Finally, though the children in Pangai and Tongatapu are primarily Pila and Leti's responsibility, all the adults in the four households help regularly in terms of economic, social, and emotional supports. Providing for children in dispersed settings like this is a challenge for a great many households in the village.

Tani and Mele, for instance, do not have the sort of support that Pila and Leti do. When the school term starts, Mele moves to Pangai with their children (five sons and one daughter). The oldest child is just finishing high school, while the youngest is just beginning. Tani splits his time between Ha'ano, where he works in his garden, and Pangai where he helps Mele care for the children. Mele stays in Pangai during the school year, taking care of the children, and weaving when she can. Tani provisions the family, regularly bringing food, fish, and pandanus fibres from Ha'ano for Mele to weave. Though the household is not isolated, and does give and receive help from various people to whom they are socially tied, they have no close cooperating households either in Pangai or Ha'ano. In part this is because neither Mele or Tani have close kinspeople living nearby. At the peak of the dependency cycle (i.e., the lowest producer-to-consumer ratio), Mele and Tani must struggle to keep the children in school and meet their various church and social obligations. Once the oldest children finish school, this situation would gradually reverse itself, but in 1992 the demands on Tani and Mele were immense.

The numbers of children in school in Pangai, Tongatapu, and elsewhere in Tonga are given in Table 5.1.[7] The children attending school in Tongatapu all stay with relatives or board at their schools. Most of those attending school in Pangai stay with a related adult from Ha'ano Island who has relocated temporarily to Pangai. These adults are almost exclusively women.[8]

Table 5.1: Persons Temporarily Absent from Ha'ano Island for Education-Related Reasons by Village

Village	Children at School: Pangai	Children at School: Tonga	Children at School: Elsewhere	Adult Care-givers	Preschool Children in Pangai
Fakakakai	14	24	1	3	2
Ha'ano	22	6	0	4	11
Muitoa	15	2	0	3	2
Pukotala	13	11	4	3	6
Total	64	43	5	13	21

Delineating the Household/'Api

Individuals within an *'api* share *most* resources, but they do not share all resources, and they do not have coterminous material and social interests. This is the case in almost every configuration of *'api* membership. Wives do not have the same social responsibilities, kinship connections, or kinship obligations as their husbands; marriage does not merge the *kāinga* of husband and wife. Children have different *kāinga* than either their mother or father; that is they are *kāinga* to both their mother's side *and* their father's. Even siblings, though they may remain within a common household well into adulthood, also develop diverging social ties. Church membership, one of the most intense sites for the development of social relationships and connections, frequently varies within a particular household (Decktor-Korn 1977, 197). Variation in the social ties of individuals within a household is manifest at different junctures. On an everyday basis there may be little which points to multiple and sometimes competing interests, but in the more structured and public performance of ceremonial exchange, the appearance of any overarching *'api* unity can dissolve.

In the example of Pila and Leti's household given earlier, the closely cooperating households described are linked through Pila (Finau and Sione's households) and Leti (Vili's household) respectively. In addition to the ties formed through Pila and Leti, the social configuration is held together by people's common commitment to the children (that is the children of Pila and Leti) who are *kāinga/famili* to everyone involved.

In terms of the discussion regarding the relationship between *kāinga* and *famili*, the configuration I have just described is interesting (and by no means atypical), in that even the term *kāinga* is only sensible when focussed. Each of the four households, and indeed each of the individuals within, have different *kāinga*. Though I will refer again to the "configuration" of households formed around Pila and Leti, it is vital to note that the unit I thereby describe is an artifact of my focus. Were I to focus instead on one of the other households, a different configuration would emerge. At all levels the patterns of interrelationship are ego-based and overlapping rather than corporate.

Within the household, the most profound lines of cleavage run through the marriage bond. Contrary to Gailey (1980, 1987), women have not been transformed into wives and mothers alone, but maintain roles, responsibilities, and privileges as sisters and daughters within their natal families throughout their lives; in a similar vein men generally maintain linkages to their natal families regardless of post-marital residence choices. Husband and wife are never fully integrated socially, and the key to what common interests they do possess is not their marriage, but their *children*. The material consequences of these relations are investigated in depth later (chapter 7).

Again, in analytical terms, the delineation of separate households that cooperate closely, and households made up of multiple components is a difficult issue in the Tongan context. Obviously if conjugal pairs have competing interests and different social bonds, then individuals within extended family households have even more divergent interests. Yet at the same time a household may be linked to other households very closely in some ways. For instance some households have no garden lands, but are not usefully considered landless because regardless of the legalities of the situation, they treat certain lands belonging to individuals within other households as if they were commonly held (for instance Pila does not yet have legal tenure of land of his own, but treats Finau's land, and other allotments to which he has access through kinspeople, as his own).

Table 5.2: Mean Household Size on Ha'ano Island by Village
(n = 116)

Village	Mean Household Size (de jure)	Mean household Size (de facto)
Fakakakai	64	48
Ha'ano	51	39
Muitoa	66	51
Pukotala	62	44
All Villages Ha'ano Island	60	44

The creation of a new household generally occurs sometime after a couple has one or more children. For Methodists this coincides with the expected transition of a young adult man from a church member (frequently absent) to *malanga*, or lay preacher. Once a man becomes a *malanga*,[9] both husband and wife enter new and well-defined social categories which entail new responsibilities to the church and their families. For men especially,[10] this entails a reintegration into the fabric of the social order. Marriage and the birth of a child, however, do not necessarily lead to the rapid formation of a new household. This is especially true when the care of aging parents is an issue. On the other hand, if a new household is formed, the linkages with other households remain socially and materially significant. The household/'api as a unit is both too inclusive and too exclusive to capture domestic processes in the villages.

Table 5.2 gives the mean household/'api sizes on Ha'ano Island using both de facto (i.e., counting those residing in the household at the time of the census) and de jure reckoning (i.e., counting those temporarily absent at the time of the census).

The difference in mean household size between de facto and de jure residents is over 1.5 persons. This is due to the tendency for one man to remain in the village to farm while his family is in Pangai so the children can attend school. The failure to include the segment of the family in Pangai seriously distorts subsequent analysis of the domestic economy (see for instance Hardaker et al. 1988, 20). These persons have significant impact on household economic requirements and potentials, and thus cannot be ignored. The inclusion here of the figures calculated on full-time residents only is to allow the reader to make comparisons as they desire. I however, will for the most part use the figures which include temporarily absent people. Not to do so in the context of Ha'ano Island is to seriously distort the realities which effect decisions and choices made within households and the domestic economy. Further like the emically recognized units of social structure (for example *famili* or *kāinga*), *the household is a sensible unit of analysis only when it is recognized that it is a locus of social practice, and not a bounded entity.*

Both households and *famili* are constituted primarily through kin ties. Kinship and kinship relationships are a vehicle or idiom through which resources may flow. Kinship is not determinate, but clearly it is significant. Rather than looking to the structure of kinship however, we must look to its practice, or perhaps more correctly its praxis; in the intersection of interest, emotion, and the ideology of kinship are the patterns of village life. In a similar manner external legal and economic structures cannot be viewed as determinate. The interactions between local concerns, intentions, and actions and the wider political and economic contexts in which people exist are just that, interactions.

Chapter Six

The Island Economy

T he day-to day economy of Ha'ano Island is primarily subsistence in nature. People eat the crops they grow, the livestock they raise, and the fish they catch. Although some food is purchased from the small stores which can be found in almost every village, or from the larger retailers located in the regional centre, the vast bulk comes from the land and the surrounding sea. Traditional forms of wealth, primarily woven pandanus mats, pork and certain types of root crops produced on the island, also retain cogency in terms of the gift exchange system. There are, however, significant linkages between the island's economy and that of the nation and beyond. People sell copra and fish; they trade pandanus mats for both cash and other forms of traditional wealth; they send their children to school; they send people to the capital and overseas, and receive gifts of cash and goods from the same places; and some people are engaged in waged labour. People also buy a small amount of foodstuffs, sundries, and from time to time, significant amounts of construction material or consumer goods.

Much of the following is empirical and descriptive. In analytical terms the data presented shows quite clearly that despite the fact that the actual production processes are largely individuated, significant amounts of material flow between households on a regular basis. Here I look at the

Notes to chapter 6 start on p. 182.

economic activities of households, and to the informal day-to-day reciprocities which knit households together. These movements are in turn related to formal exchange practices described later.

The island itself is almost a stereotype of a South Pacific atoll. Approximately four kilometres long and one wide, it rises only fifteen metres above sea level. Most of the soils are quite rich, though some poorer coral soils dominate the areas along the lee shore. The main gravel road, made of crushed coral, runs along this shore, connecting Muitoa on the northern tip, to Ha'ano, Pukotala, and finally Fakakakai at the Southern end. The entire island, with the exception of the four village sites, is planted with neatly spaced coconut trees. These garden lands are webbed by small roads and paths. Actual gardens are spread across the island, interspersed with land in various stages of fallow. A variety of fruit trees and other useful plants can be found throughout. Roads and gardens are often bordered with pandanus plants which are used to make fine mats.

The lee shore is protected from the worst wave action, and the reef there harbours an abundance of fish, shellfish, and other marine life. Gaps in the reef allow access to moorages at Ha'ano, Pukotala, and Fakakakai, though the best mooring sites, those easily accessible even at low tide, are at Ha'ano. The windward shore, called the *liku* (or cliff) is not accessible to boats and, though rich in edible seaweeds (sea grapes or *limu*), is much less rich in marine resources that can be accessed from land. The reef slope is fished, as are adjacent undersea mounts, by fishers from the island, but because of the distances involved (even fishing the near reef slope requires the circumnavigation of the island and can take several hours) this only happens on extended fishing trips.

Infrastructural development is quite limited. None of the villages have electricity, though a few households have a generator which might be used from time to time. Only the district nurse, stationed at a small clinic at Fakakakai, has a motor vehicle in the form of a 100cc motorcycle. The Ministry of Agriculture and Forestry has a station midway between Ha'ano and Pukotala, which is also about the midway point of the island. There are two primary schools, one at Ha'ano (serving Muitoa as well), and one at Pukotala (which also serves Fakakakai). Ha'ano and Pukotala also have the island's two (rather temperamental) radio telephones. These provide links to the outside world through a switchboard system at the Pangai telephone exchange, but can be extremely time consuming to use. (The whole time I was on Ha'ano I used the phone only once, and unsuccessfully at that). With the exception of one rather brackish well located in Pukotala, all the potable water is rainwater collected from roofs and stored in cement cisterns. (This can be a problem during the periodic droughts that affect the region. A protracted drought in 1991 and early 1992 caused such a shortage that water had to be shipped in from Tongatapu by barge).

The villages themselves are quite similar. Each village is fenced and gated in order to keep livestock from ravaging nearby gardens. All have undergone depopulation, and thus the housing is widely dispersed. The most common house type, a wood structure about six metres by six metres and divided into two rooms, sits on half-metre stilts. Houses in this style, which also have two opposed doors and louvered windows for air flow, were part of a relief package, and built following the devastation wrought by Hurricane Isaac in 1982. Only a handful of houses survived that storm, and where traditional Tongan dwellings (thatched houses of various types) were prevalent before, only a very few were rebuilt. Each house sits on a designated house allotment (the land tenure system is described in detail later), but not all the allotments have houses on them, nor are all the houses occupied. Most houses are fenced in, and have a small kitchen house (*peito*), wash house, and outhouse at the back. In addition to the houses that dot the villages, there are a number of churches in each place, many of which have large meeting houses near by. Finally there are a number of active cemeteries, and quite a few ancient ones (which can be identified by their mounds and the occasional bone) inside the villages, and just outside as well. The overall village appearance is quite open. Although there are some large mango, breadfruit, and shade trees on the village grounds, most larger trees and shrubs are found either in the areas fenced around houses, or outside the village fences.

Agriculture

Most agriculture on Ha'ano Island is subsistence agriculture; but subsistence here must be understood as more than the production required to ensure physical reproduction. Agricultural production on the island today includes little cash cropping, but substantial surpluses are produced by many households. These surpluses are usually deployed in traditional exchange circuits, rather than sold on commodity markets. Given that the tool inventory for agriculture on Ha'ano Island is still very simple, capital expense is a minor component of the cost of production; the key ingredients of the productive process are land and labour.

Land Tenure

Much has been made of the changes in the land tenure system introduced by Taufa'ahau in the late nineteenth century. It has been claimed (primarily by Gailey 1980, 1981, 1987) that the linkage between men and their families of procreation to particular pieces of land has alienated women from control of land and the produce of land, by limiting the claims on the production of men by their sisters and sister's children (that is *fahu*). For Gailey, the wider significance of this change has been the nucleation of family units (see Gailey 1992, 55) and the commoditization of social relations. The problem with Gailey's position is that it is not at all obvious that pre-constitutional *fahu* rights extended to outright claims on lands, though it is quite clear that *fahu* did allow, and indeed continues to allow, access to the products of land (and arguably usufruct rights as well, see the discussion later). On Ha'ano Island the claims of sisters on their brothers continue to have cogency today, and though the organization of work has become individuated, the overall social relations of production have not.

There is no question that agricultural production today is in the hands of individual men or that these men tend to look after the everyday consumption needs of their own, or closely related households; for the most part individual households have their own gardens. Nor is there any question that the legal structure of the land tenure system assumes that agriculture is both a male activity, and that individual men are responsible first to their own households. Although women are not proscribed from gardening, they very rarely work in the fields. Agriculture is almost exclusively a male activity. Women who do work in the gardens do so with their husbands or male kin. A woman working in the gardens is greeted with approval. It is rare, however, for women to work regularly in the bush; even women without co-resident males to garden for them usually rely on some other man (for example a brother or nephew) to supply them with garden food. Moengangongo (1986), citing Faletau (1981), reports that women grow both market crops and raw materials for handicraft production. This is *not* the case on Ha'ano Island. It is true that both home vegetable gardens (mostly tomatoes, carrots, onions, and the like) and pandanus (the material for fine mats) are held to be owned by particular women, but they tend to be cultivated by men.

Land Law

In law (and in theory) all men over the age of sixteen are entitled to 8¼ acres of land for the support of their families. Land is technically leased from the Crown (through either a noble, the Minister of Lands, or a member of the royal family). These leases, once registered, are inheritable through rules of patrilineal primogeniture. While this is a significant change from pre-constitutional land tenure in theory, it is a less encompassing change than might be assumed.[1] The practice of land tenure is far more complex than the legal structure suggests, and it is a grave error to assume that the existence of the Land Act means the elimination of pre-legislative arrangements and customs, or precludes the development of new informal land tenure practices (see also James 1995).

Under the Land Act, on the death of a landholder his land passes first to his widow (so long as she lives, is chaste, and does not remarry). Then, following her death, it passes to *his* eldest legitimate son. Moengangongo notes that widows are rarely stripped of land because of adultery charges (1986, 96; cf. Gailey 1987, 199, who *assumes* a correspondence between legal provision and social reality). This may be because a widow's interest in land does not usually affect the long-term disposition of the land. On her death, land reverts to the first born legitimate male offspring of the previous male holder.[2] If there are no sons, then the land passes to any living brother or the sons of a deceased brother (again moving from eldest to youngest). Unmarried daughters may inherit if there are no legitimate male heirs, but, like widows, they may hold the land only as long as they remain unmarried and chaste. Land can also be acquired directly from either the noble of the area, or in the case of government estates like that surrounding Fakakakai, through the governor of the region.

Land Practice

Informal practices include purchasing land (specifically barred in the Land Act). The purchase of land is strictly illegal, but it does go on, although to what extent is unknown. James claims that, "Since the 1970s, the illegal land market has rapidly increased in volume and value in response to increasing monetisation, the modern incentives of commoditization, and the increasing rationalization of commercial ventures" (1995, 159). It is reasonable to assume that the flow of people into Tongatapu from elsewhere has created a situation in which increased pressure on land is accompanied by large numbers of individuals without the kinship connections to acquire land either permanently or temporarily. It thus follows that land purchases, or other practices of land distribution outside the Act, may be more common on Tongatapu than in other areas. Indeed, it is generally assumed by most (researchers, government officials, and the people themselves) that illegal land purchases are common in Tongatapu, but just how common is unclear, and assumptions about the prevalence of the practice should be tempered.

The purchase of land on Ha'ano Island is uncommon. Where it has occurred, it has been transacted between related individuals. In part this is because such transfer of lands must appear to be between kin in order to stand a chance of registration. Two cases of land purchase were identified on Ha'ano Island, both on the government estate around Fakakakai. Both cases involved the transfer of land between relatives, but through kinship linkages unrecognized by the Land Act. In one case the land was successfully re-registered, and in the other registration is still pending because counterclaims to the land have not been extinguished to the satisfaction of the authorities. In these two instances the transactions were specifically identified as purchases. It should be noted however that the transfer of cash or goods as part of a land transfer does not a commodity transaction make.

Lands are regularly transferred between kinspeople beyond the paths specified by the Land Act. On the lands of the Tu'i Ha'angana (the northern half of Ha'ano Island which includes the villages of Muitoa, Ha'ano, and Pukotala) these sorts of transfers require his approval, and generally involve the provision of some goods at the time of the request. This might entail a gift of a pig or fine mat. It is conceivable that a gift of cash could occur, but I know of no such transactions in spite of the fact that I asked all respondents. Even if cash is used to mediate a land transaction between noble and commoner, it is an open question whether this therefore justifies the assumption that a commodity transaction has taken place. It is unwise to assume that this sort of transaction is commodity exchange thinly veiled as tradition. When land is left vacant under the terms of the Land Act, and is therefore returned to the control of the Tu'i Ha'angana, kinship relationships to the previous holder are brought into play in subsequent decisions about the disposition of the allotment. The evaluation of these relationships extends beyond simple genealogy, to the substantive nature of the relationships involved. In the case of a land-holder who dies without heir, some consideration of who cared for the individual, and even the individual's wishes (also barred by the Land Act), may come into play. In part because of the close and free relationship between a man and his sister's children, there is a significant tendency for land to go to those children if there are no heirs prescribed by law. Thus both kinship relationships in general, and the *fahu* relationship in particular, continue to play a role in land transmission regardless of the dictates of the Land Act. These statements are empirically verified for the estate of the Tu'i Ha'angana, and consistent with other empirical work on the subject (see Moengangongo 1986, cf. James 1995). Exchange of land, like most exchange practice, is based on ongoing emotionally affective relationships, which by their nature include and valorize (rather than disguise) material interest and exchange practice.

The noble of an area does not have to follow what is in effect common practice. But for Ha'ano Island at least, it appears that he has, and what is more important he is expected to do so in the future. The present Tu'i Ha'angana is a young man, and from the villager's perspective, still an unknown quantity. When I asked people why they thought he would consider kinship and the relationships of those involved in extraordinary land transfers, the answers I got were generally of the "he's a nice guy" variety. Indeed from all appearances, he is *anga lelei* (of good nature — a nice guy). A couple of his actions in the short time I was in Ha'ano Island showed some concern for moderation in the exercise of his traditional rights to produce.

There are some practical reasons for people's expectation that he would do the appropriate thing. Contrary to the claim that nobles are being transformed into landlords (Gailey 1987; James 1993a, 223), nobles continue to rely on their people for traditional goods to meet their obligations to the royal family and other nobles. Morgan (1989) argues the ability of a noble to muster large amounts of traditional wealth is still an important facet of the public performance of title. The transfer of traditional wealth from commoners to nobles is common, and well outside of the legal obligations of tenancy. Although it is logical, and no doubt true, that some nobles block formal registration of land to ensure the flow of such wealth from their people, even families with secure registered title on Ha'ano Island contributed to the noble's projects. For instance, the present Tu'i Ha'angana was invested (*fakanofo*) in September 1991, just after we had arrived in the area. The investiture was a costly affair, involving considerable traditional wealth both female (pandanus mats and bark cloth) and male (pigs and yams); a large portion of this wealth came from the villagers on his estate. The alienation of any segment of the population of villagers is no more in the interest of the noble, than irritating the noble would be for a commoner. It is possible that on Tongatapu or in Vava'u that some nobles have developed ways around dependency on their people for traditional goods, but this is not the case on Ha'ano Island.

Landholding

A complete survey of all the tax allotments on Ha'ano Island was undertaken. This survey involved both an extensive review of the land registry for the area, and a careful accounting of the actual landholding patterns on the island. Two types of landholding were reported. First were lands actually registered (or believed to be so) to individuals within the household. Almost all of the land is registered, but the majority of registered landholders live elsewhere;[3] very little of the land on Ha'ano Island is still held by either the government, or the Tu'i Ha'angana. Frequent accusations have been made that nobles have tended to restrict official registration of land in order to hold onto some form of control over their people (S. Fonua 1975; James 1993a). This does not appear to be the case with the Tu'i Ha'angana. Only three small blocks of land were unambiguously in the direct possession of the Tu'i Ha'angana.

Second were lands which were being cared for (*tauhi*) by members of the household; these were lands registered to someone else but informally transferred.[4] Lands of this type may have been controlled by an individual or household for an extended period of time, or they may be relatively short-term arrangements; the minimum period recorded in the survey was one month, the maximum was forty-five years, and the mean was ten years. Such arrangements rarely involve a consistent or determined exchange of goods for usufruct rights, but may well entail the periodic request from the landholder, to the caretaker, for assistance.

Only one respondent reported any consistent payment for the use of an allotment (in this case a medium-sized pig with a value of eighty-one hundred pa'anga).[5] Several others reported periodic gifts to landowners however. In two cases during 1991-93 land was stripped from its caretakers because those who had given it felt that the caretakers had failed to give proper consideration in return. In one case this actually left the Ha'ano Island household truly landless (this is the only case of true landlessness recorded on the island), with only short-term gardens to rely on. Again, however, it must be recognized that although material interest is involved here, this does not necessarily mean that a de facto commodity relationship is in place (cf. Halapua 1981, 3). People on Ha'ano rarely separate the emotive and material aspects of any social relationship. The removal of these lands then was motivated by the feeling on the part of the landholder that the person caretaking the land had failed to show *'ofa*. To automatically assume that such explanations are mere material self-interest disguised in ideology oversimplifies and reduces the relationships involved to purely material ones.

Under the Land Act, tax allotments must be maintained or they can be repossessed by the Crown; this involves maintaining the land under cultivation. The major marker of this in the Act is the planting of the land in coconuts, but this portion of the act is no longer enforced. However almost all tax allotments are linked to a corresponding town allotment. Town allotments on the lands of the Tu'i Ha'angana are not consistently registered; very few are actually surveyed. There are town allotments that are customarily associated with certain parcels of land. (The names of these town allotments were often registered when the tax allotment was registered, but unlike the bush lands, the town sites have not been formally re-registered at the transfer of land that follows a death). Many registered holders do not live on the town allotment they technically own, but rather on some other parcel. This situation does not appear to be a problem for anyone; there is no shortage of town allotments. Town allotments in Fakakakai are surveyed and registered. It is possible, and not all that uncommon, to have a registered town allotment, but no tax allotment.

The villages are inspected by the civil authorities periodically, and town allotments must be kept clear of weeds and debris. The caretaking of a tax allotment entails the maintenance of its town allotment and thus represents some burden on the caretaker. To take care of a tax allotment thus involves both usufruct rights and responsibilities.

The complete cadastral survey of Ha'ano Island was not finished until 1968. It seems that at this time the formal registration of many previously informally held lands occurred. There are a total of 340 surveyed tax allotments with a total area of 553.38 hectares on Ha'ano Island. Although it is technically illegal for a single individual to hold more than one tax allotment, several of the smaller tax allotments are extensions of other holdings. The cadastral survey of the late 1960s was basically a survey of already existing customary holdings, some of these holdings consisted of two non-contiguous pieces of land; so long as the area of the two allotments together did not exceed the maximum allowable size, they were not broken up, and remained registered to one person. Thus although the mean size of the tax allotments is 1.63 hectares, mean size of registered total land holdings is slightly larger.

Fifty of the ninety-two tax allotments for which the circumstances of registration could be determined came from the holder's father's *famili*; that is through the application of the Land Act. A further sixteen parcels are held by widows, again in accordance with the Act. Sixteen of the allotments were granted directly from either the noble, or the government. The remainder, some ten allotments (or 10.9 percent of the total) were inherited through relationships which are not recognized under the Act (this is comparable to the figures given in Moengangongo 1986).

When we turn to the second type of landholding described above, that of caretaking, even greater variance from the patrilineal pattern encoded in the Act emerges (please refer to Figure 6.1). Approximately 40 percent of lands held under care taking arrangements were acquired through relationships consistent with the Land Act (that is, the "Patrilineal Relations" column); almost 35 percent were held through relationships which were contrary to the Act. The category of "Other Relations" refers to a variety of non-patrilineally based relationships. In fact, fully 11 percent of the total (approximately one third of the cases falling in the "other relations category"), were instances in which land was acquired from an individual's mother's *famili*.

Figure 6.1
Source of Land Held under Caretaking Arrangement

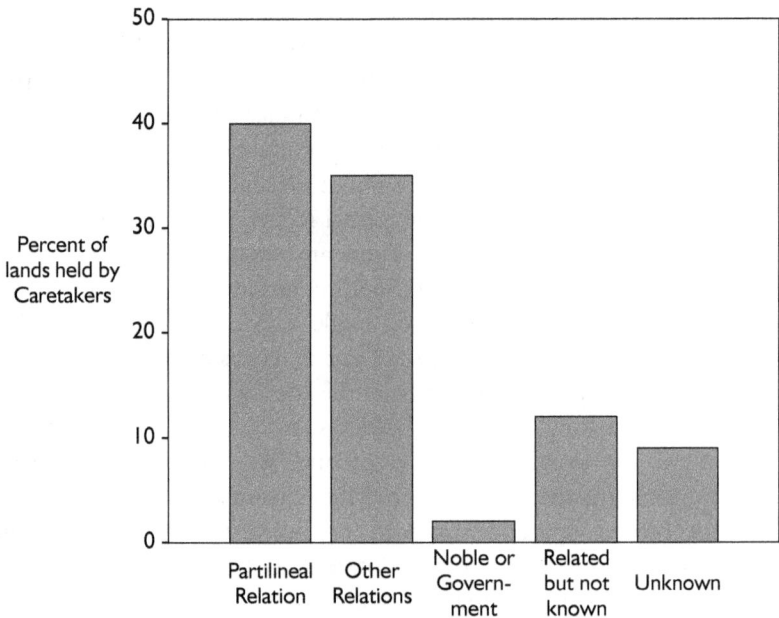

An example of how such transfers occur is warranted. A man died without a direct heir. Technically his land should have gone to the next oldest brother of his generation, or to the sons of that brother. There was in fact a living brother, but he already had land, and he himself had no direct heir (that is, sons). Rather than letting the land revert to the control of the noble, the land was transferred to the son of one of the original landholder's sisters. This occurred at the request of the sister. This sort of scenario was recounted to me several times by men who had acquired land through their mother's *famili*.

The category "Related but not known" refers to cases in which questions about people's relationship to the landholder were characterized as "*famili pe*" or "*kāinga pe*" (just related). These phrases were used by people who recognized, but could not trace, their genealogical relationships. The close patrilineal relationships referred to in the Act are without exception well within the range of any adult person's genealogical knowledge. Thus we can infer that these relationships too are beyond the Act's scope. While the Act has nothing to say about informal and temporary transfers of land, it is clear that the patrilineal bias of the Act has not been adopted within the informal arena. The non-patrilineal transfers of land under the caretaking arrangement probably approach 50 percent in total, roughly equal to those consistent with the Act.

Land Distribution

There is considerable variation in terms of the control of land from household to household. Figure 6.2 gives the distribution of land controlled (either by direct registration or caretaking arrangements) by household. Very few households do not have direct control of agricultural lands. Of the five households reporting no land, all but one were either engaged in cooperative gardening arrangements with a closely related household, or were the households of school teachers or clergy who came from elsewhere. The problem of landlessness, which is reported to be severe in other areas of the country, was not a serious problem on Ha'ano Island.

The entire discussion of landlessness in Tonga is clouded by the imposition of an individuated model of landholding on a system which operates in very different ways. Maude and Sevele (1987, 137) state that in 1984, just under fourteen thousand eligible men lacked registered land. Further they state that if all available land were distributed under the current system, the proportion of eligible men actually holding registered land would not exceed 45 percent (ibid., 129; see also S. Taliai 1975, 23). These sorts of numbers could be interpreted as indicating a state of crisis in land availability, but such interpretations assume that all men over the age of sixteen require not only land, but *registered* land for the support of their families. The nuclear family model built into the Land Act is, not surprisingly, replicated in the critiques of its operation. Given that the operation of the land tenure system is not now, and probably never was, based on the nuclear family in any simple way, such critiques overstate the problem. This is not to suggest that a problem does not exist, only that the figures used to define the problem are inappropriate.

Figure 6.2
Number of Tax Allotments Controlled by Household

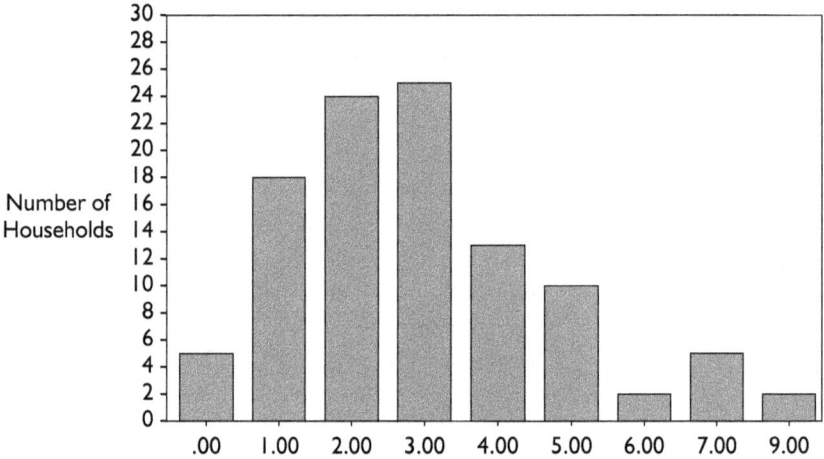

In table 6.1, the designation of "probable registration" was assigned to those for whom inheritance of land is a highly likely event, unimpeded by other possible claimants, and based on the straightforward application of the Land Act. It is somewhat ironic to note that eldest sons often attain registered land well after their younger siblings. This is because a man may inherit several pieces of land during his lifetime. For instance a man might inherit not only his father's land, but his father's father's or father's brother's land as well. When a man who already holds registered land inherits more, he cannot keep more than one parcel, but he may elect to pass one of the parcels onto a son, brother, or brother's son. The eldest son, because he is assured of his father's land, may not figure into the transfer of any lands which come into his father's possession, and must in fact wait until his father's death before gaining registered land of his own. This situation is not infrequent in the history of land transfers that I recorded.

Notwithstanding my comments above, there is a clear difference in the rates of registration (and probable registration) between different age categories on Ha'ano Island (see table 6.1).

These figures must be approached with caution. Land frequently comes open for registration, either because it falls back into the hands of the government or noble when there is no one in line to inherit, or because people closer in the line of succession have migrated, died, or do not wish to take up the land for whatever reason. The 45 individuals in the twenty- to twenty-nine-year-old category may well get an opportunity to register land at some point in their lives. Men occasionally acquire registered land late in life; one man registered the land of his brother's son (which the son turned over to him after the brother's death) well after his seventieth birthday. Given the number of allotments held under caretaking arrangements, it is likely that the vast majority will be able to at least acquire control of land in a caretaking capacity, though caretaking land need not be insecure in anything but the legal sense.

Table 6.1
Distribution of Registered Land on Ha'ano Island by Age Grade[a]

Age	No registered land	Land registered or likely to be registered
70+	2	7
55-69	1	19
30-54	24	55
20-29	45	11

a This table refers to men only, but includes men who have tax allotments on other islands.

The situation of Pila, whose household was described earlier, illustrates several of the points made above. Technically Pila is landless, because at this point in time all his access to land is mediated through his father, Finau. Pila is however Finau's oldest son, and will inherit the land registered to Finau at some point in the future (and thus would fall into the "Land registered or likely to be registered" category in Table 6.1). In addition Finau controls another three allotments in a caretaking capacity, all of which have been given to him by kinsmen. Pila, Finau, and Uili (Finau's youngest son who lives in his household) garden these lands in common. One of these allotments may eventually fall to Finau because all of the possible claimants to the land have left the island. Should this happen it is possible that Uili (who for now is in the "No registered land" category above) will be able to register one of the three other allotments.

Land Use
Land tenure and land use are distinct issues on Ha'ano Island. Farmers may have gardens on land registered to someone within the household, land controlled by someone within the household, land controlled by some other household, or any combination of the three.

When individuals use lands controlled by others, they are allowed the use of the lands for a specific garden and no more. Even where individuals are given the right to garden on the entire tax allotment, there is a qualitative distinction made between caretaking a tax allotment and short-term gardening rights. One major marker of the difference is the right to the coconuts on the land. A caretaker has the right to use the coconuts as they please: someone with only gardening rights does not. Another major difference is the gift of first fruit (*polopolo*) which goes to the owner (or caretaker) of the land after the first harvest from a garden. Usually this gift is a basket of yams. Such first fruit offerings are made when the land is granted on a short-term and limited basis.

A multi-level, multi-crop agricultural system.

There was also significant use of land under terms very similar to those of the short-term gardening type by cooperative gardening groups called *toutu'u*. The *toutu'u* on Ha'ano Island tend to be clustered around the villages (in Fakakakai two toutu'u were within the village fence on unused town allotments). The reasons for this are linked to livestock rather than land. All the villages on Ha'ano Island are fenced to keep pigs in, not out, of the villages. Within the village fence most of the pigs roam free, returning to their owner's house only for feeding at dusk (pigs are penned only in extraordinary circumstances). As a village fence ages, more and more pigs escape into the bush. Thus with an aging village fence, the garden lands close to the village are subject to an increase in the predations of foraging swine. Gardens are not usually fenced, except when they are located close to the village.

The most significant material consequence of a *toutu'u* is to provide for the collective fencing of a piece of land close by the village. Each member is responsible for providing a section of the fencing. After the fence is established each member has exclusive rights and responsibilities over a section of the garden, and except for the occasional maintenance of the fence, collective work stops. *Toutu'u* usually run for three years; after the first harvest, as in cases of short-term usufruct gardening rights, each member makes a first fruits offering to the owner/caretaker of the land.

Agricultural Production

Agricultural activity was recorded in two surveys of land under production; one in March of 1992 and one in February of 1993. The total land cropped in the first survey was 46.03 hectares; in the second survey some 56.19 hectares were under production. The slightly lower area in production in 1992 was due to the prolonged drought that affected the island during 1991-92. At the time of the first survey, farmers had already started to abandon some fields (although wherever possible these fields were recorded), and the normal cropping rotation which involves the rain sensitive replanting of gardens as first phase crops are harvested was disrupted. The survey of 1993 represents a more usual situation. The vast majority of the crops were subsistence crops in both surveys; the only significant cash crops were a couple of small plots of vanilla.

Including all gardens on Ha'ano Island in one table, the following breakdown was acquired:

Table 6.2
Area of Gardens by Control of Land (in hectares)

Survey No.	Different Household Controls Land	Own Household Controls Land	Toutu'u	Common Garden with Close Household	Government, Clergy, or Absent Household
1	11.2	21.2	5.1	0.8	3.0
2	14.6	26.9	5.5	1.9	2.6

If we remove anomalous cases, that is clergy and teachers (who generally move every three years), absent households, and government institutions like the Ministry of Agriculture and Forestry (MAF), the breakdown changes somewhat (see Figure 6.3).

Even though almost all households controlled their own lands, either through legal registration or informal caretaking arrangements, a significant percentage of the garden lands were on the lands of others. The land use pattern of the households of Pila and his father Finau are not atypical. In 1993, combined households' land in production was just over one half hectare. Of this, approximately 25 percent of these gardens is located on other people's lands (in *toutu'u* gardens). While there is a significant correlation between the area of gardens located on land under the control of the household, and total land area controlled by the household ($r = 0.41$, $n = 88$, $p < .0001$), we might well have expected a stronger correlation. There was no correlation between the percentage of land cropped on a household's own land, and total hectares controlled ($r = 0.1375$, $n = 88$, $p = 202/NS$).[6]

Figure 6.3
Garden Lands by Source (Excluding Anomalous Cases)

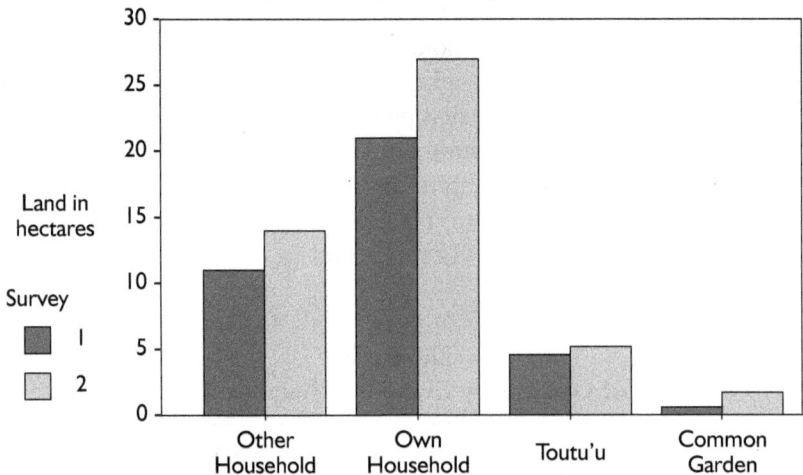

The weakness of these relations is probably due to a number of factors. Not all households have lands close to the village. Where households used other lands for gardening (either other people's land or *toutu'u* gardens), simple convenience (that is proximity to the village or other gardens) no doubt plays a role in the choice of the lands used. The availability of soil types on land controlled by the household is also a factor. Farmers on Ha'ano Island distinguish between two major soil types, *kelekele 'ua* (a rich volcanic based soil which covers about two thirds of

the island) and *'one'one* (a poorer sandy soil covering about one third of
the island); *'one'one* supports a more restricted range of crops, specifically
it is inappropriate for the highly valued yam varieties used in ceremonial
exchange, and is in general less productive.

Another reason why an unexpected quantity of gardened land is located
on other people's land may be tied up in individual farmers' concerns about
the long-term productivity of their own lands. A survey of land use patterns
conducted on Tongatapu found the lands of those who had migrated were
in fact more likely to be used than the lands of people who had not migrated (Hasan, personal communication). This result was contrary to the expectation that the lands of migrants were largely lying fallow and unproductive
(see for instance James 1993a, 217; Maude and Sevele 1987, 139). This
may imply a certain calculation on the part of those with access to lands
other than those under their direct control; that is where other land was
available, farmers used it and its *ivi* (energy), and saved their own lands. At
the very least it suggests that on Tongatapu, as on Ha'ano Island, land
belonging to absent individuals does not come out of production, but is
rather reallocated with informal mechanisms.

One farmer, who had farmed cash crops in Tongatapu, spoke to me of
ngōue fakapisinisi, or commercial farming. Referring to leased lands (that
is lands leased for cash — a practice absent from Ha'ano Island but not
Tongatapu), he suggested that agricultural practices shifted to use up the
energy in the soil as quickly, and therefore as cheaply, as possible. However, whether informal mechanisms of land redistribution on Tongatapu are
predominantly commoditized, or organized through gift exchange as they
are on Ha'ano Island, remains to be demonstrated.

Crops and Cropping Patterns

Among the factors influencing the type and amount of crops planted are
material concerns like access to planting materials, and access to lands
with the appropriate soil types. Social factors, like the anticipated subsistence and ceremonial needs, also play a role. Farmers generally plant
crops in excess of their subsistence needs in order to contribute to wider
social projects through ceremonial activity; bare subsistence is considered
pathetic. Marketable surpluses of traditional crops are sometimes a result
of conscious overproduction, but are more often the result of a particularly good growing season which leaves a surplus over and above subsistence and social requirements. There is in fact a lively internal market for
traditional crops. Markets in Nuku'alofa and Neiafu in particular (and to
a *much* lesser extent the market in Pangai, Lifuka) provide outlets for surplus production.

Almost all farmers may thus produce crops for market, but they do so almost accidentally; certainly the diversion of crops into the market rarely occurs at the expense of socially and ceremonially deployed surplus. This is a recurring problem for the Ministry of Agriculture and Forests (MAF). Part of their mandate is to encourage the production of cash crops, whether specific market crops, or traditional root crops earmarked for market. By 1991 when I arrived in Ha'apai, the regional MAF office had abandoned earlier efforts to promote traditional root crops for market (in part by providing seed corms), because they found no way to convince producers to refrain from diverting such crops into daily and/or ceremonial consumption. Instead the planting of paper mulberry, used in bark cloth production in other areas of the Kingdom, which had a strong internal market, was being promoted. In the words of one MAF officer, "You can't eat bark."

Looking to the island as a whole, some broad statements can be made. Taking the survey of February 1993, a mean of 0.082 hectares of garden land per person was attained. Excluding all atypical households a mean of 0.089 hectares per person was planted ($n = 88$). These means are an especially useful way of conceiving of production because they eliminate any distortion generated by the analytical differentiation of households; that is, sharing between closely related households, and the effect this has on planting decisions, are incorporated. The first mean is probably the more meaningful, because it includes atypical households like those of clergy and teachers. These types of households tend to rely on others for some portion of their subsistence, in part because their social rank allows it, and in part because the fact that they have less access to land and less opportunity to farm is recognized by other villagers.[7]

A fair body of work on Tongan farming systems has been produced (for instance see Hardaker 1975; Schröder 1983; Stevens 1996b; Thaman 1976), though much of this work has been concentrated on the main island of Tongatapu. Contrary to ill advised general statements about the "poor" soils of the Ha'apai region, the soils of Ha'ano Island are generally quite productive. For instance, van der Grijp (1993, 80) refers to the poor coral soils of the Ha'apai region. While this may be true of islands like Matuku (where he worked), it is not true of a substantial number of other islands like Ha'ano which have an overlay of volcanic soils (see Wilson and Beecroft 1983). It has also been suggested that the greater use of manioc [cassava] as a crop in parts of Ha'apai is a result of poorer soils compared to Vava'u and Tongatapu (Halapua 1981, 6). There is no shortage of fertile soil on Ha'ano Island, nor are there any pervasive barriers in access to rich soils. On Ha'ano Island at least, the use of manioc as a crop is more related to labour shortages than land. Although mechanized ploughs are available through the MAF on the islands of Foa and Lifuka, all agriculture on Ha'ano Island continues to be done by hand. The main tools are heavy digging spades, lighter weeding spades, and the ubiquitous machetes.

All subsistence production on the island employs a shifting cultivation pattern, and fertilizers are very rarely used. The typical rotation cycle is three years. Fallow lands are first cleared, and then a *ma'ala*, or yam garden is planted; the yam garden is usually intercropped with giant taro (*kape*). As the yams are harvested, about nine months to one year after planting, taro plants (*talo*) are intercropped with the remaining yams. By the end of the first year the garden is usually a mixture of taro, giant taro, and perhaps a few banana or plantain (*fusi*). Sometime towards the end of the second year, after most of the taro is harvested, a third crop of manioc (*manioke*) is planted. Once this crop is harvested at the end of the third year the land is allowed to return to fallow. Often the fallow has a large proportion of manioc plants which have not been fully harvested; manioc seems a perfectly good fallow cover, and it has the added advantage that some usable tubers can be harvested even from the fallow plants (this was a fairly common practice during the drought of 1991-92).

There is some variation from this "typical" pattern. Just about any crop can be added into an intercropping pattern. While most first year gardens are primarily yams and giant taro (these are the most valued crops, in part because they are so ceremonially important), gardens can incorporate a variety of plants. Sweet potatoes, corn, bananas, plantain, paper mulberry, giant hibiscus, and other varieties of food crops may be added to the mix at any point (see especially Thaman 1976 for an exhaustive study of useful cultigens cropped in Tonga). Banana and plantain are also often used as garden borders; these plants will continue to produce long after the land has returned to fallow. Monocropping of any sort is uncommon except in the third year of a garden cycle (when manioc is planted alone), although occasionally gardens may begin and end with only manioc, or perhaps sweet potato (*kumala*). Sweet potato was monocropped by a number of farmers on Ha'ano in early 1992 after the drought broke. This was because the sweet potato takes only four months to mature (as opposed to nine months to as much as fourteen months for other root crops). The drought had wiped out the previous year's harvest, and there was some urgency to produce food crops quickly.

Multi-level intercropping does occur, especially on the gardens of older men. Coconut trees are regularly spaced throughout all the tax allotments, and provide some degree of protection to the plants beneath. Food trees, like breadfruit, mango, papaya, orange, and Tahitian chestnut trees are also present in most gardens. In addition a host of other useful trees are located in strategic places on tax allotments (again, see Thaman 1976). These trees are not generally planted, but seeded by bats and birds; once seeded, however, the trees are usually protected and nurtured to maturity. The exception to this is coconut which is planted in ordered patterns. Some men in fact plant other trees, especially breadfruit, in part for their food value, and in part for the protection the trees offer other underlying crops. Farmers generally believe that yams (the most socially significant root crop, see Helu 1992) do best in full sun, but they also recognize that well-shaded gardens are resistant to drought.

Although no representative sampling was done, as a general rule (based on general observation and a small non-random sample stratified by age) it is older men who tend to have the most complex gardens. In Ha'apai, the winners of the "Best Subsistence Garden" category at the agricultural fair were invariably men over the age of sixty. These men tended to intercrop more, have greater varieties of plants under cultivation, and make greater use of tree crops. Among younger men there was a general tendency toward less variety, and while most still intercrop, the frequency of tree crops within gardens is less. There are several possible reasons for this. First, it is clear that for some men, their gardens are an abiding passion which takes up more and more of their time as they age, and other responsibilities like childrearing end. These men have both time, and the knowledge of a lifetime,[8] to expend on their gardens. Adult men with school-aged children on the other hand have considerable competing responsibilities demanding their time. As one might expect given the Chayanovian nature of village household development, both social and economic responsibilities tend to be most intense when children are of school age; everything from the generally greater subsistence production demands, to the need to acquire cash to pay school fees, to the expectation that adults at this stage in their lives will take on significant responsibilities within the church, draw upon people's time. Older men also tend to have secure tenure on land, and the experience of a time when land was not nearly as easily acquired as it is today. Tree crops of all kinds are longer-term crops than the root crops which form the bulk of agricultural production, and thus we might expect that they are more common on lands held under secure tenure than lands which might be repossessed in the short term.

Agricultural Labour

Access to agricultural land is clearly not a problem on Ha'ano Island, but labour is somewhat scarce due to out-migration. This scarcity is exacerbated by the absence of all high school students.[9] There is a strong tendency for agricultural labour to be contained within households. Very little cooperative agricultural activity takes place; what cooperative arrangements are in place are generally labour exchanges rather than labour pooling. The most common form, the *toutu'u* is described earlier. Another form of labour exchange, called a *kautaha* (sometimes glossed as "company"), seems to have been a truly cooperative venture in the past,[10] but is today a straight labour exchange. Three or more men work in turns of equal length in each other's gardens. This type of exchange is valued for both the camaraderie of group work, and for the concentration of effort which tends to occur through friendly competition. Only two such groups (one of three men, and one of five) were active during the field work period, and even these groups operated quite sporadically. Other, very informal, short-term labour exchange arrangements occurred between pairs of men from time to time.

Very few households have more than one full-time farmer. Almost 70 percent of the households had only one resident farmer, while over 90 percent had two or less; over 90 percent of all men between the ages of twenty and seventy farm, and over 20 percent of men over seventy continue to farm at some level or another. The heaviest work of gardening, the clearing of fallow lands in preparation for planting, is sometimes a cooperative activity. An older man may ask for the help of several younger men to clear some land. In exchange he might make an *'umu* (underground oven), and provide his helpers with a good meal of pork or dog. Occasionally an older man may pay a youth a small wage to help him in his gardens.

Household agricultural labour supply, rather than access to land, is the most significant factor in terms of the amount of land planted by a particular household. Land cropped to number of active agricultural labourers has a coefficient of co-variation of 0.51 (n=104, p<.0001), while the relationship of area of land cropped to land controlled was 0.30 (n=104, p<.002); the partial correlation of labour and land cropped was 0.44 (n=101, p<.0001) when controlled for the total land area in the possession of the household. The association of land cropping with the active agricultural labour was also stronger than land cropped to the total number of persons in the household (r=0.35, n=104, p<.0001). Table 6.3, which compares the mean hectares planted by the number of labourers in the household, also shows clearly that labour is a significant factor in production. Control of land in and of itself is significant only to a certain point; large amounts of land are useful only if a household has the labour to exploit it.

Table 6.3
Household Labour Supply by Land under Cultivation

No. of Labourers	Mean Hectares under Cultivation	N (total = 104)
0	0	4
1	0.38	66
2	0.68	24
3	0.89	8
4	1.33	2

Harvest Rights

Regardless of who plants a garden, the rights to harvest from a particular garden can extend quite widely. Sisters and their children maintain the right to harvest from the lands of their brothers. Although it was not possible to quantify the frequency with which this right is exercised, it was common for a man's sister's child (*'ilamutu*) to casually go to their maternal uncle's (*fa'ētangata*) garden and help themselves to what they wanted. It is expected that the garden owner be informed that crops had been taken, but in no way should this be taken to imply a granting of permission after the fact. The rights of *'ilamutu* over their *fa'ētangata* were frequently and passionately expressed in conversation; these rights extended to the use of land as well as the taking of crops. A man does not ask permission to plant a garden on the land of his *fa'ētangata*; he informs him after the fact. The erosion of the rights of a sister's children over their uncles has not noticeably occurred in Ha'ano. Rights like those described above were vigorously defended. The reason that a *fa'ētangata* should be informed that crops had been taken was so he could tell if someone else was stealing from his gardens.[11]

The nonchalance in which people harvest from the gardens of their *fa'ētangata* was, for me, remarkable. On one particular day a friend (Siua) and I were surveying gardens when we came upon the gardens of an older and particularly skilled farmer named Valu. After completing our measurements, Siua strolled over to a small stand of sugar cane (cane is only occasionally grown on Ha'ano), and proceeded to harvest about half the stand. This cane was for my daughter who had accompanied us. This surprised me because in all the time we had spent surveying, I had never seen Siua do anything even remotely like this on someone else's land. It was all the more surprising when Valu, the man who owned the garden, appeared and rather than question us about the cane we were eating, walked over to the stand, harvested the remaining stalks, and gave them to Siua. Little was said during these events. When I questioned Siua later, he was quite surprised at my discomfort with the situation, and explained patiently that Valu was his *fa'ētangata* — this he considered explanation enough.

Unlike the unreported harvests of the type described above, the theft of crops is a concern for most gardeners, and indeed for the state. Periodic inspections of garden lands by civil authorities (in the persons of the town officer and a MAF representative) are undertaken to ensure that households have adequate gardens; if a man is found to have insufficient crops for his family, he is officially warned by MAF. Delinquent farmers can, theoretically, be fined. One operating assumption behind these inspections is that a man with insufficient gardens will steal from others.

The right to harvest from certain gardens is even more widely distributed than those who are *fahu* to the owner of a garden. Brothers are also generally held to have the right to harvest from each other's gardens. In cases where a garden is on the land controlled by another individual, the landholder may harvest freely from any gardens on the allotment no matter whose gardens they may be. These crosscutting rights are held to be unlimited in everyday discourse. Whether or not there are practical social limits on the amount or frequency of harvests by those with such rights is an open question. It seems likely that excessive exploitation of the privileges of land ownership and/or kinship ties could lead to hard feelings or disputes, but I am aware of none.

These wider harvest rights are just one part of a distribution pattern of agricultural production. As I alluded to earlier, a number of households supply other households with root crops on a regular and informal basis. The interdependence of households in the area of agricultural production can be seen quite clearly in the variation of production levels from one household to the next. Figure 6.4 shows that a number of households have considerably more or considerably less land in production than would be expected if households were autonomous in terms of agricultural output. Land in production varies from 0.01 to 0.57 hectares per person; the mean production level is 0.082. Sharing between households evens out the discrepancies in production effectively. At least in terms of food crops, it simply does not make sense to speak of a poor household; *no one*, on Ha'ano Island goes hungry. Sharing of cooked food goes on between related households on a daily basis; it is neither uncommon nor unexpected. In addition food is distributed between households in the relationship of *kaunga'api* (neighbours) on a constant basis.

Figure 6.4
Variation in Per Capita Agricultural Production
between Households

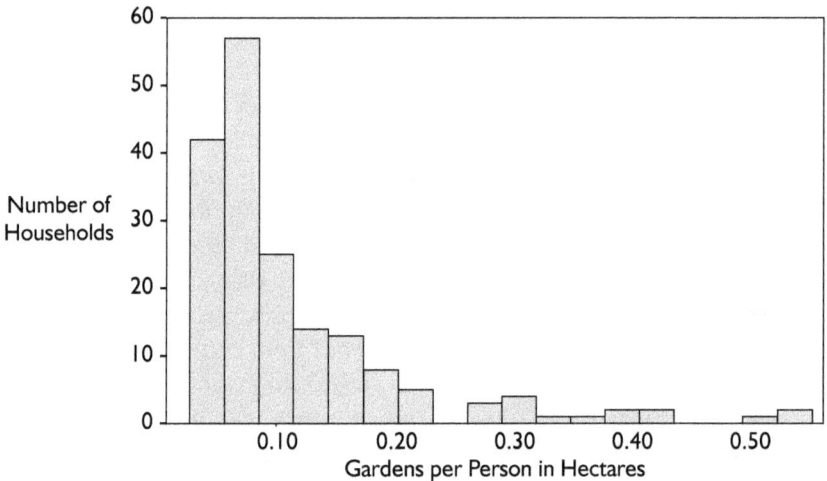

I can think of only one household in Ha'ano village which was not involved in some form of daily food exchange with at least one other household. This was an old man without either children or close relatives in the village. While he did not go hungry (in fact he had a small garden of his own), he was socially impoverished, and in a position of dependency, rather than mutual interdependence. He did have some everyday exchange relations with another household, but it was an uncomfortable relationship, and one which was unsatisfying to all concerned. This was the only individual in Ha'ano who could reasonably be described as impoverished, and he suffered from a social impoverishment, not an absolute one.

People share food in other ways as well. The phrase *"ha'u tau kai"* (come and we will eat) is familiar to anyone who has lived or worked in Tonga; it is a greeting as much as an invitation, and it is used whenever someone passes a house in which people are eating or preparing to eat.

The sharing of food in this manner is so ingrained in day-to-day sociality, that for most Tongans it is unremarkable except in its absence. This attitude to food sharing appears to be of considerable antiquity. Mariner reports that in the days that followed his capture by Tongans he had some difficulty in obtaining food. When he expressed this difficulty to 'Ulukalala (his chiefly benefactor), he was told, "when he felt himself hungry, . . . to go into any house where eating and drinking were going forward, seat himself down without invitation, and partake with the company" (Martin 1991 [1817], 67).

Some households receive most or all of their food crops from an associated household. These are usually households of either elderly people, or independent women. The elderly are generally supplied by either a son, son-in-law, or grandson. Independent women are usually supplied by one or more brothers (that is a male sibling or male cousin). For instance the household of Toa and her husband Kepueli had only a very small garden on a church toutu'u, clearly insufficient for their needs. They were supplied by the son of one of Kepueli's brothers, Tani, who lived in Muitoa. Other households have a much smaller production deficit. The existence of a small production shortfall can be a product of a number of factors, and need not be an indicator of dependency on another household.

Agricultural subsistence production in Tonga includes crops used in feasting and ceremonial activity. Thus a small shortfall may indicate a more limited engagement in such activity (or rather the mean is affected by producers who are heavily engaged in providing crops for exchange activity). Even if a household has not produced the surplus required to supply their feasting activities, it does not mean that they do not give feasts. Rather it may suggest that they get the necessary crops from other related households with large surpluses.[12] It is common, even usual, for households to ask for and receive physical and material help in putting on a feast; it is in fact rather uncommon for a household to muster the material and labour required to give a feast independently (see also Aoyagi 1966, 157-58). The configuration of four households which include Pila and Leti that I described earlier regularly contribute both resources and labour to each other's feasts. In addition, several also frequently support still more households. For instance Vili gives and receives help from the household of his brother Tiki; Lesi, Vili's wife, regularly supports the household of her sister, 'Ana Seini, and so on.

Livestock

Almost all households keep some livestock. By far the most common animal is the pig, which is a key ingredient in any feast. Many households also keep goats, chickens, and dogs; a very few households (n = 3) have cattle as well. Horses are used for both transportation and meat (for feasts), but only about 25 percent of all households possess them. Pigs are not consumed on an everyday basis, but rather are reserved for ceremonial and social occasions. Even when a pig dies by misfortune rather than design, there is reluctance on the part of the household to consume it. I know of no case in which a household actually consumed its own pigs (except after a feast), and a number of cases in which people would not. In one instance a man lost a large boar (the boar died of exhaustion while being chased down by dogs). This man and his household consumed no part of the animal. Instead a number of other households were given a share of the beast, and in exchange each gave the man a small newly weaned animal to help him make up for his loss.

Pigs are occasionally sold. As such they are one of the very few things which are sold for cash on the island itself. Most households neither buy or sell pigs. In 1992, in the village of Ha'ano, less than 15 percent of the households (sample size n = 35) sold more than one hundred pa'anga worth of pigs, and fully 60 percent sold no pigs at all. A few men are noted for the size of their herds, and will sell to those who find themselves in need of swine at short notice. This usually occurs when an unexpected death creates an immediate and acute social need because of the funerary obligations of individuals in a household. Pigs may also be purchased by a village (from cash raised on a household-by-household basis) to meet civic responsibilities like the King's Birthday. Most households will sell pigs only very reluctantly; this is especially true of larger castrated boars which are reserved for large events in which the household has a significant stake and responsibility (e.g., the funeral of a close relative or the marriage of a child).

Tongan farmers value their pigs, and treat them with far more concern and care than any other animal. In fact the treatment of pigs, especially fertile sows, approaches the manner in which North Americans treat dogs and cats, while dogs in the Tongan context are treated very poorly by North American standards. People often remarked to me that *palangai* (Westerners) treated dogs like children, while Tongans treated them like what they are — animals. Even horses, which are valued for both their capacity as beasts of burden, and the large quantity of meat they represent, are considerably less important to most Tongan farmers than pigs.

This is reflected in the price of horses versus pigs. A fully grown horse might sell for between three hundred and five hundred pa'anga, while a pig of the largest grade (*puaka toho* — today this refers to a castrated boar of the largest size) which represents a comparable amount of meat, might sell for between eight hundred and one thousand pa'anga.

Tongan farmers generally have a very pragmatic attitude to their livestock. Families do however grow attached to their pigs. A sow which has delivered several litters can have a unique place of affection in a household. One often sees pigs which are clearly far past their prime, sometimes missing legs and ears, being fed by people. These are sows which will be cared for until they die of old age because of the affection people feel for the animal, and the gratitude they feel for the service the sow has given them over the years.

Pigs, in addition to root crops (especially varieties of long yam), are *ngōue*, the produce of the land. *Ngōue* is the male counterpart to *koloa*, or women's wealth (primarily pandanus mats and bark cloth).[13] Women and children may own pigs, but most pigs belong to men, and the ceremonial gift of *ngōue*, including pigs, is a gendered male activity. Note however that like a man's garden crops, his pigs are subject to the demands of his sister and her children.

In 1992, Pila and Leti owned only one breeding sow, but the household had several piglets which were being raised to meet exchange obligations. All of these pigs were owned by the couple's children, and the use of a pig required the permission of the child concerned. No one anticipated that a child would refuse to give a pig for slaughter in the appropriate circumstances, but the child would be asked. This was part of Pila and Leti's child-rearing practices, and one that met with general approval in the wider community because of the Tongan values the practice encouraged. In 1992 the household used three small pigs for church feasts, gave one to the school that the oldest daughter attended in Tongatapu, gave one to one of Pila's close kin for use at the opening of a new church in Pangai, used one to help feed the carpenters working on the roof of the church of Pila's father, Finau, and one to help with the funeral of a kinsperson of Leti's. Pigs in particular are expressly for the giving, and Pila and Leti, like most Tongans, raised pigs because they were needed for the same things as fine mats and garden crops, that is, to participate fully in Tongan social life.

Cash Cropping

The production of specific cash crops on Ha'ano Island was limited during 1991-93. The squash pumpkin industry, which experienced explosive growth on Tongatapu from 1989 on (see James 1995, Sturton 1992), did not extend to the Ha'apai region. The history of cash cropping in Ha'apai, with the exception of copra production, has been sporadic. Over the medium and long terms, most cash crops have not been at all successful. Copra production has had the only consistent impact on the local economy of Ha'ano Island over the long term.

In September of 1991, the price of copra was stabilized at 275 pa'anga per metric tonne with the help of a fund provided by foreign aid donors. By October of 1992 however, the Tongan Commodity Board (TCB) buying station had suspended operations. This was due to problems internal to the TCB, and not the world price of copra. Interest in Tongatapu and Vava'u in copra as a cash crop has been waning over the past few years; the people of Ha'apai have been producing large amounts of copra. The per capita production of copra in Ha'apai has been the highest in the country for some time (Government of Tonga 1988, 34). Ha'apai makes up a small part of the population, and an even smaller portion of the political clout affecting government. It is likely that as farmers in Tongatapu shifted their energy to the production of squash pumpkin, the political will to maintain the copra-buying infrastructure diminished. Whether squash pumpkin production can be maintained looks somewhat doubtful (P. Fonua 1994). If production declines and the industry collapses, it will join a long line of cash crops which have had only short-term success in Tonga (see Bollard 1974). Most recently banana production, in the mid-1980s a major cash crop which seemed to have long-range potential and transformative significance (Needs 1988), collapsed so completely that production levels where insufficient to meet internal market demand in the early 1990s.

Though one household in Pukotala and one in Fakakakai grew vanilla for market, and one household in Ha'ano village grew watermelons, the only other cash crop of significance to more than one or two households was pandanus. Pandanus leaves, the raw material for fine mat production, were processed by most households for the weaving of mats, and/or for sale to others. Pandanus is interesting, partly because it is planted and tended by men, but owned by women. That is, regardless of the land laws, women are held to own particular plots of pandanus that they can use for their own fine mat production. A woman may have a plot of pandanus on the land of any male kinsman, or her husband. While people do not have protection in law for these plots (and indeed I know of one example in which an absent ex-husband returned to the village with his new wife and proceeded to harvest pandanus extensively from the plots of his first wife), they do have customary rights, and the expectation of the recognition of these rights. Both the processing of pandanus, and the production of fine mats are labour intensive, occupy a great deal of the time of adult women, and provide significant economic value in one way or another to almost every household. Even for households in which the sale of fine mats is not a significant source of cash income, the use of fine mats in the traditional exchange system remains important. Figure 6.5 shows the relative importance of the various cash crops grown in Ha'ano village.

Figure 6.5
Mean Household Income from Agriculture — Ha'ano 1992

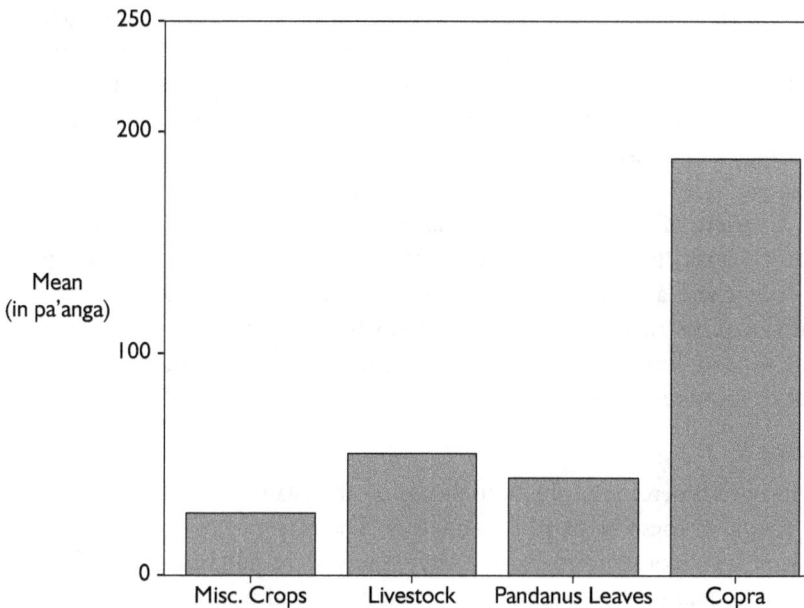

Fishing

Fishing, like farming, is primarily a subsistence activity, although for a few families significant cash earnings are generated from the sale of fish. A survey of fishing activity and the distribution of fishing capital goods was undertaken over the whole island. Most men (73.5 percent between the ages of twenty and seventy) participate in some form of fishing activity. A significant proportion of women (32.6 percent of those between twenty and seventy) harvest shellfish and octopus from the reef.

There are a number of fishing techniques used by fishers on Ha'ano Island (see Halapua 1982 for a description of several fishing techniques only alluded to here). Among the techniques employed are: deep-sea fishing off sea mounts or fishing just off the island's reef fringes (called *tau-mata'u*); trolling for species like tuna (*fakatele*); gill netting (*kupenga*) and hand netting (*kupenga sili* or just *sili*); spearfishing (*uku*); spearfishing at night (*amauku*); fishing from the shore with a simple hook and line (*lafo-lafo*); and reef collecting (*tufa*).

Fishing Equipment

The most significant capital expenditure a fisher can make is the purchase of a boat and outboard engine. Possession of a boat allows far greater opportunity to fish, and has the added advantage of providing a link to other islands and the regional centre. There are also occasions when a boat owner may make a little cash by transporting people or goods to a landing at Foa Island (which connects by road to the regional centre of Pangai). The next most expensive gear are the gill nets which people use in a variety of ways on the reef that fringes the island, and diving equipment (mask, fins, snorkel, spears, and if night diving is done, a light). Finally there are the bits of line, hooks, and weights which are used in several types of fishing. All those who fish own a little line and a few hooks and lures. Ownership of nets, diving equipment, and boats is much more restricted.

Boats

Thirty-two percent of the households on the island had a boat, although a couple of these boats had no engines. The majority of the boats on the island were constructed locally. Only a few were purchased elsewhere in Ha'apai, and only two small aluminum boats had been made somewhere besides Tonga. The cost of constructing a boat varies, but includes expenses of both cash and goods (like pigs, etc.). Cash must be used to purchase the wood and hardware for the boat, and to pay the fee to the boatbuilder (unless he is a close relative). In addition those men assisting in the construction of the boat must be fed, and generally they are fed well. A person will usually provide pigs, fish, root crops, and perhaps some store-bought meats (for example corned beef or lamb flaps) to provision workers while the boat is constructed. The mean cost in cash of the

Men build a boat . . .

. . . and sew a net.

boats for which detailed information is available was just under thirteen hundred pa'anga; in addition to this the costs in kind probably vary between three hundred and five hundred pa'anga (cash equivalents).

The outboard for the boat must of course be purchased, or acquired some other way. For instance, a number of 35-horsepower engines had been given to people as aid through the Tongan government. The mean cost of the outboards purchased, excluding those given in aid (n = 3), was just under two thousand pa'anga (a 15-horsepower engine is about 1800 pa'anga, while a 25-horsepower engine costs around 2300 pa'anga).

In addition to the larger wooden boats, several fishers also owned small dugout canoes called *popau*; there were five such boats on the island. These are constructed out of a hollowed mango log, to which an outrigger is attached. The canoes are quite useful for inshore fishing with hook and line, and for setting and retrieving nets on and around the reef. One older man in Ha'ano village, a very experienced fisher, used his *popau* for deep-sea fishing as well. These canoes are relatively inexpensive to build (between one and two hundred pa'anga paid in kind), but require a large mango log, and are thus not all that common.

The circumstances that surround the acquisition of the island fleet are in some ways metonymic of the way other sorts of material flows onto the island. The boats of Ha'ano Island and the engines that power them have been acquired in a variety of ways which include direct aid, remittances from overseas, the sale of commodities, barter, outright gifts from others, and a combination of these sources. It is worth noting that there is no relation between the ownership of boats or other types of capital equipment used in fishing, and land ownership or control.

Nets

Nylon net mesh is purchased, and then the weights, floats, and support lines are woven into the nylon. This requires some skill, and some considerable expenditure of time as well. At certain times of the year the nets are set at night and retrieved in the morning. Another type of fishing involves setting the net across an opening in the reef, and then slapping the water to drive any trapped fish into the net. Occasionally large schools of big-eye mackerel (*'otule*) come right into the reef at Ha'ano village; the gill nets are then used to surround the fish. The use of these gill nets can be quite productive and usually involves a number of men. The distribution of fish and the significance of capital equipment in this distribution is discussed next.

Thirteen households (12.5 percent had gill nets. The length of net possessed ranged from twenty metres to one household which had seven hundred metres.[14] The mean length was 140 metres, but over 60 percent of the households owned fifty metres or less of net. The cost of these nets is approximately 75 pa'anga per 25 metres. A number of households (n = 12 or 11.5 percent also have small throwing nets, called *sili*, which are used from the shoreline, and on the shallow parts of the reef.

Diving Equipment

Diving (and spearfishing [*uku*]) is a quite productive fishing activity, but tends to be confined to younger men. It is considered dangerous in both the short and long term. In the short term people worry about sharks or other hazardous marine life and drowning; in the long term diving is thought to sap the strength and health of those who do it. I know of one instance when a man quietly sold his son's diving equipment; he did this out of concern for the young man's health. The equipment is quite simple: snorkel, mask, fins, and a "shanghai" (a type of spear gun); for diving at night (*amauku*), a powerful underwater light is used to attract and stun the fish. The cost of this equipment ranges from one hundred to two hundred pa'anga depending on the quality. Thirty-two percent of households have the equipment for diving, and just over one third of these households also have the light necessary for night diving.

Other Capital Equipment

Most households have the handlines, weights, and lures necessary for handlining, either from shore or from a boat. In addition most boat-owning households have trolling equipment and lures. Handlining equipment is generally only a few pa'anga, but trolling equipment can be more expensive. Fishers interested in trolling (*fakatele*) may have several reels of line and a number of lures.

Two households in Fakakakai had a fish trap, or *pā*. A fish trap of this type is constructed out of wire mesh, and it is permanently anchored on the reef so that fish can enter when the tide is high, and are then trapped when the tide falls. Such traps provide a steady supply of fish, although quantities can vary. The cost of the trap depends on its size; generally the traps are hundreds of square feet and can cost anywhere from one to two thousand pa'anga.

Distribution of Fishing Equipment

Tables 6.4 and 6.5 detail the distribution of major fishing assets (that is boats, engines, canoes, gill nets, diving equipment, diving lamps, and fish traps). Over 60 percent of households have some major fishing asset.

Fishing Activity

Fishing is a predominantly male activity. Women very occasionally fish, usually with their husbands, but are more likely to be engaged in the collection of shellfish or hunting octopus along the reef.[15] Fishing activity by women

Table 6.4
Distribution of Fishing Equipment (n = 104)[a]

Equipment	No. of Households	% of Cases	Mean Size
Boat	33	31.7	21 feet
Engine	33	31.7	23 hp
Canoe	5	4.8	n/a
Gill net	13	12.5	140m
Throwing net	12	11.5	n/a
Diving gear	30	28.8	n/a
Night diving gear	13	12.5	n/a
Handline gear	59	56.7	n/a
Trolling gear	29	27.9	n/a
Fish trap	2	1.9	not known

a The column "% of cases" gives the percentage of households in possession of the fishing gear. Many households have more than one type of gear. Thus the total is in excess of 100%.

Table 6.5
Major Fishing Assets (n = 104)

No. of Major Fishing Assets in Household	No. of Households	% of All Households
0	41	39.4
1	21	20.2
2	25	24.0
3	7	6.7
4	8	7.7
5	2	1.9
Total	104	100

is not proscribed, but like gardening, fishing tends to be the purview of men. As part of the general economic survey, the fishing activity of all people between the ages of twenty and seventy was recorded. It should be noted that almost everyone fishes or goes to the reef looking for shellfish occasionally (once or twice a year), but many people fish more regularly; it was the people who went fishing regularly who were recorded. This said, the survey did not differentiate the levels of fishing activity.

Table 6.6 shows the breakdown of fishers on the island.

Table 6.6
Fishing Activity on Ha'ano Island by Village[a]

Type of Fishing	No. of People	% of those 20-70	% in Faka-kakai	% in Ha'ano	% in Muitoa	% in Pukotala
Handline (boat)	81	52.3	43.1	59	62.5	52.9
Trolling	32	20.6	19	33.3	12.5	14.7
Gill net	27	17.4	12.1	33.3	20.8	5.9
Throw net	14	9	12.1	7.7	8.3	5.9
Diving	45	29	31	20.5	41.7	26.5
Diving (night)	16	10.3	13.8	2.6	12.5	11.8
Total all (men)	114	73.5	72.4	74.4	75	73.5
Reef Collecting (women)	58	32.6	30	37.5	37.9	26.8

a The column "% of those 20-70" refers to Ha'ano Island as a whole. Note that because of an overwhelmingly gendered pattern in fishing activity, the figures in the last row, "reef collecting," are for women only, while for all other forms of fishing the values given are the percentage of men only. No women reported general fishing activity, and no man reported reef collecting except as a very occasional activity.

Fish Distribution

Fish is an important source of protein and food variety. It is used for everyday consumption, and provides the bulk of the *kiki* (or relish, meaning *not* root vegetables). It is also an important component of the feasting cycle, and of the day-to-day exchanges which knit households together. The sale of fish is sometimes a fairly straightforward commodity transaction, but it must be noted that these transactions are often bracketed by gift exchanges; that is the productive inputs required for generating enough fish to sell are often acquired through gifts of cash and materials from relatives living elsewhere, and the cash generated from the sale of fish is frequently turned immediately back into gift exchange processes.

An intensive survey of fishing harvests covering the period from January 1993 to December 1993 used a weekly recall technique to record the fish catch and distribution of Ha'ano village. From this survey it is possible to get not only a sense of the productivity of the fishery, but also the exchange patterns associated with it. People were asked to recall the number, size, and species of fish caught. They were also asked about the composition of the fishing party, the resources employed, and the distribution of the catch both among the fishers, and to others subsequent to this initial distribution.

Halapua (1982) discusses the distribution of fish among various groups of fishers on the Island of Tongatapu in the mid-1970s. I do a similar thing here for the purposes of future comparisons, and in order to give a sense of how people think about the relationship between material input and labour in the division of a catch. To do this I focus on two types of fishing which usually involve some degree of cooperation between fishers: handlining from a boat, and fishing with gill nets. Both activities normally involve two or more fishers.

The following refers to the activity of men only. Although I attempted to collect data on the frequency and productivity of women's reef collection/octopus hunting in Ha'ano village, I am unsure of the validity of the results, except insofar as the numbers of people reporting that they in fact engaged in reef collection (see earlier). My sense is that in terms of total weight, women's reef collection is not that significant when compared to the weight of fish generated by the fishing activity of men. This notwithstanding, for some families, and at some times, reef collection (especially of octopus) is an important source of protein, and an important and appreciated source of variety. Octopus is generally eaten at the big Sunday meal, and it is highly valued.

It is unclear to me how Ha'ano village compares to other villages and other areas in terms of the quantitative importance of reef collection. It is entirely possible that reef collection is more important in other areas, and that Ha'ano Island is atypical for two reasons. First, many adult women spend a great deal of time weaving on Ha'ano Island, especially during the daylight hours when reef collection would normally take place. The women who do spend a fair amount of time on the reef *tend* to be much older women who do not weave too much, or younger women who do not weave. For many women there is a very limited opportunity to hunt octopus. Second, male fishing activity is highly developed, and as a result fish proteins are readily available on the island. Thus the need for reef collection is likely less on Ha'ano Island than in other areas. Note however that for the households of women engaged in reef collection, this activity is a significant source of fish proteins. One older woman from Muitoa regularly supplied her household with octopus, and sold octopus out as well. Octopus has the advantage that it may be dried and preserved, and thus used when social occasions arise, or when bad weather prohibits fishing. For this reason as well those noted above, I wish to be clear that when I make the claim that reef collection is minor compared to male fishing, I mean this in the sense of relative aggregate weights and not in a social sense.

Handlining from boats

When handlining from a boat (*taumata'u*), men may fish either as a group or individually. Most fishers say that if they fish together, the total catch is divided equally with a portion going to each man, and an additional (equal portion) going to the boat (that is the owner of the boat). If the men fish separately, then each man might give the boat owner some portion of his catch. The share for the boat is conceived as covering the cost of the gas and maintenance on the boat. No one ever suggested to me anything which would indicate that consideration of the "capital costs" played a role.[16] Gill net fishing is always a cooperative activity (that is the men fish "together"); here too, the net receives a share of equal size as each individual. Again, the reason that people gave for this was the work the net owner had to do to maintain the net.

In practice the division of the catch is a bit different, and a number of factors influence any one particular distribution. If there is a guiding principle to distribution in general, it is "*feinga pe mo'o famili*," enough for the family. Before the boat gets a share of the catch, each man will take "enough" for his family. On the other hand, if a catch is good, then the boat will receive a share; if the catch is particularly good then this share might well be quite large, larger in fact than any individual's portion because each man may again take only enough for his family, leaving the rest for the boat. This is the general practice, but considerable variation is present in data collected.

For instance a number of men may go fishing to help another attain fish for a feast or other social obligation; in such cases all the fish would go to one individual. This may occur because of a specific request, or it may simply be an act of spontaneous generosity. A certain level of generosity is also expected and met even when men fish separately. If one man has caught many fish where another has caught few, it is inconceivable that some redistribution of the catch would not occur. These practices are reinforced by the fact that fishing partners are almost always related to one another, and thus there is a strong tendency for the principles of *fetokoni'aki* to come into play. Once a catch has been divided by the fishers, each person may subsequently redistribute their catch to neighbours, family, or friends. This is common; in just under 65 percent of the cases ($n = 496$) in which a man went fishing and retained a portion of the catch after the initial division, he redistributed some portion of that catch in raw form to someone from another household. I make a point of the "raw" form here because in addition to this redistribution, there is another level of distribution occurring between closely related households and neighbours which involves small quantities of cooked fish. Not surprisingly there is a clear-cut relationship between the amount of fish retained and the number of additional households who received a portion. After eliminating those cases in which some portion of the catch was sold (n = 55), the following means were calculated:

Table 6.7
Secondary Distribution of Fish in Ha'ano Village

No. of Additional Households Receiving Raw Fish	Mean of Catch Retained (kg)	No. of Cases
0	3.9	144
1	6.7	125
2	6.8	107
3	8.8	44
4 or more	13.8	21

There are a couple of material reasons for this pattern. First there are no ice-making or freezing facilities on the island. Thus fish must be either salted, redistributed, or consumed. Salting is time-consuming and it is not particularly common; fish is plentiful enough that mutual reciprocal ties will insure a consistent supply. Salting is usually done if the intention is to send the fish to people living in Tongatapu or to use it in a formal exchange. People do not salt fish to ensure future consumption. Fish in excess of consumption needs is redistributed, usually through informal gift exchanges. These exchanges usually occur within the village.[17] Fishing trips are sometimes timed to coincide with the movement of some family member to Tongatapu, or with the arrival of the inter-island boats, so that fish can be salted or iced and sent south (16 cases), usually to relatives there.

The sale of fish is relatively common, but circumscribed by expectations of generosity and reciprocity. The multiplicity of social ties between people within the village makes the sale of fish within the village problematic. If fish is sold within the village, which itself is rather rare, it is sold only to people who are unrelated. Ironically these are the same people to whom marriage ties are possible. In smaller villages like those on Ha'ano, marriage opportunities are limited (see the earlier discussion of marriage among commoners), and thus so is the pool of potential fish buyers. In order to sell fish, people generally take it to one of the small stores on Foa or Lifuka which purchase fish (at 1.50 to 2.50 pa'anga per kilogram). There is a cost involved however, in both time, gas, and land transportation, so there is a tendency to sell fish only if there is a sufficient quantity to justify the expenses.

A comparison of cases in which fish was sold to those in which it was not, yields a predictable result. The mean size of the catch retained in cases where fish was sold was almost ten times higher (60.4 kg, n = 55), than those in which no fish was sold (6.4 kg, n = 441). It is in fact relatively uncommon for a fishing trip to yield the quantity of fish necessary to justify a trip to the regional centre (just over 10 percent of all cases in which some portion of the catch was retained).

Certain types of fishing activity account for most of these cases. Over 95 percent of the trips resulting in the sale of fish involved the use of boats (75 percent) or gill nets (20 percent); the majority were in fact a result of trolling for tuna (56 percent). In 75 percent of the cases only one (44 percent) or two men (31 percent) were involved; this may be important insofar as the smaller number of men involved means a smaller number of social claims which might mitigate against the sale of the fish.

Fishing with Gill Nets

Some of the cases in which gill netting resulted in fish sales are special cases and deserve extended comment here. Ha'ano is a fishing village of some renown. There is a specific type of fishing called *taa 'atu*, which involves a highly specialized and ritualized fishing technique for catching skipjack tuna (see Gifford 1924). Ha'ano village is uniquely situated along the migration routes of the skipjack tuna (*'atu*) and the big-eye mackerel (*'otule*). Periodically schools of these species will run right up to the shoreline through a gap in the reef located directly in front of the village. Stories of the *taa 'atu* refer to fish literally jumping onto the shore. A tuna run of this type does not appear to have happened in some time, but big-eye mackerel runs occurred several times during the year and a half we were in the village.[18]

Once the fish enter the reef, gill nets are quietly deployed around the school, and then men slap the water to scare the fish into the nets. This type of fishing can yield four thousand fish (weighing about 0.5 kilograms each), but requires a large length of net, and several men to deploy the net effectively. The mesh of this net is somewhat larger than that used in other situations. The net is thus fairly specialized to larger reef fish and of limited utility for many other types of reef fishing.

The first run that occurred while we were living in the village caused great controversy, because no one in Ha'ano had nets long enough to harvest the fish effectively, and a boat from another village reaped the good fortune of the run. This upset many of the Ha'ano people who hold that fishing of the reef close to Ha'ano should be restricted to Ha'ano people, and no one from Ha'ano had been invited to fish with the other boat.[19] Immediately after the incident one of the most active fishers in the village acquired five hundred metres of net and set about sewing it. The next year when the schools came in, there were a number of Ha'ano men quickly on the water armed with this new net. The boat which had netted the last run was also in the area, and there ensued a quiet confrontation between the fishing parties. The result was a cooperative catch in which the Ha'ano net was deployed surrounding the fish, and a net from the other boat was arranged to block the entrance to the reef. The catch was then shared, but the division was controlled by the Ha'ano man who owned the net.[20] The other boat was treated generously (they received about one thousand of four thousand fish), but the entire affair established the practical control of the resource by Ha'ano village.

After this run the big-eye came another half dozen times. Each time they were met by the long net and anywhere from 6 to 10 men. The catch varied from 500 to 4,000 fish. The disposition of the fish in these cases is interesting because in some ways it was atypical. In one instance I encountered fish actually being sold in the village (the fishing harvest survey reveals that in only 7 of the 55 cases in which fish was sold, was it sold in the village).

In one case where I followed the fish from start to finish, approximately 1,000 big-eye were caught using the net, boat, and canoe of one man. Six men and four teenaged boys (home temporarily during the school break) did the fishing, which yielded about 1,000 fish, or 500 kg. Four of the men and one young man received about 50 fish each as their 'inasi (share), the rather inept but enthusiastic anthropologist received 10, and another 50 or so fish were given to two fishers who arrived after the fish had been caught and cleared from the net. The explicit reason for these last men receiving fish was that they would generally have been involved in the catch if they had been around, and that both men were skilful fishermen who had been useful additions to the fishing party in the past, and would be so in the future. The rest of the catch, about 650 fish, went to the man who owned the net (note that three of his sons were also helping but did not receive a direct share). He then sold most of the remaining fish; after about 100 of the fish had been sold in Ha'ano, we proceeded down to the next village, sold about 500 more, and then returned home.

Only two people from Ha'ano village bought fish, but one of these was a neighbour to whom the seller regularly gave fish! Given the number of fishers receiving sizable shares of fish, it is likely that many within the village consumed some of the catch without any purchase required.[21] Still, the sale of the fish marked the event as different. There are of course some practical reasons why this might have occurred. The most obvious is that the exploitation of the resource required significant outlay of both time and money in order to acquire a fairly specialized net which in fact benefited a very large number of people. This cost was born almost entirely by one man. This was generally recognized, and certainly the man who owned the net held this view.[22]

All this said, there was still an element in the sale of the fish which involved some reckoning of social ties and social distances. Fish sold at Ha'ano were sold at six for one pa'anga; fish sold at the next village went at five for one pa'anga. At Pukotala several people to whom the fishers present had social ties had extra fish thrown into their purchases, as did any church minister who purchased fish (this was explained as a gift for the blessing of the nets). Although it is possible to argue that the differences in the price of the fish are related to the cost of transporting it, this contention breaks down somewhat when it is recognized that this same fish could have been sold in Pangai or Foa for over four hundred pa'anga, when in fact it was sold on the island for just over one hundred pa'anga.

Fisheries production is a significant part of subsistence activity. In fact it is one of the key sources of daily protein; other sources, like pork or horse meat are generally available only during and after feasts. Occasionally fish is earmarked for a specific ceremonial occasion. For a few households the sale of fish also provides a significant source of cash. In general terms however, fishing is more important in terms of consumption and informal gift exchange than as a commodity. As such it stands as an excellent example of the various uses to which production can be put. Fish can be turned into a commodity, but generally it is not. Even those households which realize significant amounts of cash from fish also give large quantities away.

Even if a household has no particularly active fishers, fish is nonetheless regularly available. Within the configuration of households formed around Pila and Leti for example, Pila fished relatively infrequently, but his father Finau fished a lot, usually from his canoe (popau). Finau supplied fish to Pila and Leti's household fairly frequently. In addition, Sione had a boat and engine which he, his oldest son Maka, his distant kinsman

Vili (an older unmarried man who lived alone, but usually ate with Sione's household), and others (including Vili and very occasionally Pila) used to fish offshore. The fish from these trips was distributed widely to a number of other related households. Halamehi, an unmarried woman in her eighties, regularly got fish from Vili; Halamehi was a neighbour and though she got garden crops from her brother's son (Semisi), he rarely fished. Sione and Maka distributed fish to Pila and Leti, Vili and Lesi (Sione's wife's sister), and occasionally others as well. Again the amount of fish played a role in the breadth of the network receiving fish. Sione and Maka also occasionally sold fish, especially tuna. Finau did not sell fish, but rather distributed any surplus he caught. In the four households then, there was the capacity (in the form of adequate labour and fishing assets), and the sociological framework to ensure that all were supplied with sufficient fish for daily consumption.

The majority of households in Ha'ano were engaged in some similar arrangement, though the sociological patterns of fish distribution tend to be quite varied. Relationships based on kinship, common church membership, and neighbourliness are all played out in the distribution patterns. Like the products of agriculture (though unlike land itself), fish is used in a variety of formal and informal circumstances to forge and maintain relationships between individuals and households. While those who exchange fish tend to be related in some fashion, they are not necessarily so, and again, kinship plays a significant but not determinate role in interhousehold exchanges. Because the character of social ties are, in any one instant, a product of exchange, and because fish plays such an important role in everyday patterns of exchange, the exchange of fish both follows from, and leads to, networks of connection and mutual obligation.

Weaving

While women do not participate in much agricultural work, and exploit marine resources much less intensively than men, adult women are integral to other aspects of the economy. Reproductive labour is, like agricultural labour, not exclusively gendered, but it tends to fall to women. Men do assist in daily domestic work, but the ideological responsibility, and in practical terms much of the work, falls to women (see Kavapalu 1991, 1996; Young Leslie 1999). Child care however is frequently in the hands of young women, while older women tend to be engaged in the production of pandanus mats. These mats are integral components of both gift and commodity exchange activity.[23] The centrality of women's pandanus fine mats (called a variety of names depending on the weave — *fala* is the most common type of fine mat) and bark cloth (called *tapa* when unmarked, and *ngatu* once dyed) production was and is one of the remarkable aspects of the Tongan political economy. Indeed along with pigs, kava, and some of the more prestigious root crops, fine mats and bark cloth are key elements in almost all formal exchanges, and are frequently used as special gifts to express love and respect between people. Weaving is also the one work activity which has a gender proscription. Men do not weave (if they do the reactions of others are marked and negative). Men will help with some aspects of fine mat production (like pandanus processing for instance), but they do not weave.

Fine mats laid out for viewing before shipment to exchange partners in New Zealand.

On Ha'ano Island no bark cloth production takes place, nor has bark cloth been made on the island since the mid-1970s. Bark cloth is used, but women trade into the Tongatapu or Vava'u regions to acquire it. Usually this exchange (called a *katoanga*) is made between groups of women. Fine mats are also used in the large scale exchanges (also called *katoanga*) between women in Ha'ano and women in Tongan overseas communities — exchanges which occur every year. These exchanges of mats for money, and mats for manufactured Western consumer goods, are key sources of income for some households. In addition, women who are not involved in a *katoanga* may trade or sell some portion of their production in a less formalized context.

Figure 6.6
Levels of Weaving Activity among Adult Women
on Ha'ano Island

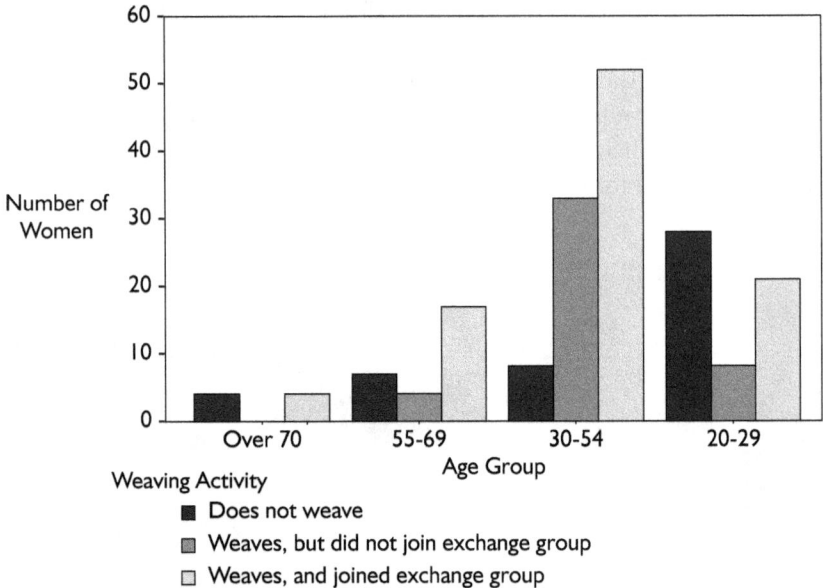

Of the women beyond school age, almost 75 percent weave (this figure includes women over the age of seventy); 25 percent of these women were involved in exchange relationships for either cash or bark cloth for a large portion of their production. By far the most heavily engaged segment of the female population engaged in weaving is that between thirty and fifty-five (some 90 percent but all categories have at least 50 percent active weavers (see Figure 6.6). Although some women weave alone or with one or two other weavers, most work in groups called *toulalanga*. These are labour sharing rather than labour pooling groups. A group of four or five women will work together on one woman's mat one day, and rotate through the group in turn. The principle of the group is that each woman receives the same amount of assistance as every other. Only accomplished weavers, mostly women above the age of thirty, can join such groups, as the quality of the work is an issue.

Again, pandanus fine mats are key components of the traditional economy, and significant in the cash-based economy as well. The cash income derived from weaving is important for many families. Although 34 percent of households sold no fine mats in 1992, almost 40 percent of households derived more than 20 percent of their income from fine mats, and for 10 percent of all households, income from women's weaving accounted for 60 percent of the household cash income. In addition to the obvious importance of mats as a source of cash, any and all significant life events, most public ceremonies, and most church-based ceremonies use some women's wealth for exchange (see chapter 7). The use of mats is one of the key markers of Tongan tradition for residents of the Islands, and especially for Tongans living overseas (see especially Morton 1998; Small 1997). Indeed it is the desire of overseas Tongans to acquire and use traditional Tongan wealth items that is responsible for the growth in *katoanga* exchange groups. For some women, participation in these groups creates social tension because mats traded to meet household income requirements cannot be used to meet kinship obligations (Young Leslie, personal communication). Because such obligations are most intense in situations that cannot necessarily be foreseen (as in the case of a sudden death), here again the ability to draw on the support of kinspeople in times of crisis is crucial.

In the household of Pila and Leti, only Leti wove. She did so in a *toulalanga* which included a number of women from the cooperating households I have already described. One of the main sources of income for Leti and Pila's household was her weaving, and so she spent a great deal of time at it. In both 1991 and 1992 she participated in a *katoanga* exchange group organized by Vili (her maternal uncle) and his sister's daughter, 'Akanesi who was living in New Zealand. The preparation of the fine mats for this *katoanga* exchange took some eight months, and each weaver received 1500 $NZ for four large mats. The mats were delivered by Pila for the group to Tongatapu, and then shipped by container to New Zealand. *Katoanga* exchange groups of these types are almost always organized by at least two well-respected older people, one in the village, and one in the overseas community. The bonds between Vili and the participants from the village (all were either kin, co-church members, or neighbours of Vili and/or his wife Lesi), the bond between Vili and 'Akanesi, and the bonds between 'Akanesi and the *katoanga* partners in New Zealand were crucial in ensuring the smooth operation of the group. In another case a long-running *katoanga* group was organized by twin sisters, one living in Ha'ano and the other in Hawaii.

Wage Income

Wage labour on Ha'ano Island is extremely limited. Wage earnings were significant sources of cash for only a few households. Just over 25 percent of households (n = 104) earned more than one hundred pa'anga, with about half of these earning more than one thousand pa'anga. There is a very limited agricultural wage-labour market with wage rates between one and two pa'anga per hour. Younger men sometimes work handling copra for the Tonga Commodities Board (TCB) at the buying station at Pukotala; wages are determined by the tonne of copra handled, and vary between ten and twenty pa'anga per day. One man in Fakakakai also worked as a watchman for the TCB and was paid about twenty pa'anga per week.

All other waged positions were connected to government. In each village one man held the position of *Ofisa Kolo* (mayor), and one man in Pukotala was *Pule Fakavahe* (regional mayor). These men received about thirty pa'anga every two weeks from the Government. A woman in Fakakakai served as the Island nurse, for which she was paid approximately 4,500 pa'anga per annum. The District agricultural officer, who lived in Ha'ano, received 2,765 pa'anga per year. A number of other individuals taught at the two primary schools on the island; their salaries ranged from 4,500 to 5,700 pa'anga a year.

Several church positions were paid, although this money was always referred to as a gift. There were two major categories of church functionary, *faifekau* and *setuata* (minister and steward); the rates of remuneration varied from church to church. Ministers received anywhere from 800 to 2,000 pa'anga, and stewards from 100 to 500 pa'anga per year.

Remittances

Cash remittances from overseas migrants are an important part of the national economy; most estimates suggest that something in the order of 50 percent of Tonga's foreign exchange earnings derive from overseas in this manner. At the level of the village economy, remittances (from both overseas and in-country migrants) are far and away the largest single source of income if the village is taken as a whole. Remittances are used in a variety of ways, but interestingly enough, the strongest correlation between remittances and other factors is that between remittances and the amount of money given by a household in the annual *misinale* donation to the church. Remittances and church donations ($r = 0.42$, $n = 24$,[24] $p < .040$) are in fact more highly correlated than total income and church donations ($r = 0.38$, $n = 24$, $p = 067/NS$).

Sign outside the International Airport in Tongatapu welcoming home migrant workers.

Remittances generally flow from children to their parents. Of the total recorded remittances in Ha'ano village (29,315 pa'anga), 18,175 pa'anga was received from children. A further 2,750 pa'anga was sent by siblings' children, 3,485 pa'anga was transferred between siblings, and some 3,000 pa'anga was sent by husbands to wives. The balance was sent by people in a variety of other relationships with the recipients. Thus, although nuclear family members are the most important sources of remittances, significant amounts come from other relatives as well. Some authors (especially James 1991b) tend to attribute an individuating function to cash remittances, and it is certainly true that remittances are not received by a kin group, but rather individuals. The way that remittances are used however, is extremely important in the reproduction of social ties.

Remittance activity is intense, but it tends to be focussed. People request remittances from their overseas kin for particular reasons. While money is sometimes sent for general purposes, it is most often the result of a specific request. School fees, funerals, and specific building projects are all reasons a person might ask for financial help. Church donations, and again especially at *misinale*, are a key way that remittances are used, and a central site for the expression of sociality. Any large construction project can also use remittances either directly or indirectly. For instance several of the fishing boats in Ha'ano were built with loans from the Tonga Development Bank; a number of these loans were then paid back by direct remittances from overseas. The act of remitting resources is itself a social one, expressing love and affection. The patterns of remittance use also have profound social consequences, perhaps because remittances tend to be used for larger projects, which necessarily involve a larger number of people and a wider network of mutual aid. In the next chapter I have a great deal more to say about remittances; they are a key element in both the material and ideological reproduction of Tongan culture and society.

Figure 6.7
Mean Household Income by Sources

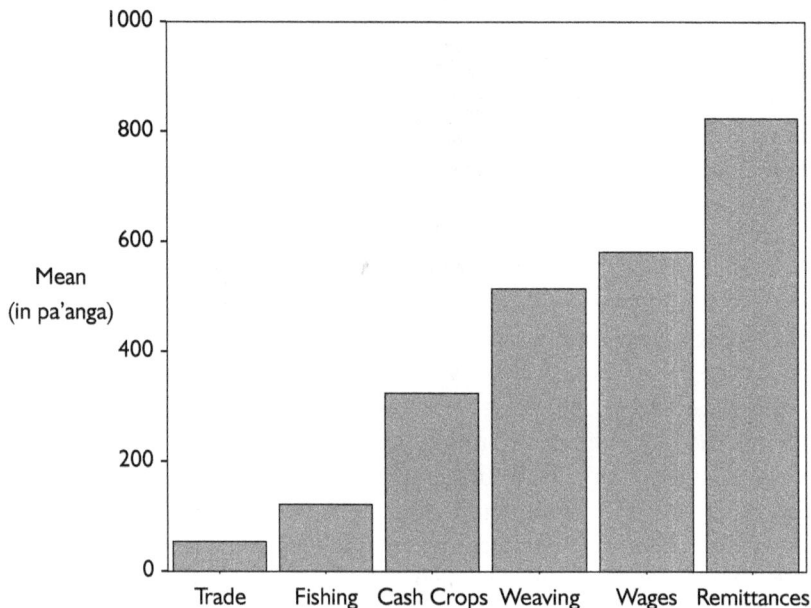

Sources of Cash

The primary sources of cash income were remittances, wages, trade, the sale of women's woven mats, and the sale of agricultural and fishing produce. Figure 6.7 details sources of the mean household cash income for the village of Ha'ano. While salaries and remittances from migrants are clearly the most significant sources of cash in the village, amalgamating households into a village obscures some important variation between households. Relatively few households had individuals who received salaries (N = 10). The levels of salaries paid, although small by Western standards, were generally large in comparison with other sources of income. The category of "trade" refers to the activities of only two households; one household ran a small store, and the other sold kava from their home. While almost all households received some remittances, the mean here was also skewed by a few households which received large sums from overseas.

The Village Economy: An Overview

The MIRAB pattern which applies to Tonga as a whole is replicated at the level of the villages; the sources of cash for people on Ha'ano Island are as expected. Remittances and wages (the majority of which are garnered from the bureaucracy) are the primary channels through which cash flows to the island. To a much lesser extent the sale of agricultural, fisheries, and manufactured wealth production (fish, copra, livestock, pandanus, and women's pandanus mats) provides cash for households on the island.

Cash, unlike other resources, does not generally flow between households on an everyday basis. The products of people's agricultural and fishing activity make up the bulk of resources which are transferred from household to household informally. Such products also make up the largest portion of local consumption requirements, and thus form an important material component of villagers' semi-autonomy. It is possible to get some sense of the structure of the island economy through an account of household production, but such an account cannot ignore the informal exchanges between households.

With a few exceptions, people do not cooperate or pool resources in day-to-day production. Even cooperative activities and institutions like the *toulalanga* or *toutu'u* are more labour exchanges than truly common ventures. Fishing does sometimes involve the cooperation of several individuals, but fishing gear is always individually owned. Land, like fishing gear, is individually controlled. This situation might well be taken as evidence that households in the villages of Ha'ano Island are nucleated or individuated, and that this is a result of changes wrought by processes of state formation and commoditization.

In order to hold to such a position however, we must ignore the prevalence of gift exchange. Land use and land tenure practices cannot be predicted by the legislation upon which they are supposedly based. Rather land tenure, the basis of both agriculture and the raw materials necessary for women's wealth production, is clearly organized through a variety of gift exchange relationships. The wide discrepancies in agricultural production also indicate that subsistence crops circulate freely between households. Finally, the empirical data garnered from my fishing harvest survey shows that households regularly disperse fish proteins to neighbours, friends, and kin.

The great variation in productive intensity and the types of activity undertaken by households is possible only because of the intensity of exchange. Such exchange is based on ties of mutual regard and ēofa; so complex are such ties that it is impossible to typify either the basis of the ties themselves, or the exact mix of material which flows between households. Although kinship can facilitate reciprocity, it does not necessitate it. Some households produce considerably more garden produce or fish protein than others, but there is no clear-cut pattern dividing gardening and fishing households. The notion that all men are farmers and fishers, and that all women are weavers overstates the situation, but provides a rough approximation of the general pattern of household production. Aside from households which have extreme gender or age imbalances, most households produce most types of wealth. There are temporary imbalances. For example, misfortune can deprive a household of pigs. The temporary migration of a woman might leave the household incapable of producing women's wealth. Such situations are generally limited, but still significant.

Production is organized within households, but households are not autonomous. Rather, resources are passed between households with great frequency. Further, these resources are used for both consumption and production. The individuation of production is not necessarily a new thing in Tonga. It may in fact be a rather old thing. What primarily facilitated control of early Tongan society was not just the chiefs' power to define productive processes but also their control over exchange, and the ideology of exchange practice. Exchange practices in Tonga have changed over the last 150 years, but as we will see, the change has been one of focus rather than type.

A large proportion of the cash acquired by individual households, I estimate approximately 60 percent on average, is used in direct donations to the church, or to pay school fees for children. The remainder is used for daily consumption, or to purchase certain types of imported food (lamb flaps, corned beef, and chicken legs for example) used in many feasts. Large sums are occasionally used to build a house or a boat, but such expenditures are uncommon, and by their nature periodic. There are no discernible trends toward capital intensification of production, and with the possible exception of investments in fishing gear (see above), people show little inclination toward anything that could be characterized as capital investment. Though cash is important, it is important primarily because of the way in which it feeds, rather than erodes, the gift exchange processes that knit people together.

Weaving, farming, fishing, and wage labour produce resources (including cash) used in a variety of ways; some are consumed directly, some are exchanged with other people informally, some are used in formal ritual exchanges, and some are exchanged for cash. Formal exchanges, the subject of the next chapter, almost always involve livestock (primarily but not exclusively pigs), garden produce (particularly certain types of yam), and fine mats and/or bark cloth. The difference between cash and these other forms of wealth is not intrinsic to the type of wealth, but rather the way in which wealth is deployed.

Chapter Seven

Gift Exchange and Ceremony

F ormal ceremonial occasions are frequent in Tonga; almost all of these events have a marked and formalized exchange component included within them. There are three basic types of ceremonial events: those focussed on life events of individuals (specifically first and twenty-first birthdays, marriages, and funerals); those associated with the church; and civic events involving the nobility, monarchy, or government. With few exceptions, ritual occasions include some form of religious observance, a kava circle of some type, and the exchange of food and traditional wealth items. The preparations for a ritual, the ritual's form, the movement of valuables within the ritual, and the movement of valuables following a ritual, all express aspects of the social relationships of the people involved.

For analysts and actors alike, the fluidity of social relations and social organization in Tongan society is such that other people's actions cannot be structurally predicted. The intentions and commitment of actors to each other and to the social groups in which they are embedded are known ultimately by action, although at times actions may be judged in terms of ideology (see Bernstein 1983; Korn and Decktor-Korn 1983).

Within each of the three types of ceremonies, people act in particular ways and construct the social groups involved in slightly different ways,

---

Notes to chapter 7 start on p. 185.

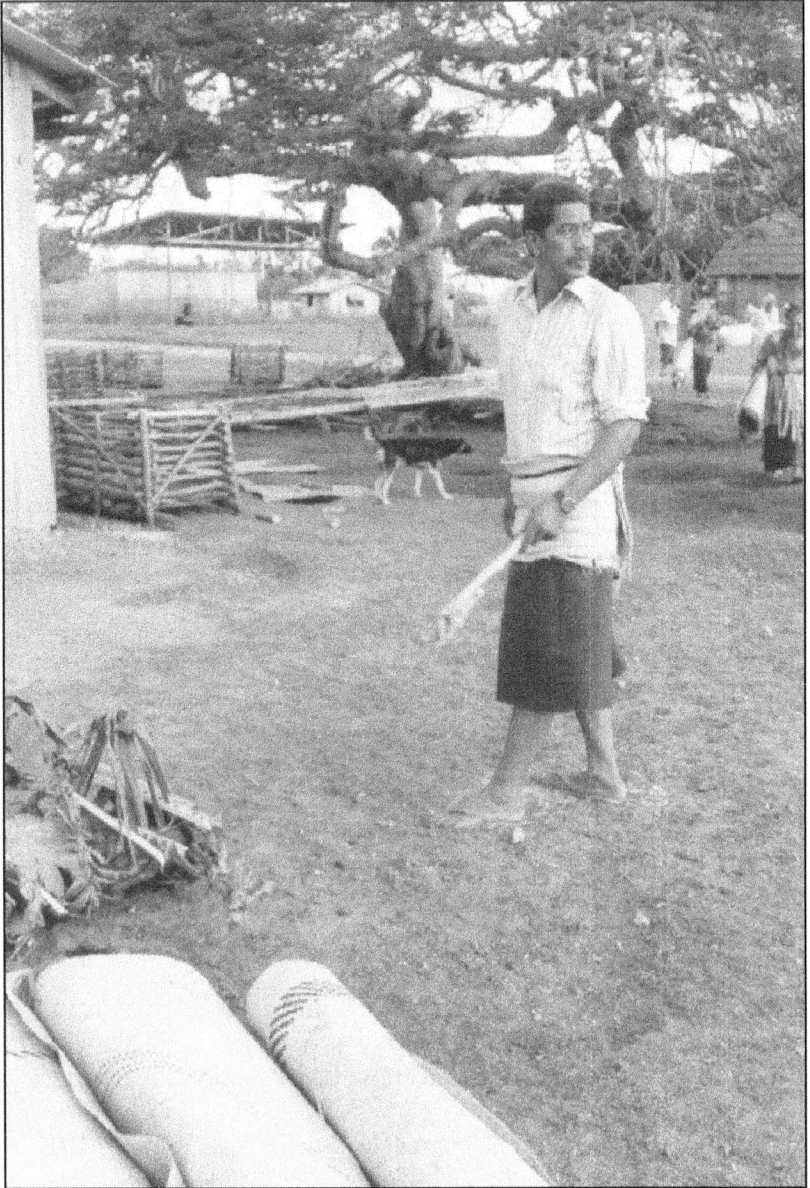

Mats, food, and kava laid out in preparation for a church exchange ceremony.

but within each type, people generate social groups of varying longevity and boundary strength by activating overlapping social ties to a particular individual or group of individuals located at the centre of the ceremony.

It is in this sense that almost all ceremonial activity in Tonga is based on ego-centred kindreds and social networks. Even where a ceremony is based on institutionally bounded entities, like church congregations for instance, the kindreds of the individuals directly involved still play a major, if informal, role.

Ceremony and the Modern Nation State

Civic ceremony is the most diverse of the three categories. It includes all ceremonies that focus on the nobility and royalty, and all those related to institutions of government. At the highest and most inclusive level are ceremonies and events for which the central figure is the King: for instance, such occasions as the King's birthday and the annual agricultural fair. These events may well encompass the entire Kingdom. For people living on the land of a noble or for those in some way related to a noble, any life transition of that noble, or any ceremonial event involving the noble, may draw people together into a group in a supporting capacity.

Whether in support of a noble or the King, people form a social group in reference to the 'eiki (high person) by providing material wealth and labour. Initially the process consists of individuals or individual groups contributing time and wealth as such, but in the enactment of the ceremony, the individuated social entities come together in relationship to the person at the centre of the event.

Events surrounding the Annual Agricultural Fair will help illustrate. Every year each of the main island groups (Tongatapu, Vava'u, and Ha'apai) host the King and a number of other nobles and high government officials. At each fair[1] the villages of the island group are each assigned two stalls at a large fairground. One stall is to display agricultural produce and/or fish (ngōue), and the other is for wealth items like baskets, bark cloth, pandanus mats, and perhaps fine clothing (koloa). There is a clear and gendered division of types of wealth.

In the days leading up to the fair there is a great deal of activity as people gather up produce and wealth, and transport it to the regional centre. The wealth of these individuals is then arranged in the stalls, and presented as the wealth of the village. While people from within the village might be able to identify the individual contributions, others not directly associated with the collection of the wealth items can not.

On the day of the fair, once all is ready, people walk around the fair looking at the various stalls while waiting for the arrival of the King. Once the King arrives, he sits on a raised dais at the head of the crowd.[2]

The ceremonies are opened with a series of prayers. Then all present are entertained with dances and music. Awards are then given by the King for the best entries in several categories like the best yam gardens (this is determined beforehand by the MAF staff). Once the awards are finished, the King gives a speech to the people, and then circles the fairground to inspect the stalls. Once the circuit is finished, a final prayer is said, and the fair rapidly breaks up.

The fair is a ceremony that brings together individual households, first as villages, and then as the people of Ha'apai in reference to the King. The fair is thus the representation and enactment of the nation and civil order in which groups are formed in reference to that order. When all of the fairs are taken as a unit, the entire nation is formed within the ceremonies, and around the King. That is, the structure of the nation itself is enacted within the event. It is not an accident that villages, so rarely the basis for social action (see Decktor-Korn 1977, 222-23), act as villages only in particular circumstances and only in association with ceremonies structured by the modern nation state. People activate particular kinds of ties in the agricultural fair; those based on village and region, and those focussed on the King as the embodiment of the state. In the agricultural fair, the ideology of village, nation, and king are played out through the mobilization and display of people and their wealth.

In 1992, a number of other ceremonies and feasts occurred during the period leading up to and following the agricultural fair that shed some light on how social processes give rise to social groups at the point of ceremony and ceremonial exchange. I wish to briefly discuss two. The first occurred among the staff of the MAF, and the second between the representatives of the Tu'i Ha'angana and the Queen of Tonga.

Travelling alongside the King's party were officials of the MAF; this party included the acting director of the Ministry. In preparation for the arrival of the King the MAF Ha'apai staff were busy organizing the fair itself. During this time they also organized a small feast for the acting director and other members of the MAF administration who had come from Tongatapu. The food for this feast was garnered from the Ministry gardens and livestock herds, and from the personal resources of several MAF employees. It was prepared by the MAF staff with the assistance of several of their relatives.

Feasting (called *faka'afe*, literally to invite) has a common pattern regardless of what ceremony or event it is meant to mark. Basically one group of people give the feast, and another receive it. The boundaries of the groups depend on the occasion or the encompassing event, and are played out in the preparation, presentation, and consumption of the feast itself. Membership in the feast-giving group is marked by the contribution of material and labour in preparation. Membership in the feast-receiving group is marked by the initial consumption of food, and by the giving of speeches honouring the group giving the feast.

After all the food for the feast is laid out in a long line called a *pola*, guests arrange themselves along both sides of the food with the highest-ranking individuals at the top (note the top of the *pola* is defined in part by the presence of the high-ranking people). The spokesperson for the group giving the feast sits both figuratively and literally below the *pola* (that is, beyond the low end of the table), and acts as *matāpule* for that group. Sometimes this person is the leader of this group, and sometimes they are the *matāpule* only. It is more formal and of higher ritual status to have a *matāpule* speak for the leader rather than the political head of the group speaking themselves.

All feasts begin with a prayer,[3] usually offered by a high-ranking person at the top of the *pola*. After the prayer, guests begin to eat; while they are eating, the spokesperson for the group giving the feast welcomes the guests, and apologizes for the inadequacy of the food. This is a common theme in these speeches, and in no way actually reflects the food offered, which in my experience is always far in excess of what could possibly be consumed at the feast itself. Guests then respond to the hosts, usually complimenting their devotion to duty and responsible behaviour; the last person to speak from the guests is the highest-ranking individual. After the last speech is given, the final prayer is conducted, and the feast is concluded. The guests leave quickly. Once they are gone the people who made the feast eat, and then divide up the remaining food and distribute it to other people as the circumstances warrant.

This basic pattern was followed at the MAF feast. The regional head of the Ha'apai office acted as spokesperson for the regional staff, and the acting director of the national MAF office acted as the highest-ranking person. In their speeches, these men repeated the ideological elements described above. The regional head apologized that the food was so poor, and explained that the recent drought had made it difficult to provide the feast appropriate to honour the director and his party. In the final speech, the director lauded the regional staff for their admirable performance of duty in spite of the difficulties they faced.

The feast taken as a whole symbolized several different things. First the individuals of the regional staff acted out their membership in the regional office by providing material and labour for the feast. The regional head demonstrated his leadership by representing his group during the feast. The regional office, operating as such during the construction of the feast, played out their subordination to the national office by offering the feast in the first place. The director and his staff, formed as a group in the act of consumption and placed under the leadership of the director in the seating and speaking arrangements, accepted the subordination of the regional office.

Whatever other crosscutting ties or ranking differences between participants that existed were rendered superficial in this particular context. That is, by other criteria, rank within the church, interpersonal kinship rankings etc., the subordination/domination configuration would have shifted, and the formation of, and membership in, the groups would have varied. The feast was framed within the general MAF structure, and thus rendered that structure socially effective, and ceremonially transparent. This type of feasting activity is one of the ways in which the bureaucratic system of the Tongan government is given social form and legitimacy. The symbolism of seating and acting within the feast give old meanings to new institutional arrangements.

The second event I wish to detail is probably nearer in form and content to political exchanges of the pre-contact and early contact period (see Morgan 1994 on the preservation of form in formal exchange involving the King). In this case, several of the high-ranking commoners from the three villages of the Tu'i Ha'angana made a presentation of a large pig and *kava* to the Queen (in this context she was representing the King), at the behest of the Tu'i Ha'angana. Whenever the King travels from the capital to other parts of the Kingdom, a series of prestations begin which reflect various relationships to the King, and provision the King and his retinue while they travel. People from villages actually on land controlled directly by the King (see Morgan 1994; van der Grijp 1993, 211-14), people from government estates, and people somehow related to the King or Queen may all make prestations of food or durable wealth. In addition, and as in this case, people from the estates of particular nobles may also make prestations *through the noble*.

This does not imply that the noble is actually present; indeed in this particular instance he was not. Rather, the presentation of the gifts to the Queen was made by a number of men representing both the people on the estates of the Tu'i Ha'angana and the Tu'i Ha'angana himself. The party making the presentation consisted of two *motu'a tauhifanua* (old one who cares for the land/people), one from Ha'ano (Hiko), and one from Pukotala (Kienga), and a church minister whose area of responsibility coincided with the estate of the noble. All three of these men were local leaders of some standing; what they had in common was that their constituencies were drawn from the people of the Tu'i Ha'angana. Their gift was understood to come from the Tu'i Ha'angana. In the giving of the gift a hierarchical political relationship was expressed. First, the people of the Tu'i Ha'angana were acting as if they were just that, his people, acting under his direction and for his interests, and furthermore, acting as a group. Secondly, the Tu'i Ha'angana was indicating his subordination to the King. Thus the contemporary political structure, as it is understood in traditional political terms, was symbolized in the exchange.[4]

Life Transition Events

Birthday celebrations, marriages, and funerals are all very important times in the lives of both the individuals at the centre of the event, and those closely associated with them. These sorts of ceremonies are ego-centred; within the event an individual's social ties are arranged into patterns in both formal and informal ways. For instance, the participants in a first birthday celebration are primarily relatives of the child, and perhaps a few other individuals who because of their status in one of the churches, government, or the political ranking system, are asked to attend to *fakalangi-langi* or honour and glorify the event.

Relatives of the child are distinguished by whether they are from the mother's side (low-ranking) or the father's side (high-ranking). The types and quantities of goods these relatives will bring to the ceremony, and the types and amounts they will take away, are dependent at least in part on their kinship relationship to the child.[5] In this regard the *mehekitanga*, or father's sister, is the highest-ranking relative and will receive the largest share of any pandanus mats or bark cloth brought for the ceremony. Women's wealth of this sort is brought for the benefit of the child, but normally does not remain with the child; it is distributed for the child to ensure social and spiritual well-being.

High-ranking guests may bring no material wealth, but honour the child and call for blessings from God during the inevitable and sometimes protracted speech-making that occurs during the feast. These guests, especially the church ministers who deliver a truncated service at the event, will usually receive some portion of the wealth accumulated for the feast.

People who help with the feast, either in the making of the *'umu* (underground oven) or in the provision of food stuffs or *koloa* (mats and bark cloth), may or may not be close relatives. Although there is a tendency for close kin to assist, not all those who assist are close kin. Bonds of friendship and neighbourliness may sometimes be as important as kinship; that is, kinship is not an absolute predictor of participation. Any gift of food to help with the feast is of course acknowledged, but the acknowledgment may be quite quietly made, with no formal speechifying to mark the transaction.

When the ceremony is completed after the final prayer at the feast, lower-ranking people who have assisted in the preparation of the feast eat, and the remainder of the food is then distributed by the family of the child. This last distribution is informal. Food is simply delivered to various households with whom the family either has ties of reciprocity, or perhaps to households with whom the family might like to initiate new connections.

The focus for this sort of event is clearly an individual, that is, the child. Around the child two main groups form. The relatives (kāinga) of her/his mother and those of her/his father, taken together, are the child's kāinga. Participation in the feast thus indicates a willingness to support the child, and a recognition not only of a relationship, but the type of relationship involved (that is, either higher or lower than the child). In the same way that villages form in reference to the King at an agricultural fair, the child's kāinga (first maternal and paternal, and then both) forms within the ceremony.[6] This occurs in both ideological and practical terms.

Expectations about who will participate in a birthday celebration, and just how they should do so, outline the ideological constitution of kāinga for commoners. The actual and particular event demonstrates in individual actions the social and economic reality of an individual child's kāinga, and just who belongs where within it. Regardless of how hierarchical or constrained the structure of Tongan social organization may appear, because all social activity is voluntary (the idea of individual agency is expressed in the Tongan phrase "fei taliha koe" or "it is free to you"), relationships must be enacted in daily life and specific events.[7] We can think of Tongan gift exchange then as marking, or perhaps even making, the social structure. Ceremonies like first birthdays and funerals turn the vast array of potential social relationships encoded in a person's or persons' kinship relationships into actual linkages traced and traceable (by Tongans themselves) through the flow of material wealth.

The concepts through which these sorts of processes are referred to and understood in everyday discourse are those touched on earlier: love ('ofa), respect (faka'apa'apa), and mutual assistance (fetokoni'aki). Love and respect are not simply emotional states, but are manifest in action —

that is, in the flow of material and mutual assistance. Love and respect operate at all levels of the social system encompassing kinship relationships, relations between commoners, those between commoners, the nobility, and the King, and even relationships between Tonga and other nations.[8] The apex of the system is God, not the King. The integration of God within the exchange system is the subject of the most frequent Tongan ceremonial activities, the focus of a great deal of the church-based activity, and the topic to which I now turn.

Church Ceremony and Gift Exchange

No treatment of Tongan society can ignore the significance of the various churches at all levels of Tongan culture. The integration of the Christian God into Tongan values and social practices is profound and ubiquitous (to date the most careful considerations of the role of Christianity in contemporary social life are Decktor-Korn 1974, 1977 and Olson 1993; and see Gordon 1988 on the Mormon Church).

My discussion focuses on the ceremonial calendar of the three main Methodist churches, known in Tongan as *Siasi Uesiliana*, *Siasi Tonga Hou'eiki*, and *Siasi Tonga Tau'ataina*. There is variation between these three churches, but generally their practices and theological beliefs are quite similar. Although there were two Mormon temples on Ha'ano Island, and I did attend some services, I am less familiar with their annual cycle. Several other faiths are present in Tonga as a whole, and both the Catholic Church and the Mormon Church have practitioners in comparable numbers to the Methodist churches, but the state church (*Siasi Uesiliana*), and the other closely related Methodist churches taken as a whole are predominant.

On Ha'ano Island, most ceremonial activity is organized through the churches. No ceremony or public event, even if it is not directly undertaken by a church, is without some overtly religious elements and the participation of a cleric of some type; all marriages,[9] funerals, birthdays, and civil ceremonies, involve God and church through some earthly representative.

Most adult Methodist men are *malanga* (or lay ministers); becoming a *malanga* is in fact the last step to social adulthood. It usually occurs after a man is married and has a child. The female equivalent of this occurs when a woman is married and has a child (either physically or through adoption); this usually coincides with her husband's ordination as a lay minister. Though it is relatively uncommon, in the *Siasi Uesiliana* women can also become lay ministers. Church ministers, called *faifekau*, are professional clerics appointed by the church conference to serve in a particular area. These ministers, both lay and conference appointed, act as representatives of the church and God in the myriad social events which take place in the villages every year. They also lead most of the services and prayer meetings held within the church. In a typical week a minimum of three full church services and at least as many "prayer meetings" are held; at each one of these services one of the *malanga* will prepare and deliver the sermon.

The most important religious occasions are followed by feasts; sometimes these feasts are lavish and include a full range of meats and special foods, and sometimes they are simple "teas" consisting of hot and cold drinks, cookies, and sweet flour dumplings.

Directly church-based events are most intense at the very start of the year. On New Year's Eve each church holds a long, multi-sermoned service that ends at midnight. This begins *'Uike Lotu*, or the week of prayer/worship. Beginning the following Sunday, and continuing for the next week, church services, followed by either a feast or a "tea," are held morning and afternoon. During this week little occurs but worship, the preparation of food, and the consumption of food.

At each service one *malanga* gives the sermon, and one of the families "answers" (*tali*) with a feast. Because of the sheer numbers of sermons given on New Year's Eve, almost all the families in the church are somehow involved in either giving a feast, receiving one,[10] or in many cases, both. Throughout the rest of the week feasts are given, but these feasts are for the entire congregation and so they tend to be much larger.

During the rest of the year a number of church ceremonies and events are marked with feasts. Easter, Christmas, and Mother's/Women's Day for instance are all marked with feasts (sometimes more than one), which are provided by a particular family; in fact people and families are said to own a feast day. For instance one family had given a Mother's Day feast for over thirty years. Visiting *malanga*, usually high-ranking *faifekau*, come periodically throughout the year to give sermons. On these occasions, the entire congregation will answer his sermon. The congregation also cooperates in providing a feast at the time of the *misinale*, the yearly cash donation made by all congregations.

Once each quarter, virtually the entire congregation travels to the regional centre for three or four days of meetings, services, and feasts. At the quarterly meetings each parish/congregation takes responsibility for providing feasts on a rotational basis. At the national level, an annual conference is held; this meeting rotates between the main island groups. The region hosting the event supplies food and feasts for visiting guests which include the highest echelons of the church (see van der Grijp 1993, 200-205 for a more detailed description).

Feasting, and the Famili: Gifts to God

Gailey (1980,1987,1992), and others (Cowling 1990a; Olson 1993) have quite correctly pointed out that with Christianity has come a different set of conceptions of kinship centred on the nuclear family and the conjugal bond between wives and husbands. I have already made a number of criticisms and caveats to the position taken by Gailey above, and will not repeat myself here. Instead I wish to focus on how kinship relationships at the local level are constructed through feasts. There are two separate things going on in local feasts. First, as in the feasts described in the last section, groups and group boundaries are formed. Secondly, and for the argument below more importantly, relationships within groups are defined in terms of interrelationship and mutual responsibility.

All church feasting is part of a reciprocal relationship between God and human beings. Particular feasts are overt manifestations of individuated relationships in which a *famili* [11] faces God and community, offers a sacrifice,[12] and with the help of their guests, asks God to deliver blessings in return. In this process, the *malanga*, as the chief representative of God, God's *matāpule* in fact, acts as the focus for the ceremony, and as the chief mediator between the *famili* and God.

On those occasions when a feast follows a church event, there is a common and consistent pattern of activity in all three Methodist churches represented on Ha'ano Island. In the days before a feast the *famili* prepares by harvesting root crops, rounding up pigs, and purchasing the store-bought goods that usually accompany traditional prestige foods. As a general rule, the larger and more elaborate a feast the better, although an overly ostentatious display might result in negative comments like *fie lahi* (wants to be big) or *fie 'eiki* (wants to be a chief). In order to gather the necessary goods, and to mobilize the required labour, the majority of households must recruit assistance from other households. Usually people who help with a feast are related to someone in the feast-giving household, but a kin tie relation is not sufficient in and of itself. Assisting households and individuals are drawn primarily from those people who normally (that is on an everyday basis) practice *fetokoni'aki* (mutual assistance) with the feast givers.

The night before, those people helping with the feast spend many hours butchering animals, preparing root vegetables, cooking other

A *famili* feast.

prestige foods (like octopus, fried chicken legs, taro greens and corned beef, lamb flaps, etc.), and building a large underground oven to bake pork and root vegetables. The funds required to purchase store-bought foods may come from the household's own cash, or it may be acquired by requests to kin within the village or elsewhere. The work goes far into the night and usually requires a number of cooperating adults to accomplish it. Even in those cases that I know of in which the majority of the material was garnered directly from household resources, the labour required to prepare the feast came from beyond the household. This cooperating group is what Decktor-Korn (1977) calls the *famili*, Aoyagi (1966) identifies as the *famili* organization, and Cowling (1990a) identifies in her fifth definition of *famili*.[13] These ties are *between* the people involved however; that is, they are individuated ties and form a unit situationally.

The unit recognized overtly in the discourse of the ceremony is generally the nuclear or extended family, but the preparation of the feast entails much wider connections within the village and beyond.

After the church service (which those giving the feast may not attend because they are busy laying out the food), those attending the feast are seated according to rank along the feast table. At the head of the table sit the 'eiki of the congregation,[14] the congregation minister, any high-ranking guests, and the malanga who gave the sermon regardless of his/her relative rank according to other ranking criteria. Below these people sit the other malanga and adult men, followed by adult women, and then younger men, women and children. Although food is relatively evenly distributed along the table, the very best foods are concentrated at the head of the table. Beyond the very bottom of the table is the ranking man of the feast-giving family, who sits beside a large basket of food which will be given to the malanga at the end of the feast. The rest of the feast givers are arranged outside of the lower end of the table and will not eat until after the feast is formally concluded.

The feast begins with a prayer of thanksgiving and a blessing of the food. People then eat while they listen to the speeches which follow. The first speech is given by the ranking man of the feast givers, who welcomes people, apologizes for the poor food (again this food is not "poor"), and then explains the reason for the feast. At this level the "reason" is not directly linked to the particular church event, but rather the person or persons within the feast-giving group for whom the feast is offered. Feasts motivated by the Church calendar are given to God, but also for some member or members of the feast-giving group. This is usually, but not always, a child. Both feasting activity focussed on life crisis events, and those described here that arise in association with the Churches, have at their centre some individual or individuals. The speaker asks that the congregation recognize the humble feast offered by asking God to bless the child and family, and to bring them good things (success in an examination at school, good health, etc.).

Subsequent speakers take up this request by speaking of the feast givers' laudable actions and devotion to family and community as is evidenced by the feast. They then ask God to help the family in the future. The speakers are generally (but not always) other malanga or respected adult men. The highest ranking persons speak last. Usually it is the malanga who offers the final prayer. Where earlier speeches may have an oblique element to them, the final prayer includes a direct request to God for assistance to the feast-giving family.

The feast is then over, the guests leave, and the feast givers eat and divide up the remaining food for distribution. The informal distribution of the food following the feast is directed by the ranking adults of the *famili*, and can be seen as a direct reflection of social ties of the *famili*. The scope of the distribution depends on the amount of food remaining; three types of connections are played out. First are those ties to higher-ranking people within the village; for instance the ministers of other congregations or people of high blood rank may receive a portion. Second are ties within the village which arise from generalized exchange and mutual assistance; neighbours, other members of the congregation, resident anthropologists, and kin may all receive a portion. If there is sufficient food, ties with people beyond the village are also recognized through this distribution, though sometimes the practical opportunity for a family to send a basket of food to kin or friends living in another village can be limited by the availability of transport.

Some church feasts are undertaken by one family alone; in others all the families within the congregation contribute separate *pola* which are then arranged together.[15] The cooperative congregation-wide feasts have a basic pattern similar to the family sponsored feasts described above. The preparation and aftermath of the feast are the same, with each family looking to its own interests and responsibilities. The presentation of the feast is slightly different. The individuation of families in these contexts is secondary (but still present) to the formation of the congregation in juxtaposition to the outside church. The feast giver in these cases is the entire congregation; they are represented by the church stewards (*setuata*) who organize the layout of the food and put together the basket of food which will be presented to the visiting *malanga* or church officials. These stewards then act as *matāpule* for the congregation.

The way that social rank is constructed within church feasting is complex. Some participants are clearly of high rank; the *'eiki* and minister of the church always sit higher in recognition of their rank. Similarly the positioning of other categories of persons follows fairly straightforward patterns of age and gender differentiation, but seating within categories (especially the group of *malanga*) can be quite ambiguous. One often sees a general reluctance to sit high, rather than low. Many of the feasts I attended started with a large gap between the unambiguously high-ranking people and the body of the group. This ambiguity arises from an egalitarian subtheme within the hierarchical structure of the feast itself. For instance *malanga* as *malanga* are of equal rank;[16] differentiation of rank is situational and not absolute. Any *malanga* can represent God and thus be of very high rank, and any *malanga* can give a feast, and thus be of very low rank. *Malanga* who are neither giving nor receiving during a feast are equal in reference to both the highest participants and in reference to God (who is the highest ranking focal point to the feast). Thus while feasts always have a hierarchical structure, there is also an egalitarian space contained within. During congregation feasts, this egalitarian space is constructed by the mutual subordination of all the constituent parts of the congregation to God and the church hierarchy.

Van der Grijp (1993, 200-11) discusses church donations and feasting in a manner somewhat commensurate with the analysis offered here. Some significant difference is present however. In van der Grijp's view, church ministers (that is, conference-appointed ministers) form a kind of spiritual bottleneck in the relationship between God and other people. While it is true that church ministers are always highly ranked in church-based feasting and ceremony, they yield to *malanga* at certain points in the ceremonial activities held by the church. Van der Grijp's insistence on seeing the power to mediate between God and the people as restricted to church ministers may be because his analysis is based on an annual conference. In the annual calendar of each of the Methodist Churches, there is one large gathering at which representatives from each individual congregation and the church administration gather to discuss business, assign positions for the coming year, and so on. These meetings bring together congregations as congregations under the leadership of their ministers, and thus in this context the hierarchical nature of the churches is particularly stark. But, while van der Grijp's assessment of the power of the church may well be correct in the context of annual conferences, it is not true for all village-level practice.

Although political rank has been thoroughly integrated into the operation of the churches,[17] the egalitarian elements of church practice have begun to give impetus to calls for democratic reform in the Kingdom; 1991-93 was a period of considerable political debate about the pro-democracy movement lead by 'Akalisi Pohiva. A common understanding in Ha'ano was that the movement (which had the overt and public support of several prominent church officials) was seeking to achieve a political system which mirrored the religious system; that is that all men (and I do mean men here) would be equal under the King as they were under God. It is far too easy to assume that Tongan society is shot through with hierarchical social forms simply because rank can be situationally established; in church feasts rank is also situationally suppressed. A similar argument can be made for ceremonies which juxtapose commoners to nobles like the *'ilo kava* (that is the noble's kava circle). Although relative rank at the top of the kava circle is well known and clear, as one moves toward the bottom the clarity disappears. Rank in the *Taumafakava* (King's kava circle) is much clearer, as is rank between and among the nobles and royal family. This may be part of the reason why considerations of rank are held to be so thoroughly important in Tongan society by those authors who have studied Tonga from the top down.

Church teachings are fairly clear about rank within the family; the head of the family is the father, and parents lead their children. The family is conceived as a circle, in which the parents sit at the head, and around which mutual aid flows freely. The dyads of God/people, *'eiki/tu'a* (nobles/commoners), parents/children are all asymmetrical in terms of power, but they are ideally reciprocal nonetheless. Reciprocity between nobles and commoners is tenuous in modern Tonga, and not coincidentally the most highly contested of these relationships. The relationships between God and the people, and between parents and children however are strong, and they come together within church practice in crucial ways.

For parents and children, feasting is one of the formal contexts in which their interrelationship is outlined. Most church feasts are given for the benefit of children. In one church the minister kept a list of the sermons and feasts given at New Year's. The list consisted of matched trios of names; first the name of the *malanga*, second the name of the head of the family answering the sermon, and finally the name of the child for whom the feast was being given. The child as beneficiary is an integral part of what the feast is about.[18] The feast then is partly about a family's devotion to God, and partially concerned with the relationship between a family and their child. By giving the feast the family shows respect (*faka'apa'apa*) for God and love (*'ofa*) for their child. The expectation of the family is that both parties (that is God and the child) will thus remain within a reciprocal relationship with the family, and each other, in the future. As we will see in the next section when we look at the way children provide for their parents after finishing school, people have good empirical evidence for this expectation.

Education and the Famili: Gifts to Children

One of the blessings most sought from God for a child is educational success. There are good material reasons why parents seek to ensure that their children succeed at school. Feasting is just one avenue to this end. The other important gift that parents give their children, and another manifestation of their love for them, is access to education.

Families devote significant resources to their children's education in both direct and indirect ways. Among the most significant recurring expenditures of cash that households make are church donations and school fees.[19] Although the payments to the schools are clearly market transactions, the fees themselves mediate the relationship between children and their older kinspeople. The provision of educational opportunities for children is an important aspect of adult responsibility, but it is not simply a duty (*fatongia*). School fees are one part of a long-term relationship of mutual caring, assistance, and responsibility which extends to the death of the parents and beyond. There is good reason, given Tongan attitudes and practice, to insist that gift exchange relationships be understood to include those within the *famili*.

Given that a conjugal pair have separate responsibilities in relation to their own natal families, children are the clearest common focus within a marriage. Neither wife nor husband adopts the kinship responsibility of the other. For instance at the death of a parent or close kinsperson of the first ascending generation, a woman is responsible for the provision of women's wealth items for the funeral which follows. Her husband, however, is not expected to provide either livestock or garden produce.[20] Rather it is the woman's brothers who must take the lead in mobilizing the men's wealth required for the funeral.

The only overlap in kinship ties between husband and wife is located in the children they have together. Other kinship responsibilities have the potential to create conflict in the allocation of household resources, while resources directed toward children need not. Indeed, because children may be a common focus for not only a conjugal pair, but for their separate kindreds as well, a couple's children can and do bring the two kindreds together in common cause.

As with large feasts, it is a rare household which can manage the education of a child, especially a bright one, without the assistance of others. Again, even if access to cash is not a problem, access to all the other things necessary for a child's success are very infrequently available within a single nuclear family or household. There are thus important linkages which extend beyond the nuclear family and household which come into play in the education of a child.

In order to access educational opportunities children must leave the island of Ha'ano. Although some of the schools have boarding facilities, boarding a child is both expensive and for many people unsatisfactory because the child will be lonely, and have no one to look after her/his needs directly. For these reasons many families are split between Ha'ano

Island and Pangai. When children gain entry into a college on Tongatapu, even this option is eliminated. In some cases an entire family may relocate to Tongatapu in spite of difficulty because of shortages in housing, land, and other economic resources. Other families choose not to migrate. Instead they seek someone on Tongatapu who can care for the child while he/she is at school. Generally this someone will be a kinsperson.

The movement of a child to Tongatapu mitigates what ideological tendency there might be toward nucleation of extended kin into nuclear families because it provides a rationale for interdependence. Material flows from the island in support of the child, and to the benefit of the people caring for the child. Pigs, fish, mangos, and garden produce are periodically sent down to Tongatapu. While one of the reasons this occurs is because the child is there, nonetheless kinship ties channel and contextualize the exchange and serve to invigorate the relationships between extended kin. The pace and scope of gift exchange is not limited by the material ramifications of the child's board. What at one level may be considered a simple exchange of board for produce, is considerably complicated by ties of affection and relationships of mutual aid which extend both backwards and forwards in time. This is certainly the case for the child, but also for the other people involved as well.

For the people of Ha'ano Island, kinship connections are one means to ensure opportunities for their children. There is no evidence in the data I collected to suggest a patrilateral or matrilateral preference in terms of where children are sent. There are two rather obvious reasons for this. First the practical considerations of the exact location of the school the child attends may have some bearing on which people are approached to care for the child, or there simply may not be that many options. Secondly, the child's kin ties are ambilineal. Again, both the mother's side and the father's side have an interest in the child, and connections continue to be patterned by ambilateral kinship relations. The process through which the educational opportunities of children are insured plays into a whole complex of other relationships. These relationships do of course have material components, and one can see a certain practical logic at work, but this logic is no more determined by economic calculation than it is by kinship or kinship ideology; rather the two intersect. The result of this interplay is not the elimination of wider social ties, but their maintenance.[21]

Education and the Famili: Gifts from the Children

Education is one of the primary routes through which people from the outer islands can gain access to the resources of the state or wider regional economy. Employment in the state bureaucracy, standing in the church hierarchy, and some opportunities to migrate overseas[22] are dependent on educational success. All three of these economic options necessitate migration from the village.

Educational success is linked to a chain of gift relationships drawing together children, their parents, their wider kinship networks, the churches, and God. Empirical evidence is available to all villagers which demonstrates the effectiveness of this chain of exchange. To a limited degree the differences between households in material well-being can be attributed to remittances from children. The most striking demonstrations of wealth differentiation occur at the time of the large annual donations to the church (*misinale*).[23]

Misinale is organized nationally by each of the Methodist churches. Target donation levels[24] and specific dates are set by the Church headquarters. As the date draws near people within the church begin to plan the feast which will accompany the *misinale* ceremony, and actively search out the resources they will use for their donations. Unlike ceremonies focussed on life crisis events, women's manufactures play a limited role in the ceremony, and the two most prominent types of wealth deployed are garden produce and livestock (for the feast), and cash. The church is elaborately decorated with women's wealth during the ceremony, but this wealth is only temporarily loaned to the church. A small amount of bark cloth or a small pandanus mat is given at the feast during the *misinale*, but compared to the amounts of cash, livestock, and garden produce, these quantities are minimal. It is arguable that the role of women's wealth (as a medium of social value) in this particular exchange event has been eclipsed by the use of cash, but women's wealth is still the central wealth category in other exchange events like birthdays, marriages and funerals (cf Gailey 1992, 55).

Like the ceremonial events described above, *misinale* can be seen as concerted group action (by the local church) in which the constituent units of the group are recognized and differentiated in that action. Individual families make individual contributions, usually in the name of the most senior male.[25] All the donations are publicly made, and the size of the contributions are called out to all present. The contributions are then added up and announced. The total *misinale* is considered to reflect on the local church itself, just as individual donations indicate something about individuals and households within the church. Greater prestige is associated with large donations.

Misinale contributions can be seen as gifts to God. As such they are part of a continuing relationship between God and the givers. Elements of both thanksgiving and expectations of future blessings are present in the discourse in and around the *misinale* ceremony. The size of a particular household's contribution can be seen to reflect the vitality and viability of their relationships to God; that is, a large contribution indicates a more expansive relationship from both sides. A larger contribution implies more blessings, and more blessings imply a larger contribution. For *'eiki* people large contributions are also related to social rank. That is, the ability to give wealth in certain situations is linked to the legitimation of rank (see Morgan 1989; van der Grijp 1993, 206).

In the most general terms the size of *misinale* contributions is related to the position of the family in its life-cycle in a fairly straightforward Chayanovian way. The dependency ratio is generally highest while children are in school; this is true in terms of both cash and subsistence requirements. Children of school age require not only school fees, but also a healthy gift relationship with God, church, and community in order to ensure their success. Once children have finished school, they are available to help the family with subsistence production, market-oriented production of crops or fish, the production of women's wealth, or wage labour.

Cash can be acquired from a number of activities, but remittances are on average the largest source. There is in fact a rather striking relationship between remittances from migrants and *misinale* contributions. Given that a large proportion of remittances flow from children to their parents,[26] it is not surprising that the levels of both remittances and *misinale* contributions are higher among those with children who have migrated out. Table 7.1 compares the mean remittances received and mean *misinale* contributions made among three categories of donating units in Ha'ano village: those with grown children, those with school age children only, and those without children.[27]

These donating units are not coterminous with households. Some households consist of more than one donating unit. Young couples living with a person or persons of an ascending generation will often make separate *misinale* donations, especially if they have children of their own. Other households contained segments which belonged to separate churches. On the other hand, sometimes extended family households make their donations together. In no case, however, did separate households make common donations.

People may however "help" others. This occurs within the ceremony, after the initial donation is made. The steward, who calls out people to come and donate, will call for *tokoni* (help); at this time, people may come up and make additional contributions in the name of the initial donating unit. Usually these additional contributions come from friends and relatives from different churches. When a *misinale* follows on the death of a person, their *famili* makes their donation in the name of the deceased as a *fakamanatu*, or memorial. On these occasions such *tokoni* can be very large, and reflects the great importance of wider kinship networks mobilized at funerals.

Table 7.1: Comparison of Remittances and *Misinale* Contributions

Type of Unit	Mean *Misinale* in Pa'anga (1992)	Mean Remittances in Pa'anga (1992)	Number of Cases
All	488	728	29
With grown children	615	1027	16
With children	375	458	10
No children	188	33	3

Misinale donations are made publicly, and the relationship indicated by the table of means above is well understood by villagers themselves. The ability to give large amounts at the *misinale* ceremony is related to access to remittances; indeed requests for cash made to children or other relatives who have migrated out are quite often made specifically for the purpose of church donations. Many migrants faithfully and enthusiastically remit resources for *misinale* and other church-focussed events. But a few migrants are reluctant to give money to their parents for church donations, and would rather provide for the direct consumption of foods and other store-bought items. This has given rise to the practice of arranging a line of credit with merchants in the regional centre of Pangai. A migrant will send cash or a shipment of goods of a certain value directly to the merchant, who will in turn provide the receiving family with a corresponding amount of goods. In the one case this practice was followed in Ha'ano village, the old couple turned their children's intention on its head by taking food from the merchant and then using it primarily for church feasting. Though it is clear that some migrants are uneasy about the level of commitment of their island resident kin to the

Churches, it is both unwise and empirically unsupported to characterize this as a trend. Remittances continue to flow to and for the support of people's obligations within their congregations.

Misinale: New Forms and/or Old?

This discussion of *misinale* has focussed on parents and their children, but these sorts of relationships are not limited to only parents and children, although this is where the churches tend to focus, and this focus tends to be most evident in the *misinale* when it is organized by *famili*. *Misinale* are not always organized in this fashion, and may involve larger more inclusive groups (see van der Grijp 1993, 205-6) in which *famili* are formally submerged into *kalasi* (classes).

In a *misinale* donation organized by *kalasi*, the congregation is divided into two or more groups. Each group makes one large donation in the name of its leader. In a manner reminiscent of the exchange practices described above, the constituent *famili* in each group donate as individual *famili*, but in the public ceremony these *famili* are subsumed into the larger group. The larger *kalasi* can be of related *famili*; the periodic use of *kalasi* should temper any assumptions about the inevitable or exclusive use of *famili* ideology in church practice. In some *misinale* there is in fact only one donating group, that is the entire congregation, organized under the congregation chair (*sea*). The chair is usually the highest-ranking member of the church, that is the church *'eiki* or chief. Both the use of *kalasi* and the occasional undifferentiated congregation donation under the chair, harken back to pre-contact gift exchange practice in which the public performance of exchange subsumed *'api* and/or *fa'ahinga* under their *'eiki*.[28]

The flow of remittances from children and others to villagers is, like the flow of material at feasts, a tangible marker of the love and respect between remitters and recipients. From within the family, the relationship which starts with the social and economic activity focussed on children, is reversed (that is reciprocated) as children in turn focus their social and economic goals to the benefit of their parents. Remittances are in fact one of several ways in which children can show their love. Indeed many of the younger adults who remain in the village show love by caring for the other material needs of the parental generation. Fishing, farming, domestic care, and the production of women's wealth are all ways of showing love to those who benefit from one's work. Remittances are remarkable insofar as they primarily take the form of cash, while these other activities tend to result in the production of subsistence and traditional wealth. All these forms of wealth, including cash, can be and are turned toward the reproduction of social relationships through the gift exchange process. At one level these relationships have undergone a historical shift and now centre on smaller social groupings organized around the Christian ideology of the family and the now individuated *'api* land tenure system. But this shift is embedded within a much wider ideology of mutual assistance among kin, and a gift exchange system which continues to implicate wider networks of individuals and groups in the well-being of individuals, households, and *famili*.

Migration is one way in which Tongans seek to help their families. Those remaining in the village have good empirical evidence to suggest this strategy is an effective way to gain access to resources beyond village boundaries. The processes of development in Tonga, of which migration and remittances are one aspect, must be understood in terms of the intentions and objectives of Tongans themselves. The relationship between *misinale*, church feasts, and remittances is one example of how gift exchange practice in the village affects the actions of Tongans both within and beyond the rural area. Furthermore, although the family is the focus of this sort of church-based activity, it should also be clear that the family is not isolated by these processes. The ideology of the family embedded in church practice, while significant, does not negate wider social ties.

Chapter Eight

Conclusion — By Their Actions
Ye Shall Know Them

> The exploitation of the world may well be an enrichment of
> the local system. Even if there is a net transfer of labour power
> to the metropole through unequal exchange rates, the hinter-
> land peoples are acquiring more goods of extraordinary social
> value with less effort than they could in the days of the ances-
> tors. There follow the greatest feasts, exchanges, and sing-sings
> that ever happened (cf Gregory, 1982; Lederman, 1986;
> Strathern, 1979). . . . the whole process is a *development* in the
> cultural terms or the people concerned.
>
> It is not "backwardness" — except from a Western-bour-
> geois perspective. Nor is it just conservatism. Surely there is
> cultural *continuity*. . . . "Neo-traditional development" might
> be the appropriate term, given the evident paradoxes in har-
> nessing custom to commerce.   — (Sahlins 1988, 7)

The general process that Sahlins alerts us to here applies across the
Pacific, and arguably (certainly he would argue) across the globe.
Articulation with the World System necessarily results in change, but
need not imply a transformation governed by external powers or their
rationales. While in some places and at some times the impact of the

---

Notes to chapter 8 start on p. 187.

World System can be all but overwhelming, it does not therefore follow that this must be the case always and everywhere. Tonga is an example of one society which has pretty much been insulated from some of the more horrific affects of global integration, and the case study presented here can tell us a lot about how people can cope when the main agents of change are markets rather than muskets. No direct military intervention, no outright seizure of the means of production heralded the Tongan entry into the World System. Tonga was never directly colonized, nor was there any significant alienation of land into plantations or other capitalist economic forms. A complex process of social transformation occurred which had, and indeed continues to have, profound continuities with pre-existing social forms and relations.

Part of this process was the introduction of cash crops (initially and until quite recently, primarily copra) destined for the world market. There is little question that Tonga has long been integrated into the World System; the production of commodities for world markets began quite early in Tonga, and it has continued at varying intensities to this day. The manner in which commodity production was introduced and pursued in the Kingdom of Tonga was however, historically particular, and the shape of villagers' participation in the World System today is explicable in terms of this particularity.

The way that villagers reacted and adjusted to the entry of church, state, and the world market into their lives is not simply a product of the nature of these initially external institutions. It is reasonably clear from the earlier discussion of the pre-contact and contact periods that while the social organization of commoners shifted, this shift was one of focus not type. Where people had once participated in the hierarchical structures of the Tongan Chiefdom through their activities within localized kin groups and in support of their chiefs, they now began to organize in a more flexible fashion in support of the churches and the reformulated hierarchy of the state. The growth in commodity production was linked to new constellations of gift exchange relationships, not in the replacement of such relations through the medium of commodity exchange.

As new land laws were operationalized, and chiefly politics became somewhat attenuated from local village level politics, the older corporate kin groups dissolved into more optative groups formed through new forms of reciprocal relations. The media of exchange within groups and between them grew to include cash, but traditional wealth items remained important in both formal and informal exchange. Land, one of the primary components of the means of production, was not commoditized. Although there were distinct (if gradually realized) changes in land tenure practices, there was no significant alienation of lands from producers. Production was individuated, but the distribution of production and productive resources was still mediated by social ties experienced and understood within an ideology of love, respect, and mutual assistance. This ideology encompassed not only kinship relationships, but also the social ties between commoners and chiefs (now nobles), and commoners and God. State and church were incorporated into particularly Tongan understandings of social relationships, rather than fundamentally revolutionizing those understandings.

The results of these changes in conjunction with a shift toward a MIRAB economic structure from about the 1960s on, can be seen clearly in the productive system of Ha'ano Island today. Again, although there is very little cooperation beyond the household in terms of production, the nucleation of production is mitigated by an intense and frequent movement of goods between households. This is clear from both the data presented regarding the variation in levels of production in agriculture, and from the frequency of interhousehold sharing of fish. The major sources of cash in the village are derived from migration and remittances, and limited (primarily bureaucracy-based) wage labour opportunities within the village, but the manner in which people gain access to externally located resources is itself a product of the way interpersonal relationships within and between households are managed. Migration for the purposes of education, and subsequently in search of cash producing opportunities, is motivated and facilitated by relationships formed through both ceremonial and everyday exchange practice.

Formal ceremonial activity is central to the formation of a number of different types of social groups. The monarchy, elements of the state bureaucracy, and commoners' relationships with their nobles are all expressed by various sorts of ceremonial activity, and the flow of material before, during, and after such ceremonies. One set of relationships, between children, their senior kinspeople, and God, is a crucial part of the way people interact with each other in the context of the MIRAB economy. Church-based feasting is undertaken to draw God into a relationship of mutual assistance with people generally, and children particularly. The provision of such feasts for the benefit of children in turn creates and expresses the love of older kinspeople for children, and creates bonds of mutual aid which subsequently potentiate reciprocation by children; if these children are migrants, they often show their love by sending cash. That this cash is frequently used in *misinale*, that is given to God, is neither accidental nor inconsequential. The maintenance of effective gift exchange relations with God and others is the mark, and the result, of social competence and prestige. Any explanation of the actions of the people who remain in the village, and those who migrate out, must be aware that the intentions of both groups are created and expressed within these terms.

Shankman's (1976) very influential monograph on Samoa suggests that migrants' intentions may be known by their actions, and that Samoan migration amounts to a rejection of traditional Samoan society. The problem with Shankman's thesis is that if Samoans are voting with their feet, the vote is split. The patterns of migration, large flows of remittances from overseas, and the vibrancy of linkages between dispersed Polynesian communities, seem to suggest that something more complex than a simple rejection is going on. The dependency thesis is not so much wrong as it is inadequate. Shankman is right, migration does create and maintain the dependency of Pacific nations on aid; underdevelopment understood as a process working on and through the nation State is assured by present conditions. But it is also necessary to recognize that another type of dependency has been created. Tonga is dependent on the 'ofa of migrants for their kinspeople at least as much as it relies on the 'ofa of donor nations like Australia and New Zealand. In the context of transnational migration, the motivations and goals of migrants and their kin are at least as important as those of governments and quasi-government institutions like the World Bank or International Monetary Fund.

The work of Wendy Cowling (1990a, 1990b) serves as an excellent example of how otherwise careful and detailed ethnography can be affected by the common predilection to assume the transformative power of capital and the World System. Cowling (1990a) provides a detailed treatment of migration and development in Tonga which examines the actions and intentions of Tongan commoners. Her treatment of the "motivations for Tongan migration" is instructive. Cowling is one of the few scholars who has conducted extensive research with both Tongan residents and Tongan migrants. Cowling writes: "The reason most commonly given for emigration by both household members remaining in Tonga and individuals who have emigrated to Sydney was that the move overseas was motivated by the desire 'to help the family'" (ibid., 298). Fully 87 percent of her sample drawn from those in Tonga gave some variant of the answer "to help the family." It is unclear what percentage of the Sydney sample gave this answer, except insofar as it was the "most common" one. Yet in spite of this we are told that,

> While Tongans living in Sydney stressed that they had moved because they needed work, or were landless, or had felt oppressed by the opera-

tion of the social system in Tonga, including the sharp class differentiation between nobles and commoners, their relatives in Tonga spoke of the migration of family members as motivated by the desire to "help the family," "improve the standard of living of the family," "contribute to family pride," "to enable the family to increase its giving to church and village projects," "to demonstrate the love of the children for their parents," or "to assist the development of the Kingdom."(Ibid., 298-99)

In what appears to be some sort of amalgamation of her Sydney and Tongan data, Cowling then goes on to list a number of other reasons for migration (ibid., 299). The top three in ranked order are: to help the family; to sidestep the Tongan social order; to obtain English language education for children overseas.[1] According to Cowling, migration for the purposes of capital accumulation and education are one commoner strategy to escape the demands and domination of the Tongan elite (ibid., 296-97).

Cowling also stresses that migration is necessitated by the underdeveloped nature of the Tongan economy, especially in outer islands like Ha'ano. For instance Cowling states:

It has to be recognized that those leaving Tonga are not just seeking personal and family economic goals, but are expressing the belief that they cannot achieve even relatively modest aims in Tonga, such as improved housing or even a clean water supply, without seeking to obtain money from outside the local economy. (1990b, 204)

This statement is interesting in part because it focuses attention on consumption, rather than social uses to which remittances are put (although both are arguably economic). In Ha'ano a large proportion of remittances finds its way into overt and formal gift exchange activity, and is not used exclusively for consumption. While Cowling is aware of this (see Cowling 1990a, 98), her construction of the "economic goals" of migrants marginalizes this aspect of their activity. A related shift in focus is evident in two tables labelled "Reasons for Departure" as well (1990a, Table 10.2, Table 10.3). In these tables, the category "to help the family" does not appear; rather categories like "No job in Tonga," and "For better paid work" dominate.[2] This is on the one hand curious, and on the other somewhat justified. While migrants are clearly leaving to help their remaining kin, one of the primary forms of this help is cash. I am not claiming here that the consumptive use of remittances is unimportant, just that this is not the only, or perhaps even primary way remittances are used.

What is not defensible is Cowling's subsequent emphasis on the dominance of the "cash nexus" in the Tongan economy. In a sort of shadow dialogue with "senior Tongan bureaucrats" who claim that migration is a voluntary act of self or family improvement, Cowling writes:

> Tonga is a cash economy. People cannot live without sources of cash, and capital is required to initiate almost any cash-producing primary production activity. Exchanges in kind for household maintenance and the economic support of extended family members is now virtually non-existent. (1990a, 310)

This is not true. Exchanges in kind and various forms of support for extended kin are far from "virtually non-existent"; such exchanges are ubiquitous (see chapter 6). It is true that cash-producing primary production activities generally require capital to begin. This is considerably less true of secondary production; that is the production of women's wealth. Fine mats were, during the early 1990s, a very significant source of cash in addition to their value in traditional exchange. Fine mat production does not generally require capital, at least on Ha'ano Island where pandanus production is more than adequate to meet people's needs. Further, it is not true that the major requirement for cash is *as* capital; cash is more than capital, and less, it is quite often a gift. I am not claiming here that cash is never used as capital; this would be as misleading as the assertion I am disputing. It is the position that cash can only be one type of thing, and its use have only one inevitable result, that I seek to disrupt.

In a general sense people require access to cash for a variety of purposes, including capital investment in things like boats and housing. The underlying issue however, is the ramification of these needs. Cowling writes:

> The values of church and state, which united "tradition" with a Protestant work ethic, emphasising the individual's duty to family and the Kingdom, have been well absorbed. However, social relations are inevitably altering. Traditional values implicit in *fetokoni'aki*, which primarily involved the sharing of food within the *kāinga*, are being transmuted into beliefs that love and duty are primarily expressed by the giving of cash. Emigration is seen by many as the only way to attempt to amass large amounts of capital. There is still great deference offered to "tradition" in Tonga and among Tongans overseas. It seems unlikely that the invocation and enactment of tradition as a formula to contain change in social relationships and in social roles and behaviour will be effective against the *inexorable influence of the cash nexus*. (Cowling 1990b, 205, emphasis mine)

What is being presaged here is just this, the dissolution of extended kin and social ties and the nucleation/atomization of Tongan society, in a word, commoditization. It is difficult to determine what lies behind this prediction. The empirical discussion which precedes it is dominated by demonstrations of the efficacy of "tradition." While one sometimes gets a sense of grim foreboding, the inexorability of the cash nexus seems to be located in the future rather than the present. Here then in the work of Cowling, like other works or writing about development processes, dependency, and the affects of the World System, an elision of global proportions is going on. As Sahlins (1993) points out, this elision threatens to replicate the very system being critiqued.

From the vantage point of Ha'ano Island, it makes little sense to speak of the "cash nexus." Nor is it advisable to speak of the cash economy as if this is the central organizing axis of social life, and gift exchange is epiphenomenal. Although people need cash, and although people wish for some of the things that cash can bring, these needs and desires are intertwined with a far more powerful nexus of relationships founded on gift exchange. Cash is generally used within the village prestige system, rather than in attempts to escape it. The transfer of cash from migrants to their remaining kin, steeped as it is in the idioms of love and respect, suggests an abiding commitment to social relations understood in traditional terms, yet mediated by a new good (that is cash).

Nonetheless, the operation of social networks centred on Ha'ano Island occurs within a regional economy which is structured by external forces. Certainly the Tongan economy is underdeveloped, and the economy of Ha'apai and islands like Ha'ano are even less developed. To the degree that cash, or the modern commodities cash can buy, is required or desired, migration is generally the most rational of the economic opportunities available over the long term. Migrants are more dependable than the world price for copra, and a great deal more cost effective to transport. Regardless of the intentions and desires of the national government, rural villagers have relied on their emotional ties with migrants to effectively gain access to resources beyond the bounds of village and Kingdom. In the context of Tonga's MIRAB economy migration is a rational economic choice, though it is not a choice without costs. At some junctures, and for some Tongans, the results of the interaction of the system of gift exchange with capitalist markets, especially in the migration process, are ambiguous. The people who actually migrate and their kinspeople remaining in the Kingdom of Tonga face significant challenges to traditional expectations and values because of the material realities of migration (James 1991b, Morton 1998, Small 1997). Migrants find themselves embedded in wage-based economies, constrained by new regimes of work, yet at the same time freed of some of the social dictates of traditional Tongan culture. Families remaining in Tonga must adjust to both increased flows of cash from remittances, and a corresponding decrease in locally available assistance due to massive levels of migration of young people. Long-term absences exact social and emotional tolls (Cowling 1990b). Nonetheless, when viewed from the village, the gift exchange system allows for the exploitation of capitalist markets by Tongans, and not simply the reverse.

The macroeconomic factors which have made migration the logical choice for cash-seeking Tongans are of course products of the World System. Tonga is geographically challenged in the same way as most Polynesian nations.[3] Tongan producers have long experience of the rise and fall of markets and market infrastructures, and are thus well acquainted with the vulnerability of price-taking producers on the periphery of the world economic system. The growth of government bureaucracy and the country's educational infrastructure in the postwar period, and its centralization in the capital Nuku'alofa, have resulted in internal migration in search of jobs and the educational opportunities required to access these jobs. Finally the growth of international labour markets accessible to Tongans has provided even wider opportunities to earn cash. Within this context the people of Ha'ano Island have left in droves (see Appendix 1). Why people have embraced either migration, or the use of cash, cannot however be assumed. For many Tongans the utility of cash is limited.

This is clear in the way that people use cash. Given the underdeveloped nature of the island economy there is little value to be derived from capital accumulation for most commoners. Even in the few areas in which capital investment is advantageous, like the purchase of fishing equipment, traditional practices of sharing and mutual aid transform the returns from such investments into social rather than purely economic benefits. The continuity of diffused rights and informal arrangements within the subsistence sector has ensured that the material necessity of wage labour is largely absent, and cannot be consistently compelled, because access to the means of production remains available to almost all. The fact that labour costs in Tonga are reputed to be among the highest in the Pacific (Government of Tonga [GOT] 1991c, 123) suggests that commoditization has not created a pool of desperate rural proletarians. A dispossessed underclass has yet to emerge for the simple reason that rural producers have yet to be dispossessed. Access to the primary requirement for subsistence production, land, has not been commoditized, and remains largely determined by bilateral kinship ties. Legal frameworks for dispossession have been mitigated by social ties.

As Cowling suggests, the use of cash in gift exchanges from migrants homeward predominates. But it is not true that cash therefore dominates Tongan gift exchange. Traditional exchange items like women's durables, garden produce, and pigs remain important in gift exchange; cash alone is insufficient. Cash is simply one sort of gift; although cash may have the theoretical potential to transform social relationships, the assumption that it *must* reach this potential may be rooted in a Western historical experience and/or perception of cash, capitalism, and commoditization.

Relationships founded and maintained through gift exchanges are required to facilitate the education of children, who will in turn migrate and remit funds. Perhaps even more importantly activities like feasts draw young people into the practice and ideology of *fetokoni'aki* and reciprocal relationships involving a variety of others. The effectiveness of these practices to imbue a sense of responsibility and commitment to *fetokoni'aki* is evident in the practices of migrants themselves.

As effective as out-migration has been as a strategy for individuals and families on Ha'ano Island over the last thirty years or so, the long term results are in doubt. Although people are clearly acting in their own interests, and although these interests are understood and shaped by notions of tradition, the rapid depopulation of the island is problematic. In other areas of the country, entire islands have been abandoned ('Epeli Hau'ofa, personal communication). When viewed from the perspective of the nation state, depopulation of the severity occurring on Ha'ano Island is counterproductive. The potential production levels of the current agricultural system are compromised by the under-utilization of land.

When viewed from the perspective of village people, there is an increase in dependency. This dependency is not directly on the World System, but rather this system mediated through dispersed kin. There is an increasing dependence on relationships with absent kin, but to some degree this is an interdependence. The flow of material is not one way. While cash moves from Nuku'alofa and overseas to people on the island, counterflows of traditional wealth and foodstuffs are shipped out (see James 1993b; Small 1987, 1995). The vitality of both ends of this stream of material is subject to potential stresses. The loss of the most economically productive segments of the village labour force can impinge on the ability to produce traditional wealth items in sufficient quantities to meet the demands of people both resident and absent. The most extreme possibility in terms of the deterioration of current conditions from the village perspective is of course complete depopulation, which would amount to the effective dispossession of people from their lands, and thus make them truly dependent. Any financial factor which impedes the ability of Tonga to maintain its bureaucracy, or impinges on the ability of overseas migrants to produce surpluses to send back to their home communities, can also have a direct effect on the material aspects on exchange. Shrinkage in the flow of wealth has negative ramifications for both the nation state, and of course for the individuals and groups receiving this wealth.

These sorts of pressures on the material aspects of the flow of wealth, while important, may however be secondary to stresses on the social links between migrants and their remaining kin. For both the people who remain on Ha'ano Island, and for MIRAB theorists like Bertram and Watters, the long-term strength and continuity of ties between dispersed kin are key to stability. Scholars like Cowling have expressed doubts about whether such stability is possible or likely.[4] While I have relatively little substantive to add to this particular aspect of the MIRAB debate, it is necessary to state again that current research shows stability, not deterioration (Brown 1998). At some level the long term continuity of both ideology and practice is an empirical question which must await answers.

The current situation on Ha'ano Island is characterized by effective use of dispersed kinship ties in the pursuit of economic goals firmly rooted in gift exchange and non-commoditized social relationships. These goals are themselves defined and practised in formal gift exchanges and the informal sociality of a fish shared or help given. Tongan gift exchange might well be thought of as a sort of localized, regional and transnational praxis, which should not be dismissed as the last vestiges of an eclipsed ideology.

Given the importance of gift exchange practice in terms of the connections that facilitate and motivate the flow of resources between people dispersed by migration processes, it would probably serve very little purpose to disrupt this system. Development policy and practice designed to overcome people's resistance to commodification, to shift people's energies away from social reproduction, and to force development framed only as capital investment and export growth could well be viewed as another attempt at colonization.

Tongan transnationalism is based on the activities of people on islands like Ha'ano. Subsistence agriculture provides not only insulation from the need to use cash for provisioning but the stuff of traditional gift exchange (pandanus mats, bark cloth, pigs, and garden crops) and thus the stuff of social ties themselves. Cash as a gift has been integrated into a system which includes a number of types of items accessible as long as the agricultural system remains viable. Thus to Bertram and Watters' prescription

that South Pacific island states move to ensure continued access to overseas aid and labour markets (1985; see also Bertram 1993), I would add
that actions designed to ensure the vitality of rural-producing communities are also appropriate.

Relationships created and maintained within these villages are the
foundation on which many Tongans have made their way successfully
into the global system, but what exactly is "success"? To the extent that
the centralizing pattern of the MIRAB structure may impede the ability
of people to participate in gift exchange by effectively removing the people from their lands (rather than stripping the land from the people), the
current situation may well be unstable in the longer term, but this insta-
bility would be the result of the purposive action of villagers, and only
tangentially the affects of the World System. That people everywhere, no
less than in Tonga, are embedded in a global system and subject to forces
beyond their control is as obvious as it is urgent. Analyses which turn
people into victims of this system, the inevitable dupes of the power of
capital, do service to no one. Success in Tongan terms is all about Tongan
notions of agency; it is about making one's way in the world, giving, taking, and above all, being an affective human being.

Appendix One

A Comparison of the Population and Demography of Ha'ano Island and the Kingdom of Tonga As a Whole

P opulation studies of the Kingdom tend to use a series of figures which begin with estimates drawn from Cook's journals and include various missionary estimates and later police censuses. The first modern census occurred in 1956; since then there has been a census every ten years. A census abstract covering the period 1956-86 was published in 1991. Demographers have argued that the Kingdom's population declined significantly during the early contact period, and then began a steady recovery from about the last decade of the nineteenth century which accelerated in the mid-twentieth century (M. Tupouniua 1956). Maude reports that between 1931 and 1956 there was an annual increase of over 3 percent (1965, 47).

Although the population of the Kingdom as a whole has continued to increase steadily since the 1956 census, some significant internal fluctuations have been occurring as well. There has been a marked decline in the population of the Ha'apai region generally, and the island of Ha'ano specifically.

In 1992, the total population of Ha'ano Island, including those who were temporarily absent, consisted of some 359 females and 336 males.[1] The population actually resident during the survey period (that is excluding those temporarily absent) was some 264 females and 250 males.

Notes to Appendix 1 start on p. 188.

Table A-1: Population Censuses, Kingdom of Tonga 1921-1986[a]

Year of Census	Population
1921	24,937
1933	30,693
1939	34,130
1956	56,838
1966	77,429
1976	90,085
1986	94,291

a Figures for the censuses from 1921-56 are from M. Tupouniua (1956, 16). Those for 1966-1986 are from the *Statistical Abstract 1989* (GOT 1991a).

Comparisons between my census and the censuses of the Government of Tonga are difficult to make. One major problem with a comparison of the more reliable census data (that is from 1956 on) is that the 1976 census was a de jure census, while the rest were de facto censuses.[2] Thus comparisons of village populations, especially villages like those of Ha'ano Island are problematic because of the large proportion of the population temporarily resident elsewhere. Table A-2 presents a village-by-village compilation of the various census figures and the results of my own survey.

Table A-2: Comparison of Census Data from
Ha'ano Island by Village

Village	1956	1966	1976	1986	1992 (de facto)	1992 (de jure)
Fakakakai	451		404	237	175	238
Ha'ano	380		361	214	148	196
Muitoa	108		147	103	81	105
Pukotala	309		262	173	110	156
Total	1248	1196	1174	727	514	695

The 1976 census figures show little overall change from 1966, but given that the census date coincided with the end of the school term (when there would be significant numbers of women and children living in Pangai or Tongatapu who would be counted in a de jure census but not a de facto one), it is likely that there is a significant inflation of the figure in comparison with the bracketing censuses. The precipitous drop in population between 1976 and 1986 is thus probably overstated; and it is likely that the 1976 figure would be considerably lower if de facto figures could be generated. Nonetheless, using the de jure census I conducted, which is comparable to the 1976 census, the population of Ha'ano Island has clearly fallen drastically over the last two decades (that is, from a population of 1,174 to 695).

Vake[3] estimated the drop in population in the village of Ha'ano from something like six hundred people in 1960, to the present day numbers (196). This estimate of six hundred may seem inflated given the official figures, but it must be remembered that the 1956 and 1966 censuses were de facto, while the estimate given to me by Vake is probably de jure. The differences are minor either way, and it is clear that the village, and the island as a whole, have experienced a rapid loss of people over the last thirty years.

The exact nature of the out-migration is of considerable importance. The movement of whole families, while diminishing the population, does not directly affect the proportion of active and productive adults in the remaining population. Labour migration of the most economically productive segment of the population has some fairly obvious consequences, especially for dependency ratios. A more detailed breakdown of the population is therefore warranted.

Detailed demography of the island was collected according to categories reflecting some differences significant in Tongan terms rather than just by raw ages, although the categories used do correspond to rough age grades.[4] The material ramifications of age are often less than those of status category within the village. Children were divided into three categories: preschool (0-4), primary school (5-10), and high school (11-19). Adults were divided into some six categories: young adults (approximately 20-29), full adults (30-54), older adults (55-69), elderly adults (70+).

While these categories may leave something to be desired by demographic standards, they reflect significant social aspects of age and status in the Tongan context. For instance, the division between primary school and high school is significant because when a child enters high school, both the necessary relocation of the child and the need to raise money to pay school fees, directly impact on the household. Adult status in Tongan society has as much to do with marriage and children as it does with raw age. The category of full adult encompasses primarily individuals who have taken up the responsibilities of adults. This usually occurs after marriage and the birth or adoption of a child, but for those who remain unmarried, it can occur as they age. In rough terms unmarried young adults who no longer attend school are referred to as *talavou*, or "beautiful," while married adults are called *motu'a*, or "old." An unmarried man or woman however does not remain *talavou* forever (except in jest). This division and the way it has been applied in categorizing individuals is a reasonable one, and one based primarily on the acceptance of responsibilities (especially ones related to church activities) by the individuals concerned.

Table A-3: Comparison of Age Grade Proportions (% of total) in Tonga and Ha'ano Island

Age Grade (Years)	0-4	5-9	10-19	20-29	30-54	55-69	+70
Tonga Males[a]	8	7	13.5	7.9	9.7	3.4	1.2
Tonga Females	7	7	12.3	7.9	11.1	3.4	1.3
Ha'ano Males (de jure)	7	6	8.6	8.8	13.2	2.9	1.3
Ha'ano Females (de jure)	6	8	7.5	9.4	15	4.3	1.4
Ha'ano Males (de facto)	9	7	0	11.1	17.1	3.1	1.8
Ha'ano Females (de facto)	7	10	0	10.3	17.5	4.7	1.9

a From the 1986 census (GOT 1991b).

A rough comparison between the population profile of Ha'ano Island and the rest of the Kingdom is possible by looking at the relative percentages for each age grade. When we compare the figures for the population of Ha'ano Island (de jure) with those for the Kingdom as a whole, rather than finding a smaller proportion of persons in the most productive age grades, the opposite is evident. The percentage of the Ha'ano Island population between 20-54 is actually higher, not lower than the national averages. The effect of out-migration on the population profile has not, as one might expect, been to skew downwards the proportion of adults or young adults. In comparison with the profile for the Kingdom as a whole, overseas labour migration has affected the entire Kingdom (see Ahlburg 1991; Gailey 1992); it does not appear however that age grade proportions have been more severely affected on Ha'ano Island than the country itself. The ages 0-19 are underrepresented on the island, in spite of the fact that the total population calculations (rows three and four) include children away at school.

One possibility is that the lower percentages of those under twenty living on the island are a result of adoption practices. According to Morton (1972, 1976), Tongan adoption patterns quite frequently involve some material calculation of the relative advantages to be gained by the intensification of kinship reciprocity which follows an adoption. From the perspective of parents adopting out a child, one such advantage is the sort of educational opportunities that adopting people can offer the child (Morton 1972, 64-65; 1976, 72). All higher learning institutions are located off the island, and most are in or around the capital Nuku'alofa; thus adoption patterns could be weighted towards people living away from the island.

Another possible explanation relates again to the emphasis Tongan families put on the education of children. The lure of the educational opportunities available on Tongatapu is strong, especially for younger families with several children. Opportunities to acquire the cash to pay school fees are also greater on Tongatapu. It is entirely possible therefore, that families with larger numbers of school-age children take advantage of opportunities to move to Tongatapu more frequently. In the discussions I had with people contemplating migration to Tongatapu, the greater educational opportunities that such a move would offer their children was always the first issue they raised. With these families go larger proportions of children, and thus the population profile would shift disproportionately in the direction evident in Table A-3.

Appendix Two

Glossary of Tongan Terms

This appendix contains some very simple definitions for Tongan words used frequently in the book. It is intended as an aid to the reader only. Many of the more important terms are discussed in depth in the text.

ako — education; study.

amauku — spearfishing at night.

angafakatonga — the Tongan way of behaviour.

angafakapalangi — the European way of behaviour.

angafakapa'anga — the way of money/commodity relations.

anga lelei — of good character.

fa'ahinga — a localized kin group.

fahu — "above the law"; position of privilege held by ego's father's sister and father's sister's children.

fakalahi — enlarge.

fakalangilangi — glorify or honour.

fakanofo — naming ceremony for titleholders.

fakatele — trolling.

faka'apa'apa — respect.

famili — family; kinspeople.

fanua/fonua — a bounded section of land and the people resident there; the land; the nation.

faifekau — church minister.

fa'ētangata — mother's brother.

fetokoni'aki — mutual assistance.

foha — son.

hau — champion, victor; type of aristocratic title.

ha'a — chiefly kinship group; tribe.

hou'eiki — plural of *'eiki*.

kāinga — bilateral kindred; kinspeople.

kāinga lotu — fellow church members.

kaunga'api — neighbours.

kautaha — company.

kiki — relish (meat or fish).

koloa — wealth, valuables; primarily women's manufactured cloth durables.

kupenga — fish net; fishing with a net.

kupenga sili — throw net; fishing with a throw net.

lafolafo — shore casting.

lotu — church; prayer.

mafai — political power.

malanga — lay preacher.

matāpule — ceremonial attendant to a chief.

matāpule tauhi fonua — matāpule-granted estates in the constitution.

ma'ala — yam garden.

mehekitanga — father's sister.

me'a 'ofa — gift.

misinale — annual Methodist church donation.

motu'a tauhifanua — localized ceremonial title; old one who cares for the land/people.

ngatu — bark cloth (dyed).

ngāue — work.

ngōue — garden produce.

nopele — noble.

ofisa kolo — villager officer or mayor.

peito — kitchen.

palangi — European.

pa'anga — Tongan currency (approximately 0.90 $CAN in 2001).

polopolo — first fruit.

popau — dugout canoe.

popula — slaves.

puaka toho — a large pig.

pule — authoritative status.

pule fakavahe — district officer.

setuata — church steward.

sino'i 'eiki — aristocratic stratum of chiefly people.

si'i — small.

tauhi — to take care of.

taumata'u — deep-sea line fishing.

tala ē fonua — Tongan traditional history.

tehina — younger brother.

tofi'a — post-constitutional land estate.

tohi hohoko — genealogy.

tokoni — help, assistance.

toutu'u — communal garden.

toulanganga — cooperative bark cloth-making group.

toulalanga — cooperative weaving group.

tufa — reef collecting.

tu'a — commoners.

tu'asina — brother's children (female ego).

tu'i — royal ranked title or chief; king.

uku — spearfishing.

'afeke — octopus hunting.

'api — household.

'api kolo — town allotment.

'api tukuhau — tax or garden allotment.

'eiki — high or chiefly person.

'eiki si'i — petty chief.

'ilamutu — sister's children (male ego).

'inasi — ancient first fruit ceremony; share or portion.

'ofa — love and generosity.

'ulumotu'a — head of localized kin group.

'umu — underground oven.

Appendix Three

Configuration of Households — Pila and Leti

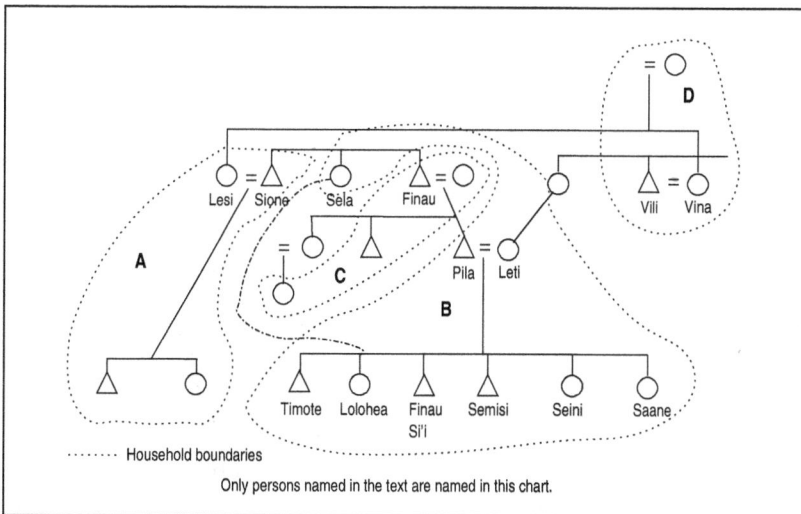

Household boundaries

Only persons named in the text are named in this chart.

Notes

Chapter One: Introduction — Recentring the Periphery

1 It is important to note that the MIRAB model is just that, a model. It is descriptive, not analytical. MIRAB is discussed in detail in the next chapter.

2 That is wealth differentiation is a result of fluctuations in consumer/producer ratios within households that shift as the core conjugal pair have children, and those children age. At the beginning of the cycle the dependency ratio is high. As the children age their productive capacity grows, and they eventually develop the capacity to create more wealth through their labour than they consume (see Chayanov 1966; Sahlins 1972).

3 Some explanation of the "we" here is in order. The fieldwork on which this monograph is based was conducted from August 1991 to March 1993. All but two months of this period were spent on Ha'ano Island. My partner, Heather Young Leslie, was also conducting fieldwork during this period. For almost the entire fieldwork period we lived together, with our infant daughter Ceilidh, in a small house in the village of Ha'ano.

4 This is a ceremonial title. It is discussed further below.

Chapter Two: Economic Development in Polynesia

1 It is interesting to note, however, that unlike earlier writers, Lockwood does not see this as a blockage to development but "just one more illustration of the Samoans' general satisfaction with things the way they are. They could change the system if they wanted to" (ibid., 207). According to O'Meara (1990), they could and did.

2 The view that migration is used to underwrite consumption rather than contribute to the pool of available capital for economic development is widely held. In the literature on the Caribbean, in many ways comparable to South Pacific island economies, similar conclusions are widespread (see Griffith 1985, 1986; Momsen 1986; Pastor 1987; Rubenstein 1983; Wood and McCoy 1985; cf. Gmelch 1987).

3 This situation is exacerbated by inflationary pressures operating on imported goods which again turn rural producers towards subsistence production rather than export production as the terms of trade worsen (Pitt 1979, 68).

4 The practice of drawing successful individuals into political and village affairs through the granting of *matai* status is widely reported (see for instance Lockwood 1971, 32); economic success can also be a direct precursor for successful political activity (see Tiffany 1975).

5 Samoans are not autonomous in the sense that they could withdraw from their participation in the overseas labour market. The overseas population is indeed proletarianized (Bertram and Watters 1985). For the villagers who remain, however, a certain distance from direct market pressures is thus obtained.

6 Market relations exist, but these relations are constrained by the salience of the social ties that mediate access to the means of production. Although merchant capital can in some circumstances have profoundly transformative effects (see for instance Sider 1986), where the basis of subsistence production remains separate and autonomous from market relations, the impact of mercantile capitalism is mitigated.

7 Land tenure practices throughout Polynesia are often offered as reasons for limited development. For instance, the edited volume *Land Tenure and Rural Productivity in the Pacific Islands* (Acquaye and Crocombe 1984) is shot through with references to the need to secure land ownership and control in the hands of individuals in order to promote agricultural development, usually as opposed to limited cash cropping undertaken within customary tenure arrangements (see for instance Mataio 1984; Sisikefu 1984). Traditional patterns of land tenure and acquisition (at least of usufruct rights) seem rather less a problem than proposed. Other authors identify instances of the use of kin ties or informal leasing arrangements by ambitious producers to expand the amounts of land they cultivate (Joralemon 1983; Marcus 1980, 90). The point here is not that traditional land tenure patterns are as efficient as possible, but that they are often efficient enough, at least when reckoned from the village level.

In a rather pessimistic appraisal of the utility of changes in land tenure in Samoa, Seumanutafa writes: "Although registration of family lands and changes in land rights may bring about minor increases in village agricultural production it seems unlikely that significant long-term increases would accrue. Emigration, remittances, and the Samoan value system would seem to militate against this. *Even if current social political and economic systems were to change radically* and an efficient infrastructure initiated it seems that the constraints of soils, climates, isolation, and dependency will probably preclude any sustained increase in village agricultural production" (1984, 154 emphasis mine).

Whether this remarkable statement is true of Samoa, it does draw attention to the fact that if development means "self-reliance" for the Samoan state,
development is likely to be difficult to realize.

8 See Marx, *Capital* Vol. I, Part One, especially Section Four (1993[1867]).

9 Alienation also arises from the objective social relations of production. For
Marx commodity fetishism was both ideology, and an accurate rendering of
the underlying relations of production.

10 Note that Appadurai (1986, 10) argues that barter and commodity exchange
have a "commonality of spirit," and that barter ought to be considered a form
of commodity exchange unmediated by money.

11 For instance Thomas (1991) shows that even during the earliest point of contact in the Pacific, the exchange of goods between Europeans and Pacific
Islanders sometimes occurred in ways that denied relationships rather than
formed them. He thus suggests caution in assuming that societies in which
gift exchange is significant, are unaware of, or incapable of denying the formation of relationships in the exchange context. Like Appadurai, Thomas
cautions against overromanticizing gift economies, and overgeneralizing the
absence of alienation in economies we typify as gift economies.

12 The term SCP was introduced to bring analytical specificity to the conceptual-
ization of "peasants" (Friedman 1978).

Chapter Three: Social Structure and Organization during the Contact and Early Post-Contact Period

1 Several early anthropologists, including Radcliffe-Brown and Lewis Henry Morgan, drew on Tongan material in the pursuit of wider ethnological issues (see
Rogers 1975, 234-35 for a synopsis). Radcliffe-Brown actually worked in Tonga
as a Colonial officer, but wrote very little about Tonga in subsequent years.

2 See Decktor-Korn 1974, 6 who casts similar doubt on the temporal control of
much of the anthropological writing done on Tonga prior to the 1970s; see
also Urbanowicz 1973 on the usefulness of ethnohistorical material in reconstructions like Gifford's.

3 According to Howard and Kirkpatrick (1989, 49) a concern for culture history and pre-contact social forms typifies most of the works sponsored by the
Bishop Museum in the 1920s and 1930s.

4 For a discussion of these "fragmented traditions," see Evans and Young Leslie
1995.

5 By this I mean the histories of Polynesians encoded in their own tradition,
not academic histories about Polynesians. Almost all scholars using the oral
history of Tonga in their work tend towards the heroic traditions encoded in
elite knowledge if only because it is more accessible, unified, and encompasses
the entire polity. Such histories are comprehensive if not complete.

6 For instance, Kaeppler (1978) criticizes Decktor-Korn's (1974) work for failing
to recognize the recent nature of commoner kinship systems. It is unclear to me,
and perhaps to Decktor-Korn, that her analysis is of a system radically different
from the past. Rather it could be that the relations Decktor-Korn describes are
contiguous with older, but poorly described, commoner interactions.

7 The pre-contact transmission of titles was probably patrilateral rather than strictly patrilineal (Gailey 1987, 50; Lātūkefu 1974, 86); this is certainly true for the Tu'i Kanokupolu title (Bott 1982, 123-24; Lātūkefu 1974, 107).

8 There was a class of leadership, called *hau*, or "champion, victor," which designated chiefs who through warfare and marriage attained political and military dominance, sometimes without associated rank or title. These men rose from time to time in various areas with varying degrees of success, but unless underwritten by access to significant titles and appropriate social rank their positions were not heritable, and they were somewhat precarious. While the primary use of the term is a relational one which juxtaposes the sacred power of the Tu'i Tonga with the administrative power of the Tu'i Ha'atakalaua and/ or Tu'i Kanokupolu (these latter titles were sometimes referred to as *hau*, see Kirch 1984, 225-26; Mahina 1992, 160-87; Morgan 1994), not all *hau* came from these titles and not all *hau* held these titles.

9 This split in the sacred and secular aspects of the kingship has correlates in the rest of Polynesia as well. See for example Hocart 1970; Marcus 1989; Sahlins 1985.

10 See Mahina 1992, 160-71 for a detailed analysis of the circumstances precipitating this development. Note that Mahina sees the reformulation of the nature of the Tu'i Tonga title as fundamentally linked to the development of the principles of *fahu* (see below).

11 Many titles have the word *tu'i* within them; for instance the title from the area in which I worked, Tu'i Ha'angana. Such titles are not, however, of the same stratum as the three discussed above.

12 The use of the term *'eiki* for an individual was both relative, and situational. That is an individual could be called *'eiki* depending on who else was present on any particular occasion (see Bott 1982, 60-61). This point is revisited later.

13 Note by extension, through *fahu*, these rights were held by the sister's children as well.

14 Bott (1982, 86) views *ha'a* likewise, and suggests that they may be considered to be grouped maximally in association with one or another of the three *tu'i* lines (see also Nayacakalou 1959, 95).

15 Later ethnological treatments of Polynesian kinship drew into question the appropriateness of conceptualizing Polynesian societies as patrilineal (see especially Davenport 1959; Firth 1957, 1963; Goodenough 1955).

16 They in fact refer to the work of Gifford and Martin as "models of their kind" (Beaglehole and Beaglehole 1941, 3).

17 See Rogers (1975, 235-36) for a further critique.

18 But see also Sahlins (1985, 45) who seems to suggest that the lack of lineage identification among "underlying populations" [commoners] is a pre-contact phenomenon linked to the "heroic" nature of Polynesian hierarchy.

19 In Martin's glossary (1827 [1817], V.2, App.1:liii) the word is translated as: *Cainga.* [*kāinga*] A relation; a kin; one of the same party or interest. Both of the meanings are implicit here.

20 Maude has to some degree ignored the disagreements contained within the literature, nonetheless I, like Gailey, take his reconstruction to be a reasonable (if somewhat overgeneralized) distillation of the literature. The scheme is also consistent with evidence collected in ethnohistorical research within the vil-

lage of Ha'ano (in conjunction with Heather Young Leslie). For other slightly varying reconstructions see Bott 1982, 69-77; Maude 1965).

21 In Maude's 1965 work he uses the term *kāinga* to refer to the unit of social organization called *fa'ahinga* in his 1971 work. The term *fa'ahinga* seems to come from Lātūkefu (see Maude 1965, 29).

22 Note such relationships can be lateralized a considerable genealogical distance.

23 *Fanua* is the older form of *fonua* (Churchward 1959, 140), and was the term used in Ha'ano in 1992.

24 Note however that Gailey maintains that this formation was incipient, not realized; see also Gailey 1985.

25 Note that the first *matāpule* associated with the Tu'i Tonga were "from the sky," as of course was the patrimony of the Tu'i Tonga himself (Biersack 1990, 49).

26 Rogers 1975, 61-66 reports that the titleholders of Niuatoputapu have been converted from *matu'a* (*motu'a tauhifanua?*) to *matāpule* to the king over the last hundred years or so.

27 See Stevens (1996a) for a persuasive example of how some current land boundaries can be linked to the way local kinship groups were organized under the *'eiki* through their *'ulumotu'a*.

28 This is the process which seems to give rise to the so-called *'eiki si'i* (petty chief) titles, which may well be a subset of the *motu'a tauhifanua* class of titles. Ethnohistorical research in Ha'ano revealed evidence that just such a process occurred there (see also Bott 1982, 110-12, 160; Mahina 1992, 167-68 for other examples).

29 This is also an example of the reversal of the more usual chiefly marriage practices in which the marriage of high ranking women into a particular title could elevate the title and subsequent titleholders (i.e., her sons), but did not negate patrilateral transmission of the title.

30 *Hou'eiki* is the plural of *'eiki*.

31 Note Mahina is obviously not too concerned here about the precise reconstruction of the nomenclature of these units and this list should not be taken as definitive. His inclusion of the term *famili* in his discussion may indicate a belief that there is a semiotic and symbolic continuity between pre-contact and present day ranking systems (see Mahina 1992, 175; and see discussions later).

Chapter Four: European Contact and the Transformation of the Traditional Polity

1 See Lātūkefu 1974 for the constitutional documents referred to here.

2 These were titles which recognized political supremacy in these regions and not any genealogical history.

3 Except that land could not be sold to foreigners (ibid., 234).

4 This was a right of consultation only, but it has effectively meant that nobles have the right to approve land grants. Current practice requires the signature of the noble on the registration certificate of new land grants. A noble must simply refuse to sign in order to effectively block registration. In one case I know of from the 1970s a noble was ordered by the Land Court to sign a

land grant, but repeatedly failed to do so. The claimant eventually simply gave up, and never took possession of the land.

5 The earliest recorded date which appears in the Land Registry for Ha'ano Island is not until 1910.

6 The early legislature contained thirty nobles, thirty people's representatives, and members of the privy council appointed by Taufa'ahau. In practice the thirty people's representatives were drawn from the non-noble chiefs (Wood Ellem 1981, 81).

7 Records from Ha'ano Island show that 1928, not coincidentally following the Land Act of 1927, was a watershed year for allotment registrations. The registration of lands, restricted as it was to allotments of a limited size, forced the breakup of whatever customary holdings remained. On Ha'ano Island, this process was completed with the cadastral survey of 1966-67.

8 The term *fa'ahinga* today refers to rather loosely defined groups of people closely enough related to one another that marriage within the *fa'ahinga* is proscribed. Commoners at least consider marriage between any individuals who are in any way identified as consanguineal kin as incestuous. Such marriages do occasionally occur, but may result in both gossip, and a complete reordering of kinship relationships and kinship networks.

9 The traditional *ha'a* system is not however the only structuring component of elite kinship or politics today (see Marcus 1980).

10 See Olson (1993, 92-108) for a good summary of pre-contact beliefs and practices.

11 Both focus on the use of the term *famili* as a loose confederation founded in day-to-day exchange between the members of a sibling set and their nuclear families, although Decktor-Korn recognizes the use of the term as I have outlined above.

12 This process is ongoing, and at times larger units come into play. This issue is discussed later.

13 At first the tribute paid to the churches was in the form of subsistence products, later copra and coconut oil (then sold by the church for cash), and then finally cash itself (Bollard 1974).

14 Again, it is problematic to assume that because the state levied taxes on individual men, that these taxes were paid by these men. Gailey (1980) makes this assumption, but given the very poor fit between legal documents and social practice in Tonga (then and now), this is naive textualism.

15 See Gordon 1988 for a discussion of the partial transformation of Tongan *famili* in the context of Mormonism.

16 Note however that this competitive aspect had pre-contact antecedents in the form of the first fruits ceremony called '*inasi*. Olson (1993, 104) suggests that the provision of material to the god Hikole'o, through the Tu'i Tonga, by chiefs and their *kāinga* was tied to the prestige system. Ideologically the '*inasi* ceremony was linked to the notion that chiefly responsibilities included the regeneration of the world. The '*inasi* had integrative aspects as well. The parallels between this form of exchange and current exchange practices within the churches are compelling.

17 This shift should probably tell us something about the state's limited ability to collect the taxes and fines it imposed.

18 James (1988, 33-34) correctly points out that not all *koloa* was produced by women and not all of women's production was considered *koloa*. Note however that the control and exchange of the types of *koloa* which were produced by women was an essential part of elite politics, and perhaps all politics as well.

19 Campbell (1992, 64)) argues that "private capital investment and [government] policies directed thereto are post-1970 phenomena." Thus the "accumulation and investment at home" to which Gailey refers was presumably not that of capital.

20 Note that Gailey seems to suggest that all traditional wealth items were replaced by commodities. This is simply not true (see James 1988). Traditional *koloa* is exchanged alongside new wealth items — it is in fact quite rare to find any exchange that does not involve either *koloa* or *ngōue* (men's garden produce).

21 See O'Meara (1990, 195) on the utility of *cash as a gift* in modern Samoa.

22 Appadurai (1986, 9) in an attempt to dissolve the exclusive association of production-for-exchange with production for *market* exchange argues that we need to redefine "a commodity as any thing intended for exchange," and thus problematizes what he sees as an overdrawn distinction between gifts and commodities. While such an approach may have some merit, this strategy may obscure as much as the incorporation of gift exchange into production-for-use. My point here is that however this issue is approached, it must not collapse local intentions and constructions of the exchange processes into an encompassing structure, be it the World System or the capitalist mode of production (see also Gregory 1997, 42-46).

23 Note that *'ofa* is sometimes translated as "love," but should be translated as "love *and* generosity" (Gordon 1988; Young Leslie 1999).

24 See Torens (1989) for a similar opposition drawn by Fijians.

25 It is important to recognize that the Tongan household is not corporate, and that the relationships within the household, like those beyond it, are expressed through gift exchange.

26 The complex and multiple meanings of this term are taken up later.

27 Again, this is partially correct. First, the types of goods desired by the Tongan elites were patterned by their own categories of wealth (see Sahlins 1988 for a detailed description of this in Hawaii). In addition, the flow of traditional wealth items was not, and has not been, eliminated from the commoner-state, commoner-noble, or commoner-church relationships.

Chapter Five: Contemporary Social Organization among Village Commoners

1 That is limited to their participation in the provision of material support for the chiefly political project of the nobles to whom they are related by blood or tenancy (cf. Cowling 1990a, 119-25; cf. Kaeppler 1971, 188-89).

2 Definition v. originates in Decktor-Korn (1977).

3 The following discussion refers to the *famili* in the sense outlined in Cowling's fifth definition.

4 In fact there is little to distinguish van der Grijp's concept of *maison* from Decktor-Korn's *famili* except the former's references to Lévi-Strauss.

5 All the names used here and in other descriptions of household activities (all of which come from the situation as it existed in 1992) are pseudonyms.

6 I will return to the households described here by way of example of points made later (see the kinship chart in Appendix 3 for a graphic representation of the relationships).

7 This table was compiled from data collected in March and April of 1992. This same data was used to develop the demographic analysis of Ha'ano Island presented in Appendix 1.

8 When a woman moves to Pangai to care for her children entering high school, she is normally accompanied by all of her primary school and preschool children. She may also care for the high-school children of closely related households.

9 Only one of the Methodist churches allows women to become *malanga*.

10 Tongan men between the period after their education stops and before they are married enter a life stage in which they have considerable freedom. Behaviours inappropriate for adults (alcohol consumption, dancing, fighting, and the theft of livestock or garden foods, for instance) while not condoned, are not surprising to anyone. Young men are almost beyond the bounds of propriety during this period (see Cowling 1990a, 172). Young women also enter a period of greater freedom during this life stage, but remain more responsible to their families (see Cowling 1990a, 150 who disputes Decktor-Korn's 1977 contention that a Tongan youth, especially a young woman may "please oneself").

Chapter Six: The Island Economy

1 See W. Rodman (1985). He makes the very simple but profound observation that state law and common practice are not by any means necessarily the same.

2 It should be noted that Moengangongo is basing her statement on land court records (in Hunter 1963 as well as her own research); it is entirely possible that when a widow is no longer chaste, she gives up her land long before the issue reaches court. I know of two cases in which widows simply allowed the land to pass on to the next heir, without any legal wrangling. The public discussion of a woman's morality which would no doubt follow a land court case centred on her "adultery," probably leads many women to refrain from opposing an attempt to take land she holds as a widow.

3 Note that the survey was focussed through the households resident on Ha'ano Island. This removes the data one step from the actual land registry, so that although almost all the land is registered, only a portion of it is held by those living on the island. The following tables reflect this.

4 Note that these lands are not necessarily given over by their registered owners. For instance lands held by widows may be under the de facto control of one of her sons. The land might even be farther removed from its registered owner. The long-term processes of out-migration have resulted in the transfer of land rights from one usufruct holder to another; in such cases the current caretaker may not even know who the registered owner is.

5 The Tongan pa'anga was valued at approximately $0.90 Canadian in 1993. The purchasing power of the pa'anga is roughly equivalent to the Canadian dollar, though in the context of village Tonga, the robust subsistence economy and informal exchange mechanisms make such comparisons slightly misleading as the need for cash is much less.

6 The category of "common garden" requires some additional discussion. The database used to generate these figures was set up on the basis of individuated households. Some households were distinguished as separate because although they had common lands and sometimes common gardens as well, they had separate kitchens and usually cooked and ate separately; in two instances father-son pairings were involved, and in one a father-in-law/son-in-law bond. In cases where common land was involved, the legal and customary control was in the hands of the senior male, but the land was thought by all concerned to be common land. Although analytically separate, the separation is just that — analytical. The class of garden referred to above as "common garden" refers to gardens of the junior male on these common lands. To group such gardens as on the lands of "other households," while technically correct, is substantively misleading.

7 A quick check of these figures is possible by multiplying the total population, 695, by the mean hectares planted (from the 104-household sample of 626 persons) of 0.082, which results in a total of 56.99 hectares. The actual total amount of land planted at the time of the second survey was 56.19 hectares. The twelve households excluded from the first sample contain a disproportionate number of clergy and teachers because these tend to be the most mobile households and therefore represent a higher portion of households excluded because of their absence during one of the surveys. As these households tend to have less land planted per person, the slightly lower result is to be expected.

8 An older man known to be a competent gardener talking about yam gardening is one of the events at a kava circle which will result in immediate quiet.

9 See the discussion of the population profile of Ha'ano Island in Appendix 1. The most productive age grades on the island had not been depleted (relative to the Kingdom's population profile) by labour migration. Migration for educational reasons has however resulted in a dearth of children between the ages of ten and nineteen. This is not insignificant in terms of dependency ratios. Children in this age grade can make significant contributions to the domestic economy, but given that on Ha'ano Island these children are absent, a greater proportion of a household's labour requirements fall to the adults who remain. Note also that the entire Kingdom suffers from a drain of the population of adults because of external labour migration, and thus both the Kingdom as a whole, and Ha'ano Island have high absolute dependency ratios.

10 See Cathy Small's (1987) excellent description and analysis of the transformation of cooperative *kautaha* to the labour-exchanging *toulanganga* (making bark cloth) groups in the production of bark cloth. The *kautaha* may have been the last vestiges of a productive function for kinship groups larger than *famili*.

11 There is no way to effectively guard gardens. Farmers do however mark the spots where crops have been taken without their consent. This is done by

driving a stick into the ground where the theft has occurred. This is a message to the thief that his activity has been noted.

12 There may be a sort of specialization going on here. That is, between two closely cooperating households one may produce pigs or fish a lot, but have limited gardens, while the other might have extensive gardens but few pigs. Two such households might supply the exchange items needed in a reciprocal manner.

13 See James (1988) for a discussion of the gendered aspects of wealth. She offers a good repudiation of Gailey's contention that only women's manufactures need be considered wealth in Tonga.

14 Five hundred metres of this was one long net used specifically for fishing the big-eye scad, and had been purchased and constructed for that specific purpose. The circumstances surrounding this particular net are detailed later.

15 I am indebted to Heather Young Leslie for the observation that searching for octopus on a reef looks a great deal more like hunting than "collecting."

16 I do not claim here a definitive statement on whether something recognizable as "capital costs," or perhaps more appropriately the opportunity cost of using resources to acquire a boat or net, plays a role in the logic of the division of a catch. I would note however, that the measure of a share is conceived in proportion to a fisher, and not in relation to the objective cost of the resources used during a fishing trip.

17 In 25 cases (5 percent) fish was sent to Pangai for members of the household staying there; this is by my framework intrahousehold exchange.

18 The ritual *taa 'atu* has not occurred for almost twenty years. However it seems that a tuna run occurred in 1985, but that most of the run was caught in a fish trap which sat on the foreshore at the time, and the ritual techniques were ignored.

19 There is no basis for this belief in law, and I am unsure of its roots or antiquity. Nonetheless it is a view passionately held by many people. A village-based resource management system is currently (2001) under consideration by the Ministry of Fisheries.

20 This man led both the actual fishing and the division afterward. This was not simply because he owned the net however, but also because he was a very experienced fisherman.

21 I think it very likely that the neighbour who purchased the fish would have received some as a gift if she had not sent a message to the beach that she wanted some fish. I am unsure of the dynamics here.

22 In other contexts this same man would ensure that anyone on the beach when fish was landed would receive a share. Hanging around when fish is landed is in fact an indication that you would like some fish, and it is difficult and rude for the fisher not to offer some. This can produce some tension though, because a request made in this manner cannot be lightly denied, and no request can be lightly made either. This was a recurring problem for me when I was trying to weigh fish that were landed. In spite of my protestations that I wanted only to weigh the fish, my presence made people uneasy in part because they had to offer fish, and paradoxically, because I then tried to refuse their offer. I received two lectures and several pained looks for refusing to take a share of a catch.

23 For a fuller discussion of the significance of women's wealth production see Gailey (1980, 1981, 1987), Small (1995) and Young Leslie (1999).

24 The units of analysis here are households; note that some households have more than one section which made *misinale* donations in 1992. Where this is the case the sections have been aggregated.

Chapter Seven: Gift Exchange and Ceremony

1 This description refers specifically to the Ha'apai fair, but the basic structure is the same at all three fairs. Each one is organized and administered by the MAF.

2 Other authors have linked the agricultural fairs to the traditional *'inasi* ceremony of the Tu'i Tonga (Bataille 1976, 85 cited in van der Grijp; van der Grijp 1993, 211-14). While this position clearly has merit, the spatial arrangement of the stalls, the dais, and the people of various ranks is a replication of the spatial arrangements of a kava circle. The King's dais is at the top of the circle, high-ranking people and matāpule are arranged on either side, and then the village stalls form a circle descending around the dais. The people sit in front of the King in the centre of the fairgrounds.

3 Some feasts actually incorporate a full or partial church service.

4 For further discussion of the construction of the nation from the local level up through ceremonies juxtaposing nobles and the King, see Morgan (1989).

5 Bott (1958, 61) working in the 1950s says the father's side provides food, while both sides bring mats and/or bark cloth with the emphasis on the mother's side. Kavapalu (1991, 81) reports that "both families may contribute food." In cases I know from Ha'ano Island, there was a tendency for the father's side to give food, and the mother's side to give *koloa*.

6 There is an overt connection between these two levels of organization. Wood-Ellem (1987) reports that all of Tonga was considered Queen Sālote's *kāinga*.

7 These points are presaged in Decktor-Korn's works in which she talks about Tonga as an example of "loose structure."

8 Foreign aid is referred to as a *me'a 'ofa* (gift), and held to demonstrate the *'ofa* (love) of other nations.

9 Purely civil marriages are not possible in Tonga; no marriage license can be issued without the signature of a church minister.

10 When a *malanga* receives a feast given in response to a New Year's sermon, usually only the *malanga* themselves actually attend, but a large basket of food is sent to the *malanga*'s household shortly afterwards.

11 Gailey (1992) uses "family" to refer to the church-based constructions of relationship which emphasize the nuclear family. While Gailey recognizes the great variation in people's practice, she uses the term to emphasize the ideological pressures exerted by church teachings. In this Gailey may be ascribing a power and pervasiveness to the ideology it does not possess; this usage systematically marginalizes variation in ways which Tongans do not. This said, Gailey's point has some merit. There is a tendency in most ceremonies associated directly with the church, for the overt unit of ceremony to be the nuclear or extended family.

12 I am indebted to Heather Young Leslie for pointing out that feasts are indeed referred to as sacrifice (*felaulau*).

13 It is problematic to identify these constellations of cooperating kin as stable groups. The membership can change fairly significantly from event to event, and the assistance of a particular individual at one feast does not guarantee their cooperation at the next. I differ here with Decktor-Korn in emphasis, where she sees structure, I see process. Furthermore people who co-operate in this way may well be neighbours or friends, and not necessarily kin.

14 This is the highest-ranking member of the congregation reckoned through the traditional political ranking system (that is through blood rank) and its post-constitutional reformulation (that is noble status — which may in fact conflict with blood rank sometimes). This person may be male or female, in Ha'ano village two of the three church *'eiki* are in fact female.

15 This sort of feast is common when a *malanga* or high-ranking church official visits, or when the congregation (or set of congregations) is responsible for a feast at the quarterly meetings.

16 The churches do in fact have different ranks of *malanga*, but these are not individuated personal rankings. Within each class, the *malanga* are of equal rank.

17 For instance through the spatial differentiation of the highest-ranking individuals from the bulk of the congregation during church services, and their placement at church feasts.

18 This is of course also the case in feasts and ceremonies for children's first and twenty-first birthdays.

19 Note also that church donations subsidize church-run colleges. The majority of the colleges in Tonga are run by one church or another.

20 He may of course make a contribution. If he does help, it is in addition to what might be demanded, and often a reasonably modest donation.

21 Gailey (1992), in what amounts to a partial retraction of some of her earlier work (especially Gailey 1980, 1987), makes a similar point in the reference to migration and remittances as they affect households in Tongatapu.

22 While not all migration opportunities are linked to educational achievement, most are facilitated by the same sorts of kinship linkages as those referred to above.

23 Wealth differences can also be played out during feasting activity, but wider kinship connections effectively mitigate gross differentiation insofar as most households can draw on others for the traditional wealth items required in feasts. In addition feasts are dispersed through time, so pooling is an effective strategy.

24 It is rather too easy to denigrate people's commitment to *misinale* as a misguided allocation of scarce resources to a rapacious church hierarchy. In simple material terms it is important to recognize that people receive direct benefit from a sizable portion of their donations. The disposition of the donations varies from church to church, but in the majority of cases church members see immediate returns from approximately two-thirds of what they contribute. This portion either stays with the local church, or is used to support the church schools.

25 But note, sometimes the donation is made in the name of the most senior female. If there is no male of the most senior generation in a household, then the donation is made in the name of the senior woman. If the most senior man is of inferior social rank to his spouse, then the donation is made in her name. At one *misinale* for which I have records, all the donations were made in the name of the most senior female. In one other instance at which we were present, a woman made an additional donation to that of her family in her own name as a form of *tokoni* or assistance.

26 This argument must be tempered with the knowledge that significant remittances flow between siblings, especially brothers and sisters. Remittances are not solely about families (that is parents and their children) as defined by the church. See also Gailey 1992.

27 The categories involving children include people with active adoptive relationships.

28 The original formation of the Tongan churches involved the integration of *'eiki* leadership within congregations. The early history of church schisms seems to be related to *'eiki* politics as well (Rutherford 1971). The occasional re-emergence of church ceremonial exchange under *'eiki* is thus not surprising (see Borofsky 1987 for an example of re-emergence of seemingly archaic Pukapukan social forms), although denominational diversity today has more to do with commoner-driven processes than *hou'eiki* ones (Decktor-Korn 1978).

Chapter Eight: Conclusion — By Their Actions Ye Shall Know Them

1 English language is the key to post-secondary education and of course to participation in the national bureaucracy. It is worth note here that this implies that people may look to the return of their children to Tonga as the result of migration.

2 Compare Lafitani (1992, 122), who never overtly raises the issue of migrants' desire to help their families, and simply discusses people's reasons for migration under such categories as "low wages" or "no job."

3 The recent boom in squash pumpkin production for a niche market in Japan suggests that the disadvantages which Tonga faces in terms of production and export may be overcome (Sturton 1992). But recent developments have cast doubts that squash production will be any different than the string of temporary cash crop successes of the past (P. Fonua 1994). More importantly at a theoretical level, it has yet to be demonstrated definitively that the returns from squash production were turned towards significant levels of capital accumulation by farmers. In fact the recurrent use of loans by many farmers to finance production costs suggests otherwise.

4 Note however that Cowling recognizes the current cogency of such relationships. Hayes (1991) identifies a substantial body of literature which systematically negates the significance of reciprocal ties between migrants and their home communities.

Appendix One: A Comparison of the Population and Demography of Ha'ano Island and the Kingdom of Tonga

1 By temporarily absent here I refer to all dependent children (that is those attending school elsewhere, but supported financially by the household), all those visiting elsewhere over the short term, and all those supporting dependent families from overseas on either a short term or long term basis. This includes migrants with wives, husbands, or children in the village, who continue to support their families with remittances, and for whom return to the village is expected; I do not include unmarried children whose return is not expected, even if they remit money to their families.

2 That is, the 1976 survey counted people normally present within a household, while the 1956, 1966, and 1986 censuses counted those actually present in the household on the census day (in 1966 and 1976 this was November 30, in 1956 and 1986 it was November 29 (GOT 1991a, 1).

3 Vake was the village mayor in 1960; his estimate is an informed one. 1960 is a benchmark date because of a hurricane in that year. Vake traces the beginning of the acceleration of out-migration to the effects of the storm.

4 These corresponding ages are approximations.

References Cited

Acquaye B. and R. Crocombe, eds. 1984. *Land Tenure and Rural Productivity in the Pacific Islands*. Suva: University of the South Pacific.

Ahlburg, Dennis. 1991. *Remittances and Their Impact: A Study of Tonga and Western Samoa*. Canberra: Research School of Pacific Studies, Australian National University.

Aoyagi, M. 1966. "Kinship Organization and Behaviour in a Contemporary Tongan Village." *Journal of the Polynesian Society* 75, 2: 141-76.

Appadurai, Arjun. 1986. *The Social Life of Things*. Cambridge: Cambridge University Press.

_____. 1996. *Modernity at Large: Cultural Dimensions in Globalization*. Minneapolis: University of Minnesota Press.

Bataille, Marie-Claire. 1976. "Le salon de l'agriculture aux îles de Tonga et sa relation avec le passé." *Journal de la Société des Océanistes* 32: 67-86.

Beaglehole, E. and P. Beaglehole. 1941. *Pangai: A Village in Tonga*. Wellington: The Polynesian Society.

Bernstein, Louise. 1983. *Ambiguity and Informal Social Control in a Tongan Village*. PhD Thesis, Berkeley, University of California.

Bertram, Geoffrey. 1986. "'Sustainable Development' in Pacific Microeconomies." *World Development* 14, 7: 809-22.

_____. 1993. "Sustainability, Aid, and Material Welfare in Small South Pacific Island Economies, 1900-1990." *World Development* 21, 2: 247-58.

_____. and R.F. Watters. 1985. "The MIRAB Economy in South Pacific Microstates." *Pacific Viewpoint* 26, 3: 497-520.

Biersack, A. 1990. "Blood and Garland: Duality in Tongan History," in *Tongan Culture and History*. Canberra: Research School of Pacific Studies, Australian National University.

Bollard, A. 1974. "The Impact of Monetization on Tonga." MA Thesis, University of Auckland.

Borofsky, Robert. 1987. *Making History: Pukapukan and Anthropological Constructions of Knowledge*. Cambridge: Cambridge University Press.

Bott [Spillius], Elizabeth. 1958. "Report on a Brief Study of Mother-Child Relationships in Tonga." Central Planning Department, Nuku'alofa, Tonga.

Bott, Elizabeth. 1981. "Power and Rank in the Kingdom of Tonga." *Journal of the Polynesian Society* 90, 1: 7-81.

Bott, Elizabeth, with Tavi. 1982. *Tongan Society at the Time of Captain Cook's Visits*. Wellington: The Polynesian Society.

Brown, Richard P.C. 1994. "Migrants' Remittances, Savings and Invest-ment in the South Pacific." *International Labour Review* 133, 3: 347-67.

_____. 1996. *Examining the Validity of the Remittance Decay Hypothesis from Survey Data on Pacific Island Migrants in Australia*. Canberra: The Australian National University, Centre for Economic Policy Research.

_____. 1998. "Do Migrants' Remittances Decline over Time? Evidence from Tongans and Western Samoans in Australia." *The Contemporary Pacific* 10, 1: 107-51.

Burley, David V. 1994. "Settlement Pattern and Tongan Prehistory: Reconsiderations from Ha'apai." *Journal of the Polynesian Society* 103, 4: 379-411.

_____. 1995. "Mata'uvave and 15th Century Ha'apai." *Journal of Pacific History* 30, 2: 154-72.

Campbell, I.C. 1992. "A Historical Perspective on Aid and Dependency: The Example of Tonga." *Pacific Studies* 15, 3: 59-75.

Chayanov, A.V. 1966. *The Theory of Peasant Economy*, edited by Daniel Thorner, Basile Kerblay, and R.E.F. Smith. Homewood, Illinois: R.D. Irwin.

Churchward, C. Maxwell. 1959. *Tongan Dictionary*. Nuku'alofa: Govern-ment of Tonga.

Clifford, James. 1988. "On Ethnographic Authority," in *The Predicament of Culture*. Cambridge: Harvard University Press.

Comaroff, Jean. 1985. *Body of Power, Spirit of Resistance*. Chicago: University of Chicago Press.

Connell, J. 1986. "Population, Migration, and Problems of Atoll Development in the South Pacific." *Pacific Studies* 9, 2: 41-58.

Cowling, Wendy E. 1990a. "On Being Tongan: Responses to Concepts of Tradition." PhD Thesis, Sydney, MacQuarie University.

————. 1990b. "Motivations for Contemporary Tongan Migration," in *Tongan Culture and History*, edited by Phyllis Herda, Jennifer Terrell, and Niel Gunson. Canberra: Australian National University.

Davenport, W. 1959. "Nonunilinear Descent and Descent Groups." *American Anthropologist* 61: 557-72.

Decktor-Korn, Shulamit R. 1974. "Tongan Kin Groups: The Noble and Common View." *Journal of the Polynesian Society* 83: 5-13.

————. 1975. "Household Composition in the Tonga Islands: A Question of Options and Alternatives." *Journal of Anthropological Research* 31: 235-59.

————. 1977. "To Please Oneself: Local Organization in the Tongan Islands." PhD Thesis, Washington University.

————. 1978. "After the Missionaries Came: Denominational Diversity in the Tonga Islands," in *Mission, Church, and Sect in Oceania*, edited by Boutilier et al. ASAO Monograph No. 6, Ann Arbor: University of Michigan Press.

Escobar, Arturo. 1995. *Encountering Development: The Making and Unmaking of the Third World*. Princeton: Princeton University Press.

Evans, Mike and Heather Young Leslie. 1995. "Historical Representation and Local Autonomy: the Kingdom of Tonga." Paper presented at the Power/Culture/History Seminar, Centre for Peace Studies, McMaster University, January 1995.

Fairbairn, Te'o I.J. 1985. *Island Economies: Studies from the South Pacific*. Suva: University of the South Pacific.

Faletau, M. 1981. "Roles of Tongan Women in Rural Areas in Reproductive and Economic Activity." Report to the Central Planning Department. Nuku'alofa: Government of Tonga.

Finney, B.R. 1973. *Big-Men and Business: Entrepreneurship and Economic Growth in the New Guinea Highlands*. Honolulu: University Press of Hawaii.

Firth, R. 1957. "A Note of Descent Groups in Polynesia." *Man* 57: 4-8.

————. 1963. "Bilateral Descent Groups: An Operational Viewpoint," in *Studies in Kinship and Marriage*, edited by I. Schapera. R.A.I. paper 16.

Fisk, E.K. 1962. "Planning in a Primitive Economy: Special Problems of Papua New Guinea." *Economic Record* 38, 84: 462-78.

———. 1964. "Planning in a Primitive Economy: From Pure Subsistence to the Production of a Market Surplus." *Economic Record* 40, 90: 156-74.

Fitzpatrick, P. 1980. *Law and the State in Papua New Guinea*. London: Academic Press.

———. 1983. "Law, Plurality and Underdevelopment," in D. Sugarman, ed. *Legality, Ideology and the State*. London: Academic Press.

Fonua, Pesi. 1994. "Squash: Soil Destruction Causes Crisis on the Farms." *Matangi Tonga* June-July: 11-13.

Fonua, Siosiua, ed. 1975. *Land and Migration*. Nuku'alofa: Tonga Councils of Churches.

Frank, Andre Gunder. 1967. *Capitalism and Underdevelopment in Latin America: Historical Studies of Chile and Brazil*. New York: Monthly Review Press.

Friedmann, H. 1978. "Simple Commodity Production and Wage Labour in the American Plains." *Journal of Peasant Studies* 6, 1: 71-100.

———. 1980. "Household Production and the National Economy: Concepts for the Analysis of Agrarian Formations." *Journal of Peasant Studies* 7, 2: 158-84.

Gailey, Christine Ward. 1980. "Putting Down Sisters and Wives: Tongan Women and Colonization," in *Women, and Colonization: Anthropological Perspectives*, edited by M. Etienne and E. Leacock. New York: Praeger.

———. 1981. "Our History is Written . . . in Our Mats: State Formation and the Status of Women in Tonga." PhD Thesis, New School for Social Research.

———. 1985. "The Kindness of Strangers: Transformations of Kinship in Precapitalist Class and State Formation." *Culture* 5, 2: 3-16.

———. 1987. *Kinship to Kingship: Gender Hierarchy and State Formation in the Tongan Islands*. Austin: University of Texas Press.

———. 1992. "A Good Man is Hard to Find." *Critique of Anthropology* 12, 1: 47-74.

Geertz, Clifford. 1973. *The Interpretation of Cultures*. New York: Basic Books.

Gifford, E.W. 1923. *Tongan Place Names*. Bernice P. Bishop Museum, Bulletin 6.

―――――. 1924. *Tongan Myths and Tales*. Bernice P. Bishop Museum, Bulletin 8.

―――――. 1929. *Tongan Society*. Bernice P. Bishop Museum, Bulletin 61.

Gmelch, George. 1987. "Work, Innovation, and Investment: The Impact of Return Migrants in Barbados." *Human Organization* 46, 2: 131-40.

Goldman, I. 1970. *Ancient Polynesian Society*. Chicago: University of Chicago Press.

Goodenough, W. 1955. "A Problem in Malayo-Polynesian Social Organization." *American Anthropologist* 57: 71-83.

Gordon, Tamar. 1988. "Inventing Mormon Identity in Tonga." PhD Thesis, Berkeley, University of California.

―――――. 1992. "Review of *Kinship to Kingship*." *American Ethnologist* 19, 3: 601-4.

Government of Tonga. 1988. *Ha'apai 1988/1995 Regional Plan*. Nuku'alofa: Central Planning Department.

―――――. 1991a. *Statistical Abstract 1989*. Nuku'alofa: Statistics Department.

―――――. 1991b. *Population Census 1986*. Nuku'alofa: Statistics Department.

―――――. 1991c. *Sixth Five-Year Development Plan, 1991-1995*. Nuku'alofa: Central Planning Department.

Gregory, C. 1982. *Gifts and Commodities*. London: Academic Press.

―――――. 1997. *Savage Money: The Anthropology and Politics of Commodity Exchange*. Amsterdam: Harwood Academic Publishers.

Gudeman, Stephen. 1992. "Remodelling the House of Economics: Culture and Innovation." *American Ethnologist* 19, 2: 141-54.

Gudeman, Stephen and Alberto Rivera. 1990. *Conversations in Columbia: The Domestic Economy in Life and Text*. Cambridge: Cambridge University Press.

Griffith, David. 1985. "Women, Remittances, and Reproduction." *American Ethnologist* 12, 4: 676-90.

―――――. 1986. "Social Organizational Obstacles to Capital Accumulation Among Returning Migrants: The British West Indies Temporary Alien Program." *Human Organization* 45, 1: 34-42.

Halapua, Sitiveni. 1981. "The Islands of Ha'apai: Utilisation of Land and Sea." Consultancy Report for the Central Planning Department. Nuku'alofa: Government of Tonga.

―――――. 1982. *Fisherman of Tonga*. Suva: University of the South Pacific.

Hannerz, Ulf. 1996. *Transnational Connections: Culture, People, Places*. New York: Routledge Press.

Hardaker, J.B. 1975. "Agriculture and Development in the Kingdom of Tonga." PhD Thesis, Armidale, University of New England.

Hardaker, J.B. et al. 1988. *Report of the South Pacific Smallholder Project in Tonga, 1984-85*. 2d ed. Armidale: South Pacific Small Holder Project, University of New England.

Hayes, Geoffrey. 1991. "Migration, Metascience, and Development Policy in Island Polynesia." *The Contemporary Pacific* 3, 1: 1-58.

Helu, Futa. 1992. "The Ethnoscience of the Cultivation of the Frail *Kahokaho*." Paper presented at the South Pacific Island Peoples Science in Suva, Fiji, 1992.

Herda, Phyllis. 1983. "A Translation and Annotation of the Journals of the Malaspina Expedition During Their Stay on Vava'u, Tonga, 1793." MA Thesis, Auckland, University of Auckland.

Hocart, Arthur M. 1970. *Kings and Councillors*. Chicago: University of Chicago Press.

Howard, Alan and John Kirkpatrick. 1989. "Social Organization," in *Developments in Polynesian Ethnology*, edited by Alan Howard and Robert Borofsky. Honolulu: University of Hawaii Press.

Hunter, D.B., ed 1963. *Tongan Law Reports, Vol. II*. Nuku'alofa: Government Printer.

Huntsman, Judith, ed. 1995. *Tonga and Samoa: Images of Gender and Polity*. Christchurch: Macmillian Brown Centre for Pacific Studies.

Hyden, Goran. 1980. *Beyond Ujamaa in Tanzania*. London: Heinemann.

James, Kerry. 1988. "O Lead Us Not into 'Commoditisation'." *Journal of the Polynesian Society* 97, 1: 31-48.

_____. 1990. "Gender Relations in Tonga: A Paradigm Shift," in *Tongan Culture and History*, edited by Phyllis Herda, Jennifer Terrell and Niel Gunson. Canberra: Department of Pacific and Southeast Asian History, Research School of the Pacific Studies, Australian National University.

_____. 1991a. "The Female Presence in Heavenly Places: Myth and Sovereignty in Tonga." *Oceania* 61, 4: 287-308

_____. 1991b. "Migration and Remittances: A Tongan Village Perspective." *Pacific Viewpoint* 32, 1: 1-23.

_____. 1992. "Tongan Rank Revisited: Religious Hierarchy, Social Stratification and Gender in the Ancient Tongan Polity." *Social Analysis, Journal of Cultural and Social Practice* 31: 79-102.

_____. 1993a. "Cutting the Ground from under Them? Commercialization, Cultivation, and Conservation in Tonga." *The Contemporary Pacific* 5, 2: 215-42.

————. 1993b. "The Rhetoric and Reality of Change and Development in Small Pacific Communities." *Pacific Viewpoint* 34, 2: 135-52.

————. 1995. "Right and Privilege in Tongan Land Tenure" in *Land Custom and Practice in the South Pacific*. Cambridge: Cambridge University Press.

Joralemon, Victoria Lockwood. 1983. "Collective Land Tenure and Agricultural Development: A Polynesian Case." *Human Organization* 42, 2: 95-105.

Kaeppler, Adrienne. 1971. "Rank in Tonga." *Ethnology* 10: 174-93.

————. 1978. "Me'a Faka'eiki: Tongan Funerals in a Changing Society," in *The Changing Pacific. Essays in Honour of H.E. Maude*, edited by Neil Gunson. Melbourne: Oxford University Press.

Kavapalu (Morton), Helen. 1991. "Becoming Tongan: An Ethnography of Childhood in the Kingdom of Tonga." PhD Thesis, Canberra, Australian National University.

————. 1996. *Becoming Tongan: An Ethnography of Childhood*. Honolulu: University of Hawaii Press.

Keesing, Roger M. 1975. *Kin Groups and Social Structure*. New York: Holt, Rinehart, and Winston.

Kirch, Patrick. 1984. *The Evolution of Polynesian Chiefdoms*. Cambridge: Cambridge University Press.

Korn, F. and S. Decktor-Korn. 1983. "Where People Don't Promise." *Ethics* 93: 445-50.

Lafitani, Siosiua. 1992. "Tongan Diaspora: Perceptions, Values, and Behaviour of Tongans in Canberra." MA Thesis, Canberra, Australian National University.

Lātūkefu, Sione. 1974. *Church and State in Tonga*. Canberra: Australian National University Press.

Lederman, R. 1986. *What Gifts Engender*. Cambridge: Cambridge University Press.

Lévi-Strauss, Claude. 1984. *Paroles données*. Paris: Plon.

Lockwood, Brian. 1971. *Samoan Village Economy*. Melbourne: Oxford University Press.

Macpherson, Cluny. 1985. "Public and Private Views of Home: Will Western Samoan Migrants Return." *Pacific Viewpoint* 26, 1: 221-41.

————. 1988. "The Road to Power is a Chainsaw: Villages and Innovation in Western Samoa." *Pacific Studies* 11, 2: 1-24.

Mahina, 'Okusitino. 1992. "The Tongan Traditional History: Tala-ē-Fonua." PhD Thesis, Canberra, Australian National University.

Marcus, George E. 1977. "Contemporary Tonga — The Background of Social and Cultural Change," in *The Friendly Islands: A History of Tonga*, edited by Noel Rutherford. Melbourne: Oxford University Press.

———. 1980. *The Nobility and the Chiefly Tradition in the Modern Kingdom of Tonga*. Wellington: The Polynesian Society.

———. 1981. "Power on the Extreme Periphery: The Perspective of Tongan Elites in the Modern World System." *Pacific Viewpoint* 22, 1: 48-64.

———. 1989. "Chieftainship," in *Developments in Polynesian Ethnology*, edited by Alan Howard and Robert Borofsky. Honolulu: University of Hawaii Press.

Martin, John. 1991 [1817]. *Tonga Islands: William Mariner's Account*. 5th ed., Vols. 1-2. Tonga: Vava'u Press.

———. 1827 [1817]. *Tonga Islands: William Mariner's Account*. 3d ed., 2 vols. Edinburgh: John Constable.

Marx, Karl. 1993 [1867]. *Capital*. Provo, Utah: Regal Publications.

Maude, Alaric M. 1965. "Population, Land and Livelihood in Tonga." PhD Thesis, Australian National University.

———. 1971. "Tonga: Equality Overtaking Privilege," in *Land Tenure in the Pacific*. Suva: University of the South Pacific.

Maude, Alaric and Feleti Sevele. 1987. "Tonga: Equality Overtaking Privilege," in *Land Tenure in the Pacific*. 3d ed. Suva: University of the South Pacific.

Mauss, Marcel. 1990. *The Gift*. New York: W.W. Norton.

Mataio, Tere. 1984. "Cook Islands: A Perspective on Land and Productivity," in *Land Tenure and Rural Productivity in the Pacific Islands*, edited by B. Acquaye and R. Crocombe. Suva: University of the South Pacific.

Meillassoux, C. 1981. *Maidens, Meal, and Money*. Cambridge: Cambridge University Press.

Moengangongo, Mosikaka. 1986. "Tonga: Legal Constraint and Social Potentials," in *Land Rights of Pacific Women*. Suva: University of the South Pacific.

Momsen, Janet. 1986. "Migration and Rural Development in the Caribbean." *Tijdschrift voor Econ. en Soc. Geografie* 77, 1: 50-58.

Morgan R.C. 1989. "Polynesian Kingship and the Potlatch." *Culture* 9, 1: 3-12.

———. 1994. "L'efflorescence du tribut et des dons." *Culture* 14, 1: 69-77.

Morton, Helen. 1998. "Creating Their Own Culture: Diasporic Tongans." *The Contemporary Pacific* 10, 1: 1-30.

Morton, Keith. 1972. "Kinship, Economics, and Exchange in a Tongan Village." PhD Thesis, University of Oregon.

———. 1976. "Tongan Adoption," in *Transactions in Kinship: Adoption and Fosterage in Oceania*, edited by I. Brady. ASAO Monograph No. 4, Honolulu: University of Hawaii Press.

Nayacakalou, R.R. 1959. "Land Tenure and Social Organization in Tonga." *Journal of the Polynesian Society* 68: 93-114.

Needs, Andrew. 1988. *New Zealand Aid and the Development of Class in Tonga*. Studies in Development and Social Change. Palmerston North: Department of Sociology, Massey University.

Ogden, Michael R. 1989. "The Paradox of Pacific Development." *Development Policy Review* 7, 4: 361-74.

Olson, Ernest. 1993. "Conflict Management in Congregation and Community in Tonga." PhD Thesis, University of Arizona.

O'Meara, Tim. 1989. "Anthropology as Empirical Science." *American Anthropologist* 91, 3: 354-69.

———. 1990. *Samoan Planters: Tradition and Economic Change in Polynesia*. Fort Worth: Holt, Rinehart and Winston.

Parry J. and M. Bloch. 1989. *Money and the Morality of Exchange*. Cambridge: Cambridge University Press.

Pastor, Robert. 1987. "Introduction: The Policy Challenge," in *Migration and Development in the Caribbean: The Unexplored Connection*, edited by Robert Pastor. Boulder: Westview Press.

Pitt, David. 1970. *Tradition and Economic Progress in Samoa*. London: Oxford University Press.

———. 1979. "The Transition Phase in Development: The Case of Western Samoa." *Civilizations* 29: 57-78.

Rodman, Margaret C. 1987. "Constraining Capitalism? Contradictions of Self-Reliance in Vanuatu Fisheries Development." *American Ethnologist* 14, 4: 712-26.

Rodman, William. 1985. "A Law Unto Themselves: Legal Innovation in Ambae, Vanuatu." *American Ethnologist* 12, 4: 603-24.

Rogers, Garth. 1975. "Kai and Kava in Niuatoputapu." PhD Thesis, Auckland, University of Auckland.

———. 1977. "The Father's Sister Is Black: A Consideration of Female Rank and Powers in Tonga." *Journal of the Polynesian Society* 86, 2: 157-81.

Rubenstein, Hymie. 1983. "Remittances and Rural Underdevelopment in the English Speaking Caribbean." *Human Organization* 42, 4: 295-316.

Rutherford, Neil. 1971. *Shirley Baker and the King of Tonga*. Melbourne: Oxford University Press.

Sahlins, Marshall. 1958. *Social Stratification in Polynesia*. Seattle: University of Washington Press.

―――. 1972. *Stone Age Economics*. New York: Aldine.

―――. 1981. *Historical Metaphors and Mythical Realities: Structure in the Early History of the Sandwich Islands*. Ann Arbor: University of Michigan Press.

―――. 1985. *Islands of History*. Chicago: Chicago University Press.

―――. 1988. "Cosmologies of Capitalism: The Trans-Pacific Sector of 'The World System'." *Proceedings of the British Academy* 74: 1-51.

―――. 1992. "The Economics of Develop-man in the Pacific."*Res* 21: 12-25.

―――. 1993. "Goodbye to the Tristes Tropes: Ethnography in the Context of Modern World History." *Journal of Modern History* 65, 1: 1-25.

Said, Edward. 1978. *Orientalism*. New York: Vintage Books.

Schmink, Marianne. 1984. "Household Economic Strategies: Review and Research Agenda." *Latin America Research Review* 19, 3: 87-103.

Schröder, Peter et al. 1983. *Investigation of Current Yield Potentials on Tax Allotments on the Islands of Ha'apai and Vava'u, Kingdom of Tonga, South Pacific*. Berlin: Technical University of Berlin.

Seumanutafa, A'eau Tiavolo. 1984. "Western Samoa: Registration and Rural Development," in *Land Tenure and Rural Productivity in the Pacific Islands*, edited by B. Acquaye and R. Crocombe. Suva: University of the South Pacific.

Sevele, Feleti. 1973. "Regional Inequalities in Socio-economic Development in Tonga: A Preliminary Study." PhD Thesis, Christchurch, University of Canterbury.

Shankman, Paul. 1976. *Migration and Underdevelopment: The Case of Western Samoa*. Boulder: Westview Press.

―――. 1990. "Phases of Dependency in Western Samoa." *Practising Anthropology* 12, 1: 12-20.

Shils, Edward. 1971. "Tradition." *Journal of Comparative Studies in Society and History* 13, 1: 122-59.

Sider, Gerald M. 1986. *Culture and Class in Anthropology and History: A Newfoundland Illustration*. Cambridge: Cambridge University Press.

Simkin, C.G.F. 1945. "Modern Tonga." *New Zealand Geographer* 1, 2: 99-118.

Sisikefu, S. 1984. "Niue: Registration and Rural Productivity," in *Land Tenure and Rural Productivity in the Pacific Islands*, edited by B. Acquaye and R. Crocombe. Suva: University of the South Pacific.

Small, Cathy Ann. 1987. "Women's Associations and Their Pursuit of Wealth in Tonga." PhD Thesis, Temple University.

―――. 1995. "The Birth and Growth of a Polynesian Women's Exchange Network." *Oceania* 65: 234-56.

―――. 1997. *Voyages: From Tongan Villages to American Suburbs*. Ithaca: Cornell University Press.

Smith, C. 1984. "Forms of Production in Practice: Fresh Approaches to Simple Commodity Production." *Journal of Peasant Studies* 11, 4: 201-21.

Smith, G. 1986. "Reflections on the Social Relations of Simple Commodity Production." *Journal of Peasant Studies* 13, 1: 99-108.

Stevens, Charles. 1996a. Untitled paper presented at the annual meetings of the ASAO, Hawaii, 1996.

―――. 1996b. "The Political Ecology of a Tongan Village." PhD Thesis, University of Arizona.

Stevens, Charles and Mike Evans, eds. 1999. "Sustaining Islanders: Economy, Ecology, and People in the Pacific Island States." Special Issue of *Pacific Studies* 22, 3/4.

Strathern, Andrew. 1979. "Gender Ideology and Money in Mt. Hagen." *Man* 14: 530-48.

Sturton, M. 1992. *Tonga: Development Through Agricultural Exports*. Economic Report No. 4. Honolulu: PIDP, East-West Centre.

Taliai, 'O. 1989. "Social Differentiation of Language Levels in Tonga." MA Thesis, Auckland, University of Auckland.

Taliai, S. Siupele. 1975. "Theology of Land," in *Land and Migration*, edited by Siosiua Fonua. Nuku'alofa: Tonga Councils of Churches.

Taussig, M. 1980. *The Devil and Commodity Fetishism in South America*. Chapel Hill: University of North Carolina Press.

Tiffany, Sharon. 1975. "Entrepreneurship and Political Participation in Western Samoa: A Case Study." *Oceania* 66, 2: 85-106.

Thaman, R.R. 1976. *The Tongan Agricultural System*. Suva: University of the South Pacific.

Thomas, Nicholas. 1989. "The Force of Ethnology: Origins and Signifi-cance of the Melanesia-Polynesia Division." *Current Anthropology* 30, 1: 27-41.

_____. 1991. *Entangled Objects: Exchange, Material Culture, and Colo-nialism in the Pacific*. Cambridge: Harvard University Press.

Torens, Christina. 1989. "Drinking Cash: The Purification of Money through Ceremonial Exchange in Fiji," in *Money and the Morality of Exchange*, edited by M. Bloch and J. Parry. Cambridge: Cambridge University Press.

Tupouniua, M. 'Uli'uli. 1956. *Report on the Results of the 1956 Census*. Nuku'alofa: Kingdom of Tonga.

Tupuoniua, P. 1977. *A Polynesian Village: The Process of Change in the Vil-lage of Hoi, Tongatapu*. Suva: South Pacific Social Sciences Associa-tion.

Urbanowicz, Charles. 1973. "Tongan Culture: The Methodology of an Ethnographic Reconstruction." PhD Thesis, University of Oregon.

Van Binsbergen, Wim and Peter Geschiere, eds. 1985. *Old Modes of Pro-duction and Capitalist Encroachment*. London: Routledge and Kegan Paul.

van der Grijp, Paul. 1993. *Islander of the South*, translated by Peter Mason. Leiden: KITLV Press.

Vason, George. 1840 [1810]. *Life of the Late George Vason of Nottingham [An Authentic Narrative of Four Years at Tongatapu]*. London: John Snow.

Ve'ehala and Tupou Posesi Fanua. 1977. "Oral Tradition and Prehistory," in *Friendly Islands: A History of Tonga*, edited by Noel Rutherford. Melbourne: Oxford University Press.

Wallerstein, Immanuel. 1974. *The Modern World System*. New York: Aca-demic Press.

Walsh, A. 1970. "Population Changes in Tonga: An Historical Overview and Modern Commentary." *Pacific Viewpoint* 11, 1: 27-46.

Warry, W. 1987. *Chuave Politics: Changing Patterns of Leadership in the Papua New Guinea Highlands*. Canberra: Australian National Uni-versity.

Wilson A.D. and F.G. Beecroft. 1983. *Soils of the Ha'apai Group, Kingdom of Tonga*. NZ Soil Survey Report 67. Lower Hutt: New Zealand Soil Bureau.

Wolpe, H. 1975. "The Theory of Internal Colonialism: The South African Case," in *Beyond the Sociology of Development*, edited by Oxaal, I., T. Barnett, and D. Booth. London: Routledge and Kegan Paul.

Wood, A.H. 1932. *A History and Geography of Tonga*. Nuku'alofa, Tonga: C.S. Summers.

Wood, Charles and T. McCoy. 1985. "Migration, Remittances, and Development: A Study of Caribbean Cane Cutters in Florida." *International Migration Review* 19, 2: 251-77.

Wood Ellem, Elizabeth. 1981. "Queen Sālote Tupou III and Tungī Mailefihi: A Study of Leadership in Twentieth-Century Tonga (1918-41)." PhD Thesis, Melbourne, University of Melbourne.

————. 1987. "Queen Sālote Tupou of Tonga as Tu'i Fefine." *Journal of Pacific History* 22, 4: 209-27.

————. 1992. "Customary Landholding in Tonga after the 1975 Constitution." Paper presented at the Tongan Culture and History Conference at Hawaii, 1992.

Young Leslie, Heather. 1999. "Inventing Health: Tradition, Textiles, and Maternal Obligation in the Kingdom of Tonga." PhD Thesis, Toronto, York University.

Index

www.ingramcontent.com/pod-product-compliance
Lightning Source LLC
Chambersburg PA
CBHW072122020426
42334CB00018B/1684